What's Behind the Numbers?

A Guide to Exposing Financial Chicanery and Avoiding Huge Losses in Your Portfolio

John Del Vecchio, CFA

Tom Jacobs, JD

New York   Chicago   San Francisco   Lisbon   London   Madrid   Mexico City
Milan   New Delhi   San Juan   Seoul   Singapore   Sydney   Toronto

The *McGraw-Hill* Companies

1 2 3 4 5 6 7 8 9 0   QFR/QFR   1 8 7 6 5 4 3 2

ISBN: 978-0-07-179197-7
MHID: 0-07-179197-3

e-ISBN: 978-0-07-179198-4
e-MHID: 0-07-179198-1

This publication is designed to provide accurate and authoritative information in regard to the subject matter covered. It is sold with the understanding that neither the authors nor the publisher is engaged in rendering legal, accounting, or other professional service. If legal advice or other expert assistance is required, the services of a competent professional person should be sought.
—*From a Declaration of Principles Jointly Adopted by a Committee of the American Bar Association and a Committee of Publishers and Associations*

Library of Congress Cataloging-in-Publication Data
Del Vecchio, John.
    What's behind the numbers? : a guide to exposing financial chicanery and avoiding huge losses in your portfolio / by John Del Vecchio and Tom Jacobs.
        p. cm.
    ISBN 978-0-07-179197-7 (alk. paper) – ISBN 0-07-179197-3 (alk. paper)
  1. Stocks–Prices. 2. Securities–Prices. 3. Securities fraud. 4. Investments.
5. Portfolio management. I. Jacobs, Tom, 1956- II. Title.
    HG4636.D45 2012
    332.6–dc23
                        2012014943

McGraw-Hill books are available at special quantity discounts to use as premiums and sales promotions, or for use in corporate training programs. To contact a representative, please e-mail us at bulksales@mcgraw-hill.com.

This book is printed on acid-free paper.

To my parents Barbara, John, and Allen—JDV
To my partner Vilis Inde—TJ

Contents

PART 2: Avoid Huge Losses

Acknowledgments

We thank our agent, Bob Mecoy, for his steady hand, unfailing confidence, and sense of humor and our sponsoring editor Stephanie Frerich at McGraw-Hill, for taking us on and being enthusiastic, patient, and good-humored. We couldn't be more fortunate with agent and editor. We also thank The Motley Fool for giving us both our starts and the freedom to grow, and for encouraging all viewpoints and strategies—never a party line. And thanks to Motley Fool colleagues and friends—analyst Alex Pape and senior analyst Michael Olsen, CFA—for taking scarce time available after their demanding jobs to provide comments and corrections on parts of the manuscript. And to technical writer, graphic artist, and fine artist Martha Hughes for manuscript preparation.

JDV: I would like to thank my parents Barbara, John, and Allen for all their love and support over the years. Special thanks to my business partner Brad Lamensdorf. Without him, The Active Bear ETF (HDGE) would not be possible. Thanks to Dean Somes, Jeff Williams, and Tom Sprunger for all their hard work on market timing. Jeff Middleswart for allowing us to use my work as case studies in this book. Tom because this book would not be possible without him. And finally to The Motley Fool where Tom and I first met and a place that spawned many opportunities for us in the ensuing years.

TJ: I would like to thank John for introducing me to the field of earnings quality early in my value investing career, asking me to do this book with him, and being a great collaborator and friend. To The Motley Fool for giving me my first and many opportunities as an investment analyst and to make lasting friendships there. To my late father, who bought me two shares of Ford Motor in 1968 to start my investing life, and taught me economics lessons (some of which I remembered and others only through mistakes). And foremost to my partner, Vilis Inde, for his many years of love, support, good humor, and patience.

Introduction: What This Book Does for You

Simple: *Show me where I'm going to die, so I don't go there.*

Many investors have owned a stock that skipped merrily on its way higher and higher, the CEO a deity, everything skittles and beer—until one day they wake up to see that stock has detonated a bomb in their brokerage account. They had whistled past the graveyard, and now they are in it. With this book, you won't be one of them. We help you find where the investing bodies are buried, so you don't join them.

Shareholders Beware

The world has never known since the earliest slingshot hawkers at the corner of Boulder and Dinosaur a time without financial chicanery. From Dutch tulipomania to the first joint stock companies, managers often devoted more energy to keeping up appearances than to keeping the books. Think of the South Sea Company bubble of the early 1700s and the railroad and canal companies of the 1800s.[1]

"Shareholders be damned" was the smug rule of managers until the Crash of 1929 and Great Depression led to their first obstacle, the 1934 founding of the U.S. Securities and Exchange Commission. Sure, the Great and Glorious Company Management Oz still tried smoke, fire, sound, and nonsense to prevent Dorothy and the shareholder gang from paying attention to what was really behind the curtain, but when the persistent Totos could finally poke their noses behind the management curtain, they did so with the watchdog SEC on their side.

The game may have become tougher in the ensuing decades, but managements have remained inventive. Some know they can placate the majority of shareholders with high-calorie, low-nourishment earnings press releases. It's then just a touch more work to distract the handful who actually listen to earnings conference calls or read the transcripts, but after that it's a breeze. Few investors even glance at company SEC filings, and only a fraction of those burrow into their seemingly objective financial statement lines and obscure notes.

This book shows you the only fine print that matters—where management most frequently hides the information that shows their chicanery. You need not turn over every stone—only those that are the best predictors of trouble. Because you are a practical investor and most likely are not planning a career as an accounting Ph.D., you don't have to memorize the minutiae in a forensic-accounting textbook. You want to avoid losing money, period. That's why we've picked out the tools most likely to find the aggressive accounting that leads to large losses. You can avoid buying those stocks, sell them, or even short them for profit. Every blowup avoided improves the performance of your portfolio: Lose less, profit more.

The Pressure to Push

With 17,000 stocks traded in the United States and at least 45,000 worldwide, you have to beware. There is no shortage of land mines. Only half of all businesses can be above average; still fewer can be great. Management faces crushing pressure to make things appear better than they are. Few execs can resist the pressure from boards, Wall Street analysts, and shareholders to meet each quarter's earnings expectations. It's a jungle out there, and the corporate beast will do anything to survive. Management tortures the numbers to "beat by a penny" and to keep the Wall Street analyst predators and their dreaded downgrades at bay. Rules and regulations allow creative companies to twist, push, knead, and tweak their way to the very edge, where the gray area of aggressive accounting can become black indeed.

Aggressive accounting may not be illegal, but it's chicanery. It's *usually* tough to catch until it's too late—when, though it's worked before, now it doesn't. The company can beat by a penny this quarter and by another penny the next—perhaps even for several quarters, by ever-thinner pennies. Sooner or later, however hard and long aggressive accounting can try to entomb the bodies, they rise like zombies, until the company misses huge and the zombies suck management brains and investor profits through stock downgrades and selling.

Stunned shareholders shake their heads and say "wha' happen'?" But the alert investor can avoid that surprise when prepared with this book's techniques. Our goal is for you to avoid or to sell the stock before it blows a hole in your financial life—and even profit from the ensuing downfall by shorting in appropriate cases.

Earnings Quality Is Job One

The job is to analyze *earnings quality*. For any line on a financial statement, a company can choose a best, good, OK, or questionable practice. The better the treatment, the better the earnings quality—and vice versa. To evaluate earnings quality is to avoid losing money when that quality is poor.

The financial media focus on earnings per share (EPS), hence "earnings quality," but there is no single indicator. This book may place revenue recognition at the top and inventory management next, but every part of the financials connects with another. "Earnings" is the financial picture taken as a whole. As every macroeconomist and Buddhist knows, everything is interconnected; no line item or footnote is an island. Revenues, inventories, operating cash flows, charges, acquisitions, margins, cost of goods sold—each must be understood in relation to the others. Many investors wish for one magic metric to rule investing. Those wishes ride hearses.

Fortunately, investors do not need advanced degrees in earnings quality, though at first glance it may appear difficult to grasp the many moving parts. Management may change the company's revenue recognition policy to raise revenue this quarter and massage inventory treatment the next, manage working capital to boost operating cash flow, obscure real earnings power with serial acquisitions, and on and on, with countless ways to use aggressive accounting to mask the real situation.

But this book's method is practical. You don't have to check off an endless list. Some forms of aggressive accounting are more aggressive than others—you will learn here which. The more management uses the aggressive accounting measures most likely to predict trouble, the lower the earnings quality. Most investors don't know *any* of the ways, let alone the most important ones, through which management can stretch the truth. Those investors ignore the risks, and inevitably own stocks that are digging deep graves in their portfolios.

This book builds on the few resources available on earnings quality—books and authors to which we owe enormous debts, including the path-breaking Thornton (Ted) O'glove's *Quality of Earnings*[2] and exhaustive (in a good way) works by Professors Charles Mulford and Eugene Comiskey.[3] Our book is different, because we augment their learning with a practical goal. With arithmetic and effort, you can use this Monday morning. You don't need to spend years and tuition at the Del Vecchio-Jacobs College of Earnings Quality (wire transfers and Krugerrands welcome). We focus on the best accounting indicators and prioritize them for you. We take you from what to look for to how to use what you find. This book is a total and practical solution that you can use to make money and avoid huge losses *now*.

From Here to Monday Morning

It's a two-part process. Part 1 begins exploding the myths of stock performance, expected returns, earnings quality, and short sellers. Then you're prepared to analyze financial statements—not to be the best accountant there is, but to be the wealthiest investor you can be. You don't need *every* indicator of poor earnings quality and potential losses—you just need the *most accurate* predictors.

For 13 years, John distilled from the universe of earnings quality issues the best predictors. These are the most serious danger signals that, when identified, will help you avoid huge losses. On the investing highway, you want to read, not all the signs, but only those that lead to your destination. John's tested these to produce a remarkable investment record.

After Part 1 arms the investor with the best financial statement predictors of poor results, Part 2 provides a tactical manual for applying them in the day-to-day real world of portfolio management. Stopping after Part 1 might earn readers an "A" in earnings-quality studies, but Part 2 shows how to go forth to make (and not lose) money.

There you will see how earnings quality analysis works with Tom's experience of long-side investing in order to make a truly effective long-short portfolio. Backed by research data and experience, our preferred strategy for the long side ("long book") is Tom's small-cap, low-valuation, asset-backed, catalyst-driven world of opportunistic value and special situations. We close with performance data showing that, if you start with earnings-quality analysis and pair Tom's long strategy with John on the short side, then, as a risk manager, you will form a long-short portfolio with less overall volatility and greater returns.

Next comes John's specific, technical analysis and market timing (neither the voodoo varieties). These added portfolio risk-management tools supplement fundamental earnings quality analysis in order to manage the short side ("short book") of the long-short portfolio. These can help you avoid a bear market in part or completely. If you do that, it really doesn't matter what you do the rest of the time.

We don't ask you to take this on faith. This book does not titillate with "*if only* you had done this, *you would have* avoided the explosions." Our examples are all real-time, including actual reports provided to clients (which you can find in full and for free, at www.deljacobs.com). Both John's Chapter 9 and Tom's Chapter 6 present hard data showing that this book's investing strategy, versus market averages, works.

Your Strong and Confident Future

While you read, you are certain to both enlarge your view of what can happen and worry more about the land mines. Be philosophical. No matter your investing style, strategy, or experience, and no matter how much you learn, you *will* encounter in your investing life companies that bring revenue forward to make today look better at the expense of the future, which only delays paying the piper. You *will* consider buying companies which say that their business is growing so much that of course it's taking longer to collect from customers—a nonsensical explanation for rising days sales outstanding or days sales in inventory, which may be the two great single indicators of trouble in the next quarter or several. And you *will* at least once, and usually many times, unwittingly own companies that reveal these and other ways they are doing anything they can to meet Wall Street expectations, putting off the day of reckoning when they have exhausted all the ways and all the time that aggressive accounting can manipulate numbers.

No investor can avoid every problem. It's impossible to have all the information, not least about the unknowable future. But you will be prepared. This book can help you avoid serious losses, so you won't wake up living a nightmare after aggressive accounting at your company stops working and the stock craters. When, for the first time, everyone sees the company without clothes as they and the stock fall into the Florida sinkhole, you'll have your eyes wide open and your feet on solid ground.

Enjoy and prosper!

John Del Vecchio, CFA   Tom Jacobs, J.D.
Dallas, Texas   Marfa, Texas
                August 2012

Website: www.deljacobs.com
E-mail: JD@deljacobs.com, TJ@deljacobs.com
Twitter: @deljacobs

PART 1

Expose the Chicanery

Chapter 1

The Real Risk of Stock Investing

Most stocks lose money. That's right, so forget about the financial services industry's mantra to buy stocks and hold them forever. Ignore the moment-by-moment media anxiety—Dow up! S&P 500 down!—that plays to the emotions of fear and greed to grab your eyes, ears, and money. Instead, stay calm and look at the data, not the marketing.

Consider the longest secular bull market most people today have ever experienced, 1983 through 2007. Blackstar Funds studied all common stocks that traded on the NYSE, AMEX, and Nasdaq during this period, including those delisted.[1] They then limited their research universe to the 8,054 stocks that would have qualified for the Russell 3000 at some point from 1983 through 2007. During this period the Russell 3000, accounting for 98 percent of U.S. stock liquidity, rose nearly 900 percent, yet:

- 39 percent of stocks had a negative total return. (Two out of every five stocks are money-losing investments.)
- 18.5 percent of stocks lost at least 75 percent of their value. (Nearly one out of every five stocks is a really bad investment.)
- 64 percent of stocks underperformed the Russell 3000. (Most stocks can't keep up with a diversified index.)
- A small minority of stocks significantly outperformed their peers.

Blackstar provides the stark reality supporting the last point: The best-performing 2,000 stocks—25 percent—accounted for all the gains. The worst performing 6,000—75 percent—collectively had a total return of 0 percent.

It's obvious that a few stocks are responsible for all the market's gains. This shows why it is essential to avoid the losers—and that there are valuable opportunities to profit from shorting, even in a bull market. But the long-only investor has it far worse: To garner real returns, that investor has to be extraordinarily lucky to pick only the outperformers and none of the portfolio-destroying disasters. The odds don't favor this.

Imagine you are reading this in 1979 and we told you that General Motors, Woolworth's, and Eastman Kodak—strong and undoubted Dow components[2]—would in 33 years all be bankrupt. You would never have believed us, yet it's all happened. Large brand-name stocks give the illusion of stability, but there is none. They join the index long after their periods of greatest growth, when their size guarantees a future of GDP growth at best. What are the odds you would have picked only the survivors, let alone the winners?

But let's assume for a moment that you possessed the extraordinary good fortune to pick only the 25 percent winners in the Russell 3000. You probably still don't win. Human nature can't take the pressure of the roller-coaster ride.

Consider Ken Heebner, whose results at Loomis-Sayles Peter Lynch called "remarkable."[3] Heebner opened his own mutual fund business, and on March 25, 2010, his CGM Focus Fund had racked up annualized returns of more than 18 percent since January 2000. That's starting *before* the 2000–2002 crash and *including* 2008. These returns are unbelievable, but what happened? Investors behaved like . . . people. They poured money in after his 80 percent return in 2007, just in time for the fund's 48 percent drop in 2008. Morningstar modeled the fund's cash inflows and outflows to find that the typical investor actually *lost* 11 percent per year, despite CGM's 18 percent annualized *gains*, selling during downturns in CGM's performance and buying at upturns.[4]

Instead of buying more during or after Heebner's or any other great investor's disastrous periods such as calendar year 2008, investors sell. Heebner's contrarian success comes with great volatility that most can't handle. Investors chase last year's winner, buying high and selling low.

If most stocks lose money and most investors' emotions get in the way of profits, why invest in stocks at all?

Inflation Kills

The conventional wisdom for investing in the stock market is to grow savings beyond the rate of inflation. While experienced investors understand the concepts of nominal (the actual number) returns and real (the number minus inflation), most investors do not make this distinction. They are happy when their stocks are up nominally and unhappy when down nominally, even though inflation and deflation make the numbers irrelevant to what that investor has actually gained or lost. Real—inflation adjusted—returns are all that matter.

The conventional wisdom is right, because inflation does destroy the purchasing power of paper money. Unfortunately, whether the stock market provides the real returns to mitigate or eliminate that threat depends on when you happen to live. Average annual real returns may or may not be positive and, even if positive, may not be for long periods. Beating inflation is likely an accident of birth. Examine Table 1.1 of the S&P 500, including dividends, from 1950 to 2009.[5]

The 1950s skew the results dramatically. That decade produced the lowest annual inflation of all. Figure 1.1 shows the table information starkly and emphasizes the flat nominal returns from 1968 to 1983 and devastating real returns. Then, the 1980s and 1990s produced truly excellent annual real returns, followed by poor ones.

The data require more analysis. Unless an investor dollar-cost averages (invests roughly equal sums at regular periods) in the S&P 500 with these dividend yields, that investor risks choosing the majority of stocks that do not produce the S&P's average and/or have lower or no yield, reducing or eliminating the benefit of reinvesting dividends.[6] Remember, most gains in the stock market averages come from a minority of stocks.

Problems with Dollar-Cost Averaging

But even dollar-cost averaging is no panacea, because incomes and savings increase with age, and age reduces the time available for compounding. It is completely random whether a person's high-wage-earning years and greater investing returns occur during high or low inflation and therefore times of high or low *real* returns. During tough economic times, income and savings may not increase with age.

Table 1.1 S&P 500 Nominal versus Real (Inflation-Adjusted) Returns, 1950–2009

Decade	S&P 500 Price Change Percentage	Dividend Rate Percentage	Average Annual Returns			
			Total S&P 500 Return Percentage	Inflation Percentage	Real S&P 500 Price Change Percentage	Real S&P 500 Return Percentage
1950s	13.2	5.4	19.3	2.2	10.7	16.7
1960s	4.4	3.3	7.8	2.5	1.8	5.2
1970s	1.6	4.3	5.8	7.4	(5.4)	(1.4)
1980s	12.6	4.6	17.3	5.1	7.1	11.6
1990s	15.3	2.7	18.1	2.9	12.0	14.7
2000s*	(2.7)	1.8	(1.0)	2.5	(5.1)	(3.4)
1950–2009	7.2	3.6	11.0	3.8	3.3	7.0

*In some cases, numbers appear not to add up, due to the effect of averaging 10 years of actual numbers whose result is rounded here. Figures for dividend distribution rates present high uncertainty, of about ±5%. Geometric averages were calculated for price changes, total returns, and inflation.
Source: www.simplestockinvesting.com, by permission.

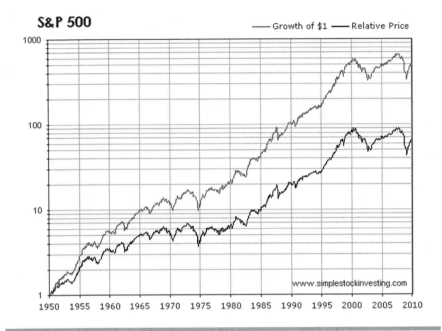

S&P 500 ——— Growth of $1 ——— Relative Price

Figure 1.1 Nominal and Real (Inflation-Adjusted) S&P 500 Returns 1950–2009.
Source: www.simplestockinvesting.com, by permission.

And human nature also puts the kibosh on dollar-cost averaging. Benjamin Graham and David Dodd[7] notably described the simple problem, captured by Jason Zweig:

> Asked if dollar-cost averaging could ensure long-term success, Mr. Graham wrote in 1962: "Such a policy will pay off ultimately, regardless of when it is begun, *provided* that it is adhered to conscientiously and courageously under all intervening conditions."
> For that to be true, however, the dollar-cost averaging investor must "be a different sort of person from the rest of us . . . not subject to the alternations of exhilaration and deep gloom that have accompanied the gyrations of the stock market for generations past."
> "This," Mr. Graham concluded, "I greatly doubt."[8]

Graham didn't mean that no one can resist being swept up in the gyrating emotions of the crowd. He meant that *few* could. To be an intelligent investor, you must cultivate what Graham called "firmness of character"—the ability to keep your own emotional counsel. Otherwise, you risk ending up like Morningstar's estimate of the average investor losing money in Heebner's super-performing CGM Focus Fund, buying high and selling low.

To preserve the purchasing power of your money against inflation and grow it at a higher rate, you must invest early, with discipline, and for a long time or earn multiples of your wages later to make up for the shorter time period available as you age. You must be the rare exception to human nature—a superhuman being that can, unflinchingly and without emotion, dollar-cost average and reinvest dividends via an index fund for decades.

> *"In the long run, we are all dead."*
>
> — JOHN MAYNARD KEYNES

All the common investment statistics used to support the case for owning stocks—as Jeremy Siegel argues in *Stocks for the Long Run*[9]—are misleading at best. Siegel asserts that 130 years of market data prove that "stocks, in sharp contrast to bonds, have never suffered negative after-inflation returns over any 20-year period or longer."[10] He further adds that 200 years of data show that selling in a bear market is always wrong: "You take the pain, you hold your position, and you will be rewarded in the future."[11]

How many investors building investments for retirement—for plain old self-sufficiency—are interested in twenty years of being *even* with inflation? Or that *over 200 years*, not selling in a bear market means you will be rewarded "in the future"?

This suggests, not that stocks are for the long run, but rather, that in the long run, we are all dead. And probably preceded by not having enough money, which more data will show us next.

Innovations Haven't Increased Household Net Worth

Tax-advantaged accounts, such as 401(k) plans, postulate that a high return on pre-tax contributions compensates for anything other than hyperinflation. But this is no solution. During tough times, companies cut back on their employer matches and employees reduce or eliminate their contributions.[12] Some people simply prefer foregoing "free" money—pretax and allowing greater future returns—to have cash now. Job loss takes away the choice of whether to have the benefits at all. Even among those who retain jobs and contribute to 401(k) plans, 22 percent had borrowed from their accounts by the end of 2010, which precludes them from further investing until they've paid off the loan.

No wonder the average balance in these accounts, for those over age 55 with ten years participation, was only $233,800 as of the end of March 2011. Overall, including those with or without a tax-advantaged plan, in 2011 the average 55- to 65-year-old had a net worth of $180,125 and the average for those 65 and older was $232,000.[13] These amounts are simply insufficient as a base for old-age support[14]—and this is for the oldest, richest group in society, the large mid-boomer age cohort.

Among those who do save and invest, most unknowingly confuse stock market expectations with the concept of "store of value," which is the notion that there is something absolutely safe—gold, real estate, timber, farmland, livestock, government debt, or stocks—that will retain value through all known and unknown events. In *Wealth, War and Wisdom*,[15] Barton Biggs studied data to determine if any investment vehicle was able to retain value through the worldwide dislocation of World War II, including inflation, periodic market closings and, in the case of eastern European countries and those absorbed into the U.S.S.R., tens of millions of investors, business owners, and landowners who endured 50-year market closes, worthless currencies, and the elimination of private property.

His conclusion? The best you can do is own some land with livestock, crops, and water. But, he emphasizes, even if you do have some, the neighboring have-nots will likely have more guns.

Most investors want both some "store of value" *and* real returns above inflation. They accept the necessity of stocks and the stock market, but they need the mindset of the short seller to manage stock risk. A short seller's approach to risk, when combined with a sound, value-managed long side, is as close to the holy grail of store of value plus real returns as is possible for stocks.

The best long strategy is small-cap value, according to research by Eugene Fama and Kenneth French.[16] The problem is that there is massive year-to-year volatility. The money manager employing this strategy alone would have had, for instance, a terrible 2008 followed by an incredible 2009. Because these peaks and troughs, even amid superior long-term performance, scare away most investors, few registered investment advisors (RIA) dare to use it, for fear of going out of business. RIAs accept the market average, also a ready defense against liability.

But investors, money managers, and clients can obtain substantial compounding of absolute and relative returns. On the long side, this requires a small-cap value strategy and catalyst-driven special situations, using liquidation value, activist investing, corporate restructurings, and more. Such a strategy was developed by Benjamin Graham and used by his student, Warren Buffett, during his hedge-fund days prior to closing the fund and running Berkshire Hathaway full time, and it is supported by extensive studies analyzed in Tweedy Browne's comprehensive overview.[17] Small-cap value (which Tom presents in Chapter 6) when combined with the short techniques in this book, grows returns better than long investing alone.

Value is well known and studied exhaustively, while risk analysis and the practices of short sellers are not. Whether we entrust our money to others, invest it ourselves, or invest client money, we need to understand and employ the tools necessary to recognize aggressive accounting. This allows investors to avoid the blowups or use them for profit and to manage risk in a long-short portfolio. Lose less, make more.

Here are just a few of the reasons why learning to recognize aggressive accounting in order to avoid losers or, like short sellers, profit from it is essential to risk management and investing profits.

Lowest Average Cost Doesn't Win

Legg Mason's Bill Miller was perhaps the best-known proponent of the view that lowest average costs wins, yet the formerly record-holding mutual fund manager blew up all his accumulated gains through individual stock cataclysms. He owned all the infamous losers in the first decade of 2000—Enron, Freddie Mac, WorldCom, Wachovia, Bear Stearns, and AIG. Value investors act contrary to the market by averaging down to gain a better price on businesses *they know well*. Miller clearly didn't know what he was buying well enough to justify taking extreme contrary positions with such large percentages of the portfolio.

The problem, to use one of his numerous disasters as the extreme example, is that, if you dollar-cost average a Bear Stearns that loses almost everything—it doesn't matter. You're finished. Do it enough times, and your pockets are inside out. The index, at least, is not going to zero, but individual stocks can. So if you dollar-cost average anything other than an index, you still have the problem of how to avoid the portfolio-destroying disasters. Repeat: With just a few blowups, Miller eliminated all his years of breaking records as the manager with the longest consistent streak of outperforming the S&P 500.[18]

To buy any individual stock, let alone take any contrary market position, you have to be able to identify earnings quality concerns in your companies' financials, and you have to stay away from anything you don't understand well enough to do so.

The Index Is No Panacea

The universal stock performance benchmark, the S&P 500, is in many ways a momentum-investing tool. It works this way: As more and more investors buy a stock, the price rises, which brings a higher market capitalization. At some point the stock may reach the size at which it moves up the ladder of market caps into the S&P 500. If the stock increases more, it carries a greater share of the S&P 500 index itself, which is market-cap weighted. At the same time, investors may desert other companies in the index. These companies then drop in market cap and eventually fall off the index, representing a smaller share of it on the way.

Therefore, stocks' greatest gains may precede entry into the august group of the top 500. The more they rise, the less they can gain on a percentage basis. If you are ExxonMobil with the number one market cap in 2011, what will it take to go up 10 percent, or 25 percent, let alone 50 percent or 100 percent? (Note: We believe that 2012's number one company, Apple, is not typical—and at writing still not all that expensive. But when it or any company becomes such an overwhelming percentage of the index and you own it, it becomes doubly important to hedge.) And if you are a large company and your stock declines, the decline is far weightier. Ten years ago Yahoo! and AOL and Cisco Systems were all near the top of the S&P 500. Not today.

There are many index options available, but each has its own issues—whether it's the broad Wilshire 5000 which, in effect, becomes an index for the economy, or an equal-weighted index, or one of the indexes of various market capitalization stocks where winners leave the index.

Indexes are the best of poor alternatives for anyone not investing in individual stocks. The minute that investors choose stocks, they have to learn about earnings quality.

The Real Investing World We Live In

Financial professionals really have no choice but to give clients what they want, like the familiar and "safe" Coca-Cola, Pepsi, Microsoft, Intel, and ExxonMobil. The RIA is hamstrung by human nature. Clients want risk-less real returns, but they don't know what that means. So Steve the RIA delivers the average, and in a bad year, he says, this is what the market did. He's the broker equivalent of the company information technology professional who buys Microsoft or IBM or Intel products because he won't lose his job if there's trouble ("everyone else has it"), but risks los-ing it if he buys a lesser-known company's better product that later causes problems.

RIAs rely heavily on modern portfolio theory and its asset-allocation practice. Most buy mutual funds representing supposed asset classes—growth, value, large cap and small cap stocks, gold, bonds, and so on—that ostensibly act differently from each other. Then they follow a strict percentage allocation among the funds and rebalance regularly—quarterly or annually—to return the funds to the correct percentage. This means that, if the mutual fund manager does well, RIAs who own the fund for clients sell that fund. No wonder mutual-fund managers are commonly compensated for being within a few percentage points of the market aver-age and not for beating the benchmark by more than a few points.

Investors must learn enough about real risk from aggressive account-ing to manage their own money, client money, or those who manage it for them, but no one really wants to hear about it. Optimism sells. From as long ago as when Edwin Lefèvre's *Reminiscences of a Stock Operator*[19] chronicled early twentieth-century shorting, and even after the accounting scandals of the boom ending in 2000, it's still considered un-American at best and criminally manipulative at worst to focus on anything negative about a company—let alone in a company's reported information—that could affect its stock. Short-side thinking seldom appears in the *Wall Street Journal* or the *Financial Times* (whatever other considerable merits we find in these fine publications). The worst you'll encounter is someone advising caution or that a stock is "overbought." True risk management—not just mediocre mimicking of the overall market—doesn't sell. Blind and baseless promotion does.

The indexes reinforce the mythical stock market where something—somewhere—is enduring, when it isn't. The indexes themselves are anything but. The retail investor is not going to pick only winners, and the indexes don't help, because of their structure and human nature. Successful professionals will have too much money under management to reap real returns on the long side alone, because they can't buy the less liquid small caps that Fama and French proved outperform. They can't accumulate big enough positions to make a difference in their returns— "move the needle"—and so are restricted to large caps that mirror the indexes and the economy. Or they will fail to employ the short-side mindset to avoid massive drawdowns. There simply are neither indexes nor individual stocks for the long term.

With the tools in this book, investors will increase their chances of achieving high real returns by weeding out or avoiding the stocks that perform so poorly that they will ruin overall returns and possibly destroy capital permanently.

Everyone will have poor performers, even among stocks with good financials and business operations. No one ever has all the information about any investment, or about the future. But poor performers with fictitious revenue or deteriorating balance sheets are different. They can be identified, sold, or avoided. Savvy investors can attempt to profit from them by shorting the stocks. We believe that no investor must short a stock—though it can enhance returns. But we do believe that the short-selling expert's tools—and the shorting mindset—can lead to successful investing, simply by avoiding the statistical basement revealed by the data.

This book does not advocate or explain shorting or selling based on overvaluation, fads, frauds, or poor business models, even though these make up the overwhelming majority of stocks sold short. Surprisingly, very bright fundamental investors—those who do bottom-up research on companies and their industries—will only short on these bases, even though they are willing to go long on stocks with specific catalysts. It's as if investors with enormous skill at ferreting out value where no one else can find it suddenly have memory loss on the short side.

Why are these poor bases for shorting? Because overvaluation can continue indefinitely. Fads can do very well against all odds for a long time, not least because those who follow the fad will buy the stock. Frauds are very hard to identify until after the fact. China frauds in 2010–2011 fooled brilliant investors who had decades of success. Trying to identify business models that will fail is extremely difficult; determining *when* they will fail is all but impossible. Doing so requires that the investor be right, even when being right is impossible to know and the risks of being wrong are devastating.

Shorting or selling on those bases is simply too hard, risky, and unnecessary. We recommend waiting until there is aggressive revenue recognition, weakening balance sheets, and deteriorating cash flow trends. It's the flip side of value-with-catalyst, which is fundamental analysis of value *combined with a catalyst for stock market buying to boost the price to realize that value* (see Chapter 6). So too, on the short side. Wait until there are negative catalysts for profits in the near future—a year or two at most, the rough time period that the value-with-catalyst investor seeks. It's easier and more effective, the equivalent of "don't fire until you see the whites of their eyes."

What They Do and What They Miss

It's useful to look more closely at why those who insist on shorting only fads, frauds, and failing business models and those whose methods mean they have to be right, are wrong.

The conventional short seller's first target is fads. This mindset says that a company like shoemaker Crocs will make money with a one-trick pony until a fickle public turns to the next thing and the stock dies. Here and elsewhere, short sellers short the stock and watch with disbelief as it rises until margin calls put them in a hospital bed.

Next come frauds, situations where short sellers are certain that fraud will send a stock to zero. How can they know? Legions of China small-cap stocks proved fraudulent in late 2010 and early 2011 and destroyed investors. Even cautious value analysts and money managers like John Paulson, famed for making billions with foresight of the housing collapse, took acid baths on these. Who knew that these and Tyco, WorldCom, Enron, and Elan were elaborately choreographed frauds until they were revealed to be? The handful that raised any questions were isolated. The media and company spin drowned them out.

The third favorite of the short investor is failure of a business model. As Netflix shares zoomed almost ten times from early 2009 to July 2011, investors all along the way were sure Netflix would fail, given the increasing cost of its content, competition from low-cost or free outlets such as Hulu, and other factors (see Figure 1.2). Well-known money manager Whitney Tilson shorted the stock and in December 2010 began a public written exchange with CEO Reed Hastings. (It was educational and riveting, and both deserve credit for putting themselves on the line.) Hastings converted him; Tilson covered his short at a loss in February 2011.

Unfortunately, Tilson's short case was eventually proven correct as shares that shot to $300 collapsed in stages to the $70s as the year came to an end.[20] Even the experienced are susceptible to human psychology and investment-world reality. How many investors shorting on the way up—a long steady rise—can withstand the broker's margin calls on during that rise until the stock crashes (see Figure 1.2)?

The last of the four flawed shorting characteristics is that of the short seller who "needs to be right." If the short seller is in the business of profiting from shorts only, rather than managing risk in a long-short portfolio through avoiding disasters beforehand, there is no choice: That short seller must be right. Professional short sellers must build substantial stakes in short bets, so even one going against them big time can destroy their business. Long-short investors can face problems when the short side of the portfolio goes seriously against them, but there is far less risk of permanently losing capital than there is for the short-only investor.

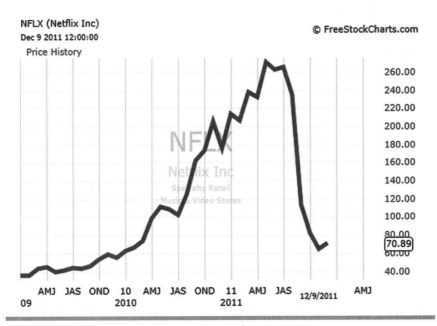

Figure 1.2 Netflix Stock 2009 to December 9, 2011.
Source: www.freestockcharts.com, by permission.

These four shorting characteristics provide no real risk management, but others can. This book's unique tools do short sellers one better by making money in both bull markets—when short sellers can have real problems—and bear markets. That's the difference between a short seller and a risk manager. Our tools manage risk in a way that works, no matter which direction the market is moving.

The case studies that follow show you how to use short sellers' tools to manage risk, how to figure out which stocks you own should go, how to avoid others, and how to short some that may have even made money for you before, investing long.

Before we look at the case studies, we should note that there's nothing magical or mysterious here. If you want to manage your risk, you need what Charlie Munger, vice-chairman of Berkshire Hathaway, defines in his characteristically blunt style as assiduity: "You gotta sit on your ass and do it." Everything in this book is about information available for anyone to read. The problem is that most people don't read it—and if they do, they don't read critically. So, while companies provide the information, there is so much there that most don't look at or know what it is that they're looking at.

The first and most superficial level of communication from companies whose stocks you own are their press releases. PR departments take management information and spin it to reinforce the investor's need to believe in an endlessly rosy future. The critical reader can glean tipoffs, but the volume of this material makes it an inefficient use of time.

Annual reports can be worse, glossy feel-good letters, rising charts, happy employees, and customers made giddy by the company's products. This is about selling, selling, selling, and obfuscation. In one startling act of marketing and hubris during the biotech boom, photographs in Human Genome Sciences' annual report for 2000 posed members of top management similarly to figures in the famous classical art behind them. (It's easy to sympathize with the analyst who called it the "cheesiest thing" he had ever seen, but despite his accuracy here we suggest he get out more.[21])

Don't be distracted! The *real* bodies aren't posing. They're buried in the footnotes.

The next level is the Wall Street analyst report. These report authors are called sell-side analysts, because they want to sell their bank's services to management, and they are cautious about writing anything critical. These include the toady analyst you hear on quarterly conference calls saying, "Great quarter, guys." The reports may contain nuggets of useful industry information, but they won't help you learn about risks for the specific company the analysts are courting.

The only information that matters comes from the company's filings with the SEC. The real information is in the actual filing's pages, and, more important, in the footnotes, where the data aren't always presented in easy-to-read tables. Even some of the best analysts' eyes glaze over at footnotes, but that's where management discloses what the law says it must. Some of the best short sellers—whether short-only or managers of a long-short portfolio—miss or do superficial analysis of these details, because they focus on fads, frauds, failures, and the need to be right.

Fads

Crocs is a great example of a fad. These colorful shoes hit the market, and within months everyone had them—from children to your least fashion-conscious friend. Among investors, just about everyone *knew* rubber shoes wouldn't survive the usual economic boom and bust—a full market cycle. By definition, a fad is going to be exciting for a while and then peter out. When that happened at Crocs, the company wouldn't have other revenue channels through which to grow the business. But none of this makes a stock a good short, because people tend to buy consumer fads, and often, in the excitement, buy the stock, and momentum investors grab on for the ride.

Indeed, Crocs catapulted over six times, from $12 to $80. A lot of people made money; fads can be very, very profitable for the upside investor if entrance and exit are properly timed. But attempts to time the market can teach you some very harsh lessons (in Chapters 7 and 8, we'll look at when market timing is warranted and can work).

There were plenty of investors shorting the stock at every price from $12 on up, and for many, this was what happened. Shorting stock requires a loan of shares from your broker. When the price of the stock you shorted (borrowed and sold) rises, your broker issues a margin call—requires you to put up cash against the loan to cover the rise in the stock's price. Many investors who were short Crocs, got margin calls they couldn't meet, were forced to cover (buy back the stock), and suffered enormous losses. This is why simply finding a fad and shorting it can never be called risk management. It's *added* risk.

Crocs did eventually drop like a Mafia victim in cement (not rubber!) overshoes, but it was only a great short when it fell from its high of

$80 back into the $50s and $60s, because that's when John's accounting analysis flagged the stock, finding the inventory issues buried in the footnotes. They also extended payment terms that got picked up in the DSO. There were crocks of Crocs in the stores and even more stacking up in their warehouse. It was foolhardy to short the stock before that, even though it was overvalued—selling for multiples of the little earnings it had—because there was no way to know that popularity wouldn't drive the stock higher. An overvalued stock can simply become more overvalued.

But when signs showed that the revenue was accelerated—the extended payment terms gave customers the incentive to take on inventory even when inventory was already piling up—the company would no longer be able to sustain its growth trajectory. The catalyst was coming. When Crocs issued earnings reports showing increasing inventory— inventory it could not sell and which clearly made the growing revenues look unsustainable—the stock was in the $50s and $60s. As Figure 1.3 shows, the market soon figured out what John had already seen, and Crocs' stock price plummeted to single digits.

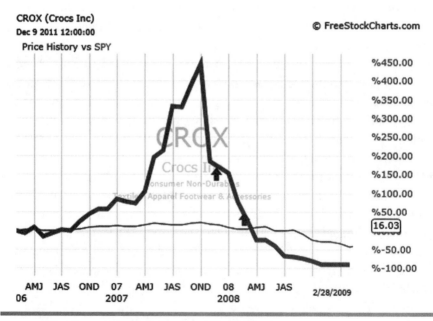

Figure 1.3   Crocs: 2006–February 28, 2009.
Source: www.freestockcharts.com, by permission.

Did it hurt anyone to wait? No, and this is one fundamental thing about short selling that is so obvious that it is confounding—and ignored. You make as much money shorting a stock that falls from $70 to $5 (93 percent) as one that falls from $100 to $5 (95 percent). Waiting for the right time isn't going to cost you money—in fact, it means you make money before the retail investor no longer props it up and the accounting issues can bring the real profits. Figure 1.3 shows this principle, where shorting at each black arrow point led to similar gains.

A likely fad stock in the making is Rovio, the Finnish company that developed the hugely popular game Angry Birds. At this writing, Rovio has raised $42 million in venture capital and plans to go public in a few years. Short sellers will be watching. If Rovio does go public, it's very possible that everyone not a child who loves Angry Birds will buy the stock. They will ignore the fact that electronic gaming is a remarkably difficult and fickle business in which to have repeat successes. It will make a lot of money for many people. But the time to short will be only when accounting analysis shows that the revenues aren't real or aren't sustainable. The Angry Birds thumb drives at Staples don't bother us— yet. We wouldn't short Rovio until seeing the whites of those Angry Birds' beady eyes—when the revenue and earnings growth can't continue.

What does this mean for you if you don't want to short? Understand why you bought a stock. Know when your love of a product or a company or the buzz about one or the other has added risk to your portfolio because you're following a fad. Avoiding the stock because it's a fad makes sense, but buying it isn't irrational when you can take advantage of the fad stock's buyers. The problem is that holding it can be terminal, if you can't or won't look to see when the fad is going the other way, such as when inventory buildup signals the end of consumer demand. When you find this, sell in order to pocket your gains or reduce losses.

Frauds

Short sellers take on unnecessary risk by focusing on fraud because frauds are preceded by accounting issues that can be identified.

Enron fell from the sky to bankruptcy in 2001, but forensic accountants weren't surprised. It was clear the revenue wasn't real if you knew where to look—and even if you didn't. When the lonely but astute analyst pointed this out in an April 17, 2001, earnings conference call, Enron CEO Jeffrey Skilling called him an unprintable name. Every major financial news organization covered this event. That should have been a red flag for every investor to start looking harder at everything Enron was saying and doing.

The problem is that constantly looking for fraud clouds your judgment. If you require a manager to be a crook, you start focusing on things you can't know—the particular details that can prove a fraud, such as actually lying about products, sales, and more. It's impossible to know when the lie is told and practiced, because people hide it. You might see indications, but if you are both wrong and short, you can lose a lot of money. If you're just trying to figure out what to hold and what to sell, you can end up selling too soon or churning your account to the point that you can't make any money.

Our process focuses on revenue. Until we see revenue problems— revenues that may be falling while inventories build and credit terms lengthen—we won't bet on whether a company is a fraud. It is rational to want to short a fraud, but the correct focus is not on whether a manager is lying, but on whether a company is practicing financial chicanery.

Business Failures

Short sellers rightly look for business models that can fail, but they can't know *when* to short without a specific catalyst that, if it materializes, will kill the company's model and let them profit (or if you own it long, destroy your wealth). What many people do is say that some company, usually one with a massively high multiple of earnings or free cash flow, can't continue. But it can, and it can do so indefinitely—that's an "open situation." A good example of the former is the municipal bond insurer Ambac, whose business model was unsustainable. Examples of the latter are Netflix, which had a high multiple that just got higher and higher until the edifice cracked, and the restaurant reservations system OpenTable.

Because the incentives to take on more debt are so great for certain businesses, and because, throughout history, credit has ebbed and flowed, spending time on the Ambac case may pay you back many times over in your investing life.

Ambac founded the municipal bond insurance (monoline) business in 1971, providing insurance to governments and companies against the possibility that the issuer of a bond they had bought would default. This would leave the insured short of assets and less able to meet its own obligations.

When buying a policy from any insurance company, the insured expects that the insurer will pay if the triggering event occurs—whether a car crash, death, medical cost, flood, or hail damage to a roof. Ambac's customers paid for protection against the event of the bond issuer's default.

Regulators require insurers to maintain capital levels against potential claims. The regulators don't require capital equal to the potential losses from all policies, just as they do not require banks to maintain capital to cover all mortgages defaulting. These businesses make money taking in more than they pay out. They make more money by evaluating risk, so that they do not face losses equal either to their current capital or capital they can raise through debt.

The industry faces a dilemma. Insurers must maintain prudent underwriting standards so as not to face losses that wipe out their capital. But to make more profits for shareholders, they must also raise capital through debt—becoming more "leveraged"—to cover more potential losses, write more policies, and collect more premiums. There is an inherent tension between underwriting standards and profits generated through more policies and more debt leverage. We know from the credit crisis that banks, for example, threw underwriting standards to the wind to lend more to anyone. When the mortgages defaulted, the banks couldn't cover their losses and blew up.

Ambac chose to raise more and more capital to maintain higher profitability. The credit rating agencies—as they did with countless others— rated Ambac highly, so lenders lent scads of money to Ambac at low cost. Because Ambac had a high credit rating, it attracted customers whose own lenders would delight at Ambac's high rating and lend to Ambac's insureds at lower rates. Everyone fed at the easy-money trough.

But Ambac went to the edge of the cliff. It insured collateralized debt obligations (CDOs), comprised of assets including mortgages. We all know what happened to all but the highest quality mortgages in the small minority of high-quality CDOs, and at this writing there is no sign that the United States or many other countries are in sight of recovery. Money is tight again.

The key point we make here is that the time to short Ambac was not when it was leveraged 125 to 1.[22] If credit had continued flowing like Niagara Falls, Ambac and countless others could conceivably have stayed on the merry-go-round indefinitely. This was the same situation that led investment banks like Lehmann Brothers to lever assets to shareholder equity as much as 30 to 1, with disastrous results.[23]

In a bull market, you can use leverage, make acquisitions, and do all sorts of things, because easy credit allows almost any business to raise money. But as we know from 2008, credit markets can seize up faster than a motor with no oil when the market turns bearish. When the money tap is turned off, a business model that depends on huge leverage suddenly dries up and becomes unsustainable. That's the catalyst and when you should short a business model. Once John saw the credit market dry up, he shorted Ambac, which eventually went bankrupt.

Until fall 2011, the most public business failure debate concerned whether Netflix was a good short. Many investors had made piles of money on its stock, which seemed only to move up. The skeptics' major arguments were that it was selling at such high multiples that growth couldn't keep up and that deals with the content providers would be renegotiated at higher rates that hurt margins, meaning that the high multiples would contract and the stock would dive.

For years, management did a brilliant job managing the transition from mailing of discs to online streaming. Netflix had more subscribers than the largest cable company, Comcast, and had increased market share and reduced the costs of sending out DVDs. All of this boosted the company's revenues and profits. There were no signs of accounting manipulation to make Netflix look better than it was.

Netflix was an "open situation." There was nothing yet to keep the stock from going up, even if in the long run it might face ruin or competition. Few businesses—even first movers like Netflix—see their advantage exist forever. But why short "hoping" for a decline in five, ten, or more years? You have to see management using accounting aggressively to mask deterioration in their business. Until then, the situation is "wide open."

Netflix shares multiplied almost six-fold in 18 months and tripled in 14 to July 2011. Those who shorted on valuation got destroyed. Meanwhile, the company continued buying back shares without regard to valuation, even as its share price exceeded bubble-era multiples. When buybacks are not opportunistic, they mask options grants or—worse—raise the question of whether they are specifically to transfer shareholder wealth to options holders and insider sellers. Worst, at the time that the buybacks continued without regard to valuation, CEO Hastings was selling under a prearranged trading program—not illegal, but not good.

On top of that, Hastings was spending valuable time engaging money manager Whitney Tilson to convince him that his Netflix short investment case was wrong.[24] Then the company bungled communications over what it might do with its physical disc business and shares plummeted. And when Netflix revealed at its third quarter report on October 24, 2011, that it had lost 810,000 subscribers[25] and admitted that it would be unprofitable for the next quarter, the stock collapsed 35 percent in one day to $77. It's hard to believe Hastings didn't see the trouble ahead when the company was buying back stock at $218 and he was making the bull case in public debating Tilson.

Another open situation was the aptly named OpenTable, debated almost as widely as Netflix. For a time, who could say that every restaurant in America that takes reservations wouldn't be using OpenTable? And then other countries? Or that some company like Amazon or eBay or Google (who knows?) wouldn't pay a huge premium to add it to its arsenal? Indeed, Google ponied up for Zagat for the first signs of competition.

Then holes began to form in the OpenTable cloth. It changed the amortization period for its software installation, using a reduced customer life—the period it retains a restaurant customer—which makes revenue and earnings look good, but only by borrowing from both down the road. Its frontloading revenue recognition was confirmed by weak deferred revenue trends. Days sales outstanding (DSO)—the time between when the company makes a sale and receives the revenue—rose dramatically, suggesting that customers had trouble paying, or that the company extended more favorable terms, or both. The stock was a profitable short in late 2011. (Later, a buyback forced a short squeeze. It was a poor company allocation of capital and a short-term fix only, so OpenTable again became a profitable short.)

The time to sell or short is not when you think a business model can't survive. The time is when the numbers suggest that management is covering up poor performance and when the stock has already begun to fall. We want to time our actions by seeing specific catalysts through our detailed financial statement analysis of revenues, inventory, accounts receivable, loss reserves, and more.

Having to Be Right

Typical short sellers have to take large positions and defend them—often publicly and for a long time—in order to make money. They are not risk managers; they are money managers who see their circle of competence—their best chance to make money—as identifying fads, frauds, and failing business models and betting big. Short sellers who do not have a long-short portfolio—who only short—cannot afford to be wrong. Thus, they are the most vocal and public promoters of their positions.

By running a long-short portfolio, managers can use shorting to manage risk and can simply close a position when it goes against them. Yet you still see them writing and presenting a "terminal short"—a short only worth it because it's "sure" to go to zero. Why do they have to short only when they see a 100 percent gain as a "sure thing" (a short can only gain 100 percent) when, at the same time, they will make a long investment in an undervalued stock with a 40 or 60 percent upside? Plus, despite having declared a "terminal short," many cover the short right away, closing the position with only a slight profit. Long investors seem to lose all sense when they turn to shorting. This deprives them of the real benefits of a long-short portfolio.

But there is a difference between being right and making money. Many very good long investors—excellent at valuation and business analysis—don't fully grasp quality of earnings and signs of aggressive accounting. They may know enough to be comfortable avoiding a stock, but they lack confidence when it comes to identifying negative catalysts to actually short the stock.

The main reason for this aversion is this: You have unlimited gains on the long side versus, at most, a 100 percent loss. But a short offers at most a 100 percent gain versus potentially unlimited losses. But show us an investor who actually holds a short that goes against them extremely. Earnings quality analysts don't short without analyzing short interest and days to cover in order to avoid the squeezes that lead to margin calls, covering at any cost, and catastrophic losses. The "unlimited losses" argument is only relevant to the unprepared short seller.

Two Metrics to Avoid Being Wrong

Whether selling a stock to avoid a blowup in your portfolio or to actively short, it's essential to know some considerations that aren't necessary to investing on the long side. If a lot of shares are sold short and the stock is thinly traded, the slightest good news could be very bad. Many people have borrowed shares, betting on a decline, after which they will return the shares to the lender and pocket the difference. If things go the wrong way and volume isn't high, they can get stuck having to cover their short (buy the shares back to deliver to the lender) at *any* price as it rockets up from increased demand. Let's look at the two key ways to avoid this pain: percentage of float sold short and days to cover.

For the first, use online sources to find the amount of shares shorted of a stock. Compare that to the float. Float means the shares that can be freely traded any given day, excluding restricted shares, insider holdings, and shares held by those with more than 5 percent ownership. The higher the percentage of shares sold short (short interest) of float, the greater the risk that any positive news can send shares soaring, because demand will exceed supply. This is a classic short squeeze. The short sellers' losses mount, they begin to cover, and their buying drives the price up further. No wonder any investor who ignores this metric often endures painful losses.

The second metric is days to cover. Here, divide short interest by average daily share volume traded. This is an indicator of how tough it would be if all the short sellers had to cover at once. If days to cover are low, there is likely enough volume to allow short sellers to exit their positions relatively easily. If days to cover are many, then the risk of not being able to exit as prices rise is too high, and the dreaded short squeeze looms again.

The best way is to focus on aggressive accounting and avoid shorting where everyone else is also doing it, such as with fads or suspected frauds. It's a head-scratcher why contrarian investors on the long side don't check to see how much company they have on the short side.

Instead of needing to be right, wait for the obvious indicator of accounting trouble and act then. You have your negative catalyst. This reduces risk and also the need to be massively right on one single position or risk serious portfolio loss through a couple of short positions in a long-short portfolio. This guarantees a two-fold edge. Tactically manage positions. Do not make massive bets on fads and ride them through a market cycle. Use fundamental and trading skills where your advantage is greatest: in accounting. You are less likely to get destroyed in any position and definitely not overall.

Sometimes, even if you are right, you still can be wrong. America Online (AOL) was making people rich before it merged with Time Warner and crashed. On October 26, 1998, AOL had a P/E ratio of 205, yet it broke out and zoomed. Anyone shorting on valuation was in a world of hurt when AOL peaked in April 1999 at a P/E of (ready?) 532! You can lose capital permanently with just one trade like that. The ambulance doesn't get there in time.

But a lot of successful short sellers didn't bet against the company on valuation, which would be bad enough, because everyone who had an

AOL account was an owner or potential buyer of the stock. There actually was an accounting issue. Sensible, sound investors shorted, based on AOL's capitalizing marketing expenses, treating them as an asset. AOL took its marketing expense off its income statement, which inflated its earnings per share.

The catch is that by the time this accounting issue of 1995 and 1996 had passed, it didn't make a difference. The company no longer needed the capitalization of an expense to appear profitable. Nothing was fictitious about AOL's revenue, which grew an astonishing 50 percent to 100 percent per quarter as the company dominated its space. The eventual small SEC fine was a mosquito bite. The short sellers did indeed identify an accounting issue. It just didn't matter.

In this book we emphasize how financial analysis prevents the mistake where an investor unearths an accounting issue but does not understand whether it matters or not in the real world. AOL was playing with accounting by capitalizing expenses, but it wasn't playing with revenue. It can be a terrible sign if a company capitalizes marketing expenses, but not when, as with AOL, demand is so explosive that revenue growth overwhelms the expense issue, just as a skyscraper overwhelms the old house next door that a recalcitrant owner refused to sell. The next chapter is on revenue recognition, because almost all aggressive accounting and earnings quality issues originate there.

That's one reason why our process helps categorize accounting issues according to the most problematic. The best situation is aggressive revenue recognition masking softening demand. Those who did not see the revenue for the capitalized expenses—the accounting forest for the trees—and shorted AOL got killed and weren't around to profit when the stock did finally collapse after the merger with Time Warner.[26]

Focus on the real accounting issues and don't let the accounting grain of sand distract you from the beach as at AOL. Keep away from the emotion of having to be right.

Minimize Loss, Maximize Wealth

The rest of this book looks at how to use the short seller's toolkit to avoid the traps and time our actions. We're going to show how we identify aggressive accounting, manage risk, and tactically manage positions.

Focusing on risk management, rather than making big profits from shorting, is a good way to manage your portfolio risk and keep growing your wealth. After all, as the tech and housing crashes have shown us, one of the very best ways to make money is by avoiding loss. Learn how to look at the fine print, and you can make and keep money passing on, selling or yes, even shorting, many stocks. We will show you when to make a change in your portfolio and how to spot that right moment. Most people see only the money they make from their successes, but the reality is that they can make as much or more by not losing it all on one stock or a bear market. Minimize risk and loss and you maximize wealth.

But what we do also works in bull markets. So bull or bear market, any investing weather, this is why the correct short-selling analysis works.

We open and close with this simple point: Most stocks lose money. Why should it be yours?

Chapter 2

Aggressive Revenue Recognition

Take It from the Top

Revenue is the top line of the income statement for a reason: It is the lifeblood of any company. Investors scrutinize trends in revenue growth to assess the strength of a company's performance. But despite revenue's crucial importance, they don't question it nearly as much as other income statement items, such as earnings per share. The conventional wisdom is that revenue is harder to manipulate than EPS, leading some to include price/sales ratios in their analysis. Yet there are many ways management can mask a slowdown by manipulating the top line.

Any investor with a few years' experience reading financial statements and a willingness to work can detect revenue manipulation. Yet most don't, because reading footnotes seems like an arduous task. So management persists in massaging revenue in numerous ways to mask underlying weakness in a company's reported results, because they can. Because the rest of the financials depend on revenue, it deserves the most scrutiny. Any doubt about the sustainability of revenue throws the rest of the financial model into question. Indeed, the financial fish rots from the revenue head.

Starting with the income statement, Figure 2.1 shows how to prioritize concerns from the top down.

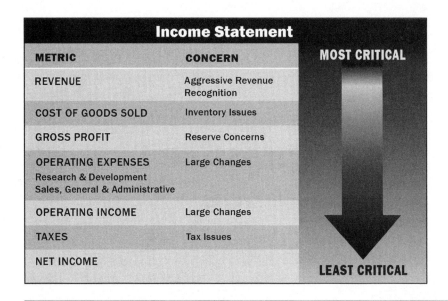

Figure 2.1 Income statement: most critical to least critical earnings quality concerns.
Source: John Del Vecchio, © 2011.

It's commonplace to hear value investors say that, of the three financial statements, the income statement is the least important and that the cash flow statement and balance sheet are paramount. But revenue is a key driver of all three statements.

Accurate revenue is crucial to confidence in cash flow, because the bottom line of the income statement—net income—is the top line of the cash flow statement. Investors read the cash flow statement in many ways, calculating Warren Buffett's owner's earnings; so-called "true" free cash flow, which includes changes in working capital; free cash flow to the firm; and more. But it is just as important to know whether revenue manipulation affects the quality and sustainability of cash flow.

Revenue affects the balance sheet, too. Consider deferred revenue, which can signal that demand for a company's products is waning or that the company aggressively recognizes revenue. Revenue ties all three financial statements together. Revenue recognition is not the only element of earnings quality analysis, but it absolutely is the most critical.

Realized or Realizable and Earned

Revenue is recognized when it is earned, but the timing is open to interpretation. The Financial Accounting Standards Board (FASB) has provided some concepts to guide management,[1] but they leave enough discretion to lead to questionable practices and results.

Revenue is "realized" when goods, services, merchandise, or other assets are exchanged for cash or claims to cash. There is a large difference between a dollar deposited in the company checking account and having a claim on one. Not for nothing do they say "a bird in hand is worth two in the bush." Claims to cash may require collection, and not everything may be collected. Revenues realized today according to this definition vary from certain to iffy.

"Realizable" is murky too. Revenues are "realizable" when the receivables are "readily convertible to known amounts of cash or claims to cash." Instead of a *claim* to cash, the company can "readily convert" to "known amounts" of "claims to cash." Management perceptions of types of claims may and do differ.

"Earned" revenues allow management the most latitude for questionable practices. Here, revenues are earned when the company "has substantially accomplished what it must do to be entitled to the benefits represented by the revenues." It doesn't take a lawyer to find room in "substantially," "must," "entitled," and "benefits" for whatever timing the company wants.

With such gray definitions, management can wiggle, especially for intangibles, such as software. Evaluating whether management sticks to the straight and narrow or pushes the limits tells you how much confidence you can have in management and whether the company's earnings quality is likely to be poor or good.

Here are some of the factors that we analyze to determine the quality of the company's revenue. And at the top is a metric you should have burned into your memory: *days sales outstanding*.

Days Sales Outstanding

A business wants to be paid as soon as possible. The longer it takes for customers to pay invoices, the more that company in essence provides no-interest customer financing—becoming a lender intentionally or not. Receivables can warn of a slowing economy, sure, but investors don't own the economy. They own specific companies that may or may not track the economy, and if they do so negatively, may want to put off showing it. Tracking receivables is crucial, because trends may show, not only poorer customer financial condition, but also that the company may be changing customers' payment terms to keep things looking good.

How many days it takes a company to be paid, on average across its customer base, is called days sales outstanding (DSO). Changes in DSO tell us a lot about whether the payment terms have shifted. More favorable payment terms often equal more aggressive revenue recognition. To calculate DSO[2]:

$$DSO = 91.25 \times (Accounts\ Receivable/Quarterly\ Revenue)$$

By tracking the receivables over several quarters—a moving average—we get a better sense of the trend. We want to compare the quarter's DSO both year-over-year (to account for business seasonality) as well as sequentially (from one quarter to the following). Changes can come from economic slowdowns, poor collection, and so on, but the practice we want to catch is a change in payment terms that borrows revenue from the future to make this quarter look better than it is.

Here is the key point that Wall Street gets wrong almost 100 percent of the time. Often, a company will report higher DSO, implying looser payment terms. Then management will comment in the quarterly conference call that the customers are of high quality, with good credit, so the company expects to collect on the receivables, and there is no risk to collection (la la la). Wall Street analysts usually take management's word for it and then regurgitate this explanation in their own research reports.

This is absolutely wrong! Higher DSO has *nothing* to do with collection but *everything* to do with revenue recognition. If the company did not offer extended terms, it wouldn't have been able to book the revenue in that particular quarter, *regardless of whether it collects on the receivables*. The company uses looser terms to pull revenue forward into the current quarter. This is called "stuffing the channel." Here's how it works.

Stuffing the Channel

A company may realize that the current quarter won't meet Wall Street expectations, which may lead investors who are focused on quarterly results to sell the stock. Management might offer extended payment terms to induce customers to accelerate the purchase of goods and services so the company can book the revenue in the current period, boost results, and avoid a stock sell-off.

This actually happens a lot more than people think. Let's say it's June 28, with two days to go in the quarter and the company has booked only 80 percent of expected quarterly revenue. It's in a bit of a jam. The CEO gets on a plane. He and his team sit across the table from you, a customer they know is all but certain to buy in the *next* quarter. That's why they pick you. Under pressure, they don't have time for a sales job, and they know you're already sold. So they lay out that if you sign before the end of the quarter, the company will discount the price and offer more favorable payment terms. This happens all the time, especially in software, where customers know or learn to wait until the end of the quarter.

Of course, this only steals revenue from future quarters when the customer would buy anyway—and likely at more normal terms. This tactic can work if a company is growing quickly and the quarter is an anomaly, but more often than not, "stuffing the channel" only means there is less in the channel later. It works, until it doesn't. The company becomes a mouse on a treadmill, and like a horror film, it ends badly.

The clearest—and rarest—indicator is if the company discloses in the Liquidity and Capital Resources section of SEC filings whether it offered special financing during the particular quarter. Good luck finding that, though. Companies that believe they have to stuff the channel to keep up appearances are hardly going to pop the balloon by revealing what they're doing.

The alert investor who spies an increase in DSO knows that this can indicate special financing. Extended payment terms by definition mean an increase in DSO. Track days of sales outstanding over the past six to eight quarters to see if there are seasonal or other trends that make this quarter normal, or whether the increase in DSO means unusual activity in accounts receivable. Code words also can reveal a lot. If management alludes to a "heavily back-end-loaded quarter," it may mean the company signed deals at generous terms near the end of the quarter in order to feed the Street. Raise your eyebrows if you hear "hockey stick growth" or "non-linear growth" for anything but a hypergrowth company. No company admits to stuffing the channel, so they use these other positive terms.

Here's a telling anecdote. Tom purchased a low-cost cloud based software product from a fast-growing company. He used it for himself only—he was not a large business customer buying the software for 1,000 seats. Yet the salesperson kept calling daily the last week of the quarter. When Tom questioned, the salesperson said this was "normal" for the end of each quarter. Indeed, stuffing the channel is rife at software companies. Tom wished he had tried to get a better price, but he did move the salesperson off company insistence on a one-time annual payment in advance. He asked for periodic payments to smooth out cash flow. Done! If a company pressures its salespeople for a deal on this puppy, it's probably offering far greater concessions to the big dogs.

A real-time case came in March 2006 when John issued this report to clients. He pointed to the risk increased DSOs posed to eResearch Technology investors:

> eResearch Technology provides cardiac safety solutions to drug and medical device makers to evaluate new products. For the quarter ending Dec. 2005, DSO jumped on both a sequential and year-over-year basis. Table 2.1 shows DSO increasing approximately four days sequentially and five days year-over-year. The increase in DSO was largely driven by increased levels of receivables, despite lower revenue year over year.

Table 2.1 eResearch Technology DSO Issues*

Quarter Ending	Dec. 2005	Sep. 2005	June 2005	March 2005
Revenue	$25.4	$20.9	$17.6	$22.9
Accounts Receivable	**$15.2**	$11.6	$11.1	$14.8
DSO	**54.5**	**50.7**	**57.4**	**59.0**
Year-over-Year Trend in DSO	↑	↓	=	↓
Quarter Ending	**Dec. 2004**	**Sep. 2004**	**June 2004**	**March 2004**
Revenue	$27.1	$28.0	$28.2	$26.1
Accounts Receivable	**$14.8**	$18.5	$17.6	$18.2
DSO	**49.8**	60.1	57.1	63.6

*Dollar amounts are in millions of dollars. DSO numbers are in days.
Source: SEC filings.

In the quarterly conference call in February 2006, CEO Joseph Esposito noted that $8 million of business was signed in "the last days of December." To the extent that certain of those revenues were booked rather than deferred, this may have indicated that the quarter was heavily loaded toward the end. And that pointed to possible aggressive terms or price discounts, either of which lowers the period's quality of earnings.

It took only two months for the revenue to come home to roost. The arrow in Figure 2.2 shows where John issued this report on March 13. On April 26, the stock closed at $13.74, and the company announced lowered guidance for the rest of the year. Shares fell steadily, until they hit $9.12 on June 12, the day the company announced that Esposito would step down. The stock bottomed in the mid-$6s in November.[3]

Helen of Troy's beauty products failed to obscure poor earnings quality when, in the first quarter of 2005, John alerted clients of concerns that the company was aggressively recognizing revenue.

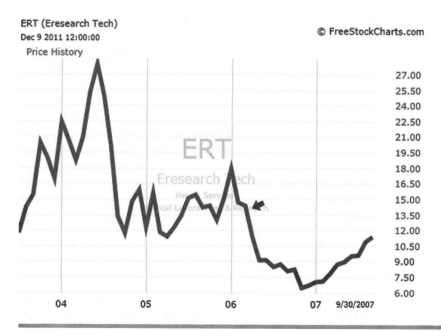

Figure 2.2 eResearch: 2004–September 30, 2007.
Source: FreeStockCharts.com, used by permission.

Increase in A/R Days Due to Extended Payment Terms
In the November 2004 period, the company experienced an increase in days sales outstanding compared with the year-ago period. At the end of the quarter, DSOs—according to the company's calculation—were 72 days, an increase of three days, year over year. The company's management attributed the increase to growth in international sales, which have longer credit terms on average. We are generally concerned about extended payment terms, as often they act to pull future revenue forward into the current period, leaving a revenue gap needing to be filled in an upcoming quarter. This increases the risk of an earnings miss in that time period, and as a result, may have an adverse impact on the stock price.

In John's experience, even just a few days year-over-year increase in DSO can signal poor earnings quality and potential trouble ahead.

Percentage-of-Completion Accounting

Percentage-of-completion accounting matches revenue earned on long-term contracts with the work performed by companies to fulfill their obligations. During each reporting period, management estimates the proportion of work completed and recognizes revenue and profits accordingly. Thus the company recognizes the revenue in advance of billing the customer.

The operative word is "estimates." Any time discretion enters into the equation, there is the opportunity to manipulate the numbers. Management may underestimate costs incurred or overestimate the proportion completed in a given period, providing a boost to current results at the expense of future reporting periods.

Aggressive revenue recognition under the percentage-of-completion method may be determined a couple of ways. If management overestimated the proportion of work performed on the contract, a sharp increase in unbilled receivables relative to revenue should alert the investor. In addition, a sharp and unexplained increase in gross profit margin may indicate that the company's management increased its estimated profits on the project.

Accelerated revenue recognition through percentage-of-completion accounting and other aggressive revenue concerns at AsiaInfo Holdings led John to release a report to clients of his Parabolix Research service on June 2, 2010. AsiaInfo shares stood at $21.54:

Company Description

AsiaInfo Holdings, Inc. provides telecommunications software solutions and information technology (IT) security products and services to telecommunications service providers, as well as to other major enterprises in China.

These two main factors lead to the conclusion that the company has deteriorating earnings quality: (1) accelerated revenue recognition and (2) likely overstated profit margins.

1. Trends in AsiaInfo's Accounts Indicate Accelerated Revenue Recognition

AsiaInfo's unbilled accounts receivables have surged in recent quarters, indicating possible revenue recognition acceleration. When a company uses percentage-of-completion accounting, it will have an unbilled receivable, which represents revenue recognized in advance of billing the customer. Aggressive managements may use the unbilled receivables as a way to front load revenue recognition from projects that are not yet completed. In essence, it is an estimated account. What's more, management may estimate the profitability of the projects prior to completion as well. Table 2.2 illustrates AsiaInfo's DSO trends.

As Table 2.2 shows, the level of DSO has increased year-over-year for four consecutive periods. However, AsiaInfo's accounts receivable levels require adjustments due to a relationship with IBM known as the "IBM Arrangement," whereby the company acts as a distributor for certain products to China Mobile, its largest client. The language from the SEC filing follows:

In addition, in recent periods we have begun to generate service revenues by acting as a sales agent for International Business Machines Corporation, or IBM, or its distributors, for certain products sold to China Mobile, or the IBM Arrangement. The service fee under the IBM Arrangement is determined as a percentage of the gross contract amount. We have evaluated the criteria outlined in guidance issued by the Financial Accounting Standards Board, or the FASB, regarding report-ing revenue gross as principal versus net as an agent, in determining whether to record as revenues the gross amount billed to China Mobile and related costs or the net amount earned after deducting hardware costs paid to the vendor, even though we bear inventory risks after the vendor ships the products to us and we bill gross amounts to China Mobile. We record the net amount earned after deducting hardware costs as agency service revenue because (1) the vendor is the pri-mary obligor in these transactions, (2) we have no latitude in establishing the prices, (3) we are not involved in the determi-nation of the product specifications, (4) we do not bear credit risk because we are contractually obligated to pay the vendor only when China Mobile pays us, and (5) we do not have the right to select suppliers.

Table 2.2 AsiaInfo Holdings' Increasing DSO: June Quarter 2008–
March Quarter 2010*

Quarter Ending	March 2010	Dec. 2009	Sep. 2009	June 2009	March 2009	Dec. 2008	Sep. 2008	June 2008
DSO	169	155	144	161	143	88	118	100
Sequential Change	9%	8%	(11%)	13%	62%	(25%)	17%	(29%)
Year-over-Year Change	19%	76%	22%	60%	1%	(13%)	(17%)	—
Four-Quarter Average DSO	157	151	134	127	112	112	115	121
Change	4%	13%	5%	14%	0.4%	(3%)	(5%)	—
A/R as a Percentage of Revenue	186%	170%	158%	176%	156%	97%	129%	110%

*DSO numbers are in days
Source: SEC filings.

Table 2.3 AsiaInfo's Increasing Unbilled Accounts Receivable, June Quarter 2008–March Quarter 2010*

Quarter Ending	March 2010	Dec. 2009	Sep. 2009	June 2009	March 2009	Dec. 2009	Sep. 2008	June 2008
Total A/R	$117.9	$129.6	$100.1	$103.2	$79.7	$52.0	$57.7	$46.2
A/R Attributable to IBM A/R	$46.7	$57.0	$21.5	$38.9	$17.9	—	—	—
A/R Net of IBM A/R	$71.2	$72.6	$78.6	$64.3	$61.8	$52.0	$57.7	$46.2
Unbilled A/R	$76.7	$72.2	$55.8	$53.7	$40.9	$28.6	$27.2	$23.7
Unbilled A/R as Percentage of A/R	108%	99%	71%	83%	66%	55%	47%	51%
Unbilled DSO	110	86	80	84	73	49	55	51

*Dollar amounts are in millions of dollars. DSO numbers are in days.
Source: SEC filings.

Table 2.3 adjusts AsiaInfo's DSO to reflect the IBM Arrangement. After adjusting for—netting—the IBM receivables, it appears as though *virtually all* [emphasis original] of AsiaInfo's increase in accounts receivables is driven by changes in unbilled accounts receivable. Not only is the trend significant, but also so is the magnitude, compounded by the fact that ASIA has a heavy customer concentration with China Mobile representing 70 percent of AsiaInfo's revenues, up from 66 percent last year and with the top three customers representing 93 percent of sales.

While AsiaInfo's unbilled A/R has been surging, deferred revenue has fallen sharply. The depletion of this account not only has served as a drain on cash flow, but also portends a slowdown in revenue in future quarters. Days in deferred revenue have dropped year-over-year for four consecutive periods. Table 2.4 shows that, as DSO have grown, the relationship between DSO to deferred revenue days (DDR) ballooned to 119 days in March 2010 from 57 days a year ago.

2. Profit Margins May Be Overstated

While percentage-of-completion accounting can lead to accelerated revenue recognition by increasing revenues booked in advance of billing the customer, it may also overstate profit margins as management estimates the profitability of the projects in the interim. Again, it's a management-estimated account.

Interestingly, while AsiaInfo's unbilled A/R has surged, so has its profitability. Table 2.5 shows the recent trends in gross and operating profit margins. Gross margin exceeded 61 percent in the March 2010 quarter, a 750 bps improvement (bps = basis points; 100 basis points = 1 percent). Operating profit margin improvement topped 1,000 bps.

Profit margins were above expectations. When sell-side analysts questioned management about the margins in order to model their future estimates, replies were ambiguous at best. CEO Steve Zhang explained that the improvement in margins was due to several factors: "I think several reasons coming together drive our first quarter strong margin improvement. I think, first of all, the top line is driven by the—our Telecom Solution revenue. On the

Table 2.4 AsiaInfo's Worsening DSO Minus DDR: June Quarter 2008–March Quarter 2010*

Quarter Ending	March 2010	Dec. 2009	Sep. 2009	June 2009	March 2009	Dec. 2008	Sep. 2008	June 2008
DDR	51	54	53	49	86	75	77	78
Deferred Revenue	$35.2	$45.6	$36.6	$31.3	$47.9	$44.4	$37.9	$35.8
Sequential Change	(7%)	4%	8%	(43%)	13%	(2%)	(1%)	(21%)
Year-over-Year Change	(26%)	3%	(3%)	(13%)	27%	53%	107%	—
Four-Quarter Average Deferred Revenue	$37.2	$40.3	$40.0	$40.4	$41.5	$39.0	$35.1	$30.2
Change	(8%)	1%	(1%)	(3%)	6%	11%	16%	7%
DSO Minus DDR	119	101	91	112	57	13	40	23
Change Sequential	18%	10%	(19%)	96%	342%	(68%)	79%	(47%)
Change Year-over-Year	108%	679%	126%	396%	35%	(64%)	(55%)	—

*Dollar amounts are in millions of dollars. DSO and DDR numbers are in days.
Source: SEC filings.

Table 2.5 AsiaInfo's Improving Margins, June Quarter 2008–March Quarter 2010: Sustainable?

Quarter Ending	March 2010	Dec. 2009	Sep. 2009	June 2009	March 2009	Dec. 2008	Sep. 2008	June 2008
Gross Margin	61.5%	57.7%	54.6%	49.1%	54.0%	53.5%	51.8%	45.3%
Change Year-over-Year	13.9%	7.8%	5.5%	8.5%	5.9%	11.4%	3.8%	—
Operating Margin	22.9%	21.5%	16.0%	10.9%	12.2%	14.5%	11.8%	8.5%
Change Year-over-Year	88.5%	49.0%	35.8%	29.2%	58.9%	17.8%	22.0%	—

Source: SEC filings.

expense side, we did experience some seasonal delay in making new hires in the first quarter. Also, in the first quarter there was this Chinese New Year and everybody took a two-week vacation, so that also decreased our total expense. I think overall its top line [is] growing faster than the expense growth."

One plausible explanation for higher top-line growth without corresponding expense is accelerated revenue recognition, as witnessed by the increase in unbilled A/R. The combination of surging unbilled receivables, declines in deferred revenues, and jump in profit margins significantly heightens the concerns with respect to AsiaInfo's earnings quality.

The relationship among the three metrics suggests that *any* slowdown in revenue may have a material impact on AsiaInfo's operations. Furthermore, on December 6, 2009, ASIA announced the acquisition of one of its competitors, Linkage Technologies (paying about $60 million in cash and issuing 28 million shares). The acquisition will only obscure AsiaInfo's growth metrics and financial comparisons further.

The quarter after the report, the stock fell 26 percent on an earnings announcement. Within 14 months the stock was in single digits. Figure 2.3 shows the downfall.

The next concept is familiar to anyone who has ever borrowed from or lent money or property to a relative or friend. At the corporate level, it's potential trouble.

Related-Party Revenue

When a company derives an increasing portion of its revenue from affiliated entities, the investor should be concerned. An outside investor cannot be sure whether the transaction is really arms-length between the parties. Be skeptical.

The notes to the financial statements disclose related-party revenue. Determine revenue without the related-party revenue and compare that to prior periods. If the revenue is not attractive without that from related parties, it's a cause for concern. Sometimes related-party revenue is so large a part of total revenues that it's a sure sign of trouble. UTStarcom (UTSI) showed this as the post–2000–2002 bull market gained momentum.

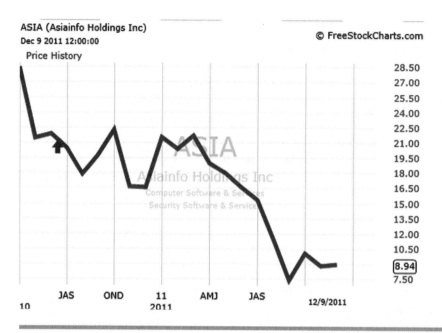

ASIA (Asiainfo Holdings Inc)
Dec 9 2011 12:00:00   © FreeStockCharts.com

Figure 2.3 AsiaInfo Holdings: April 2010 to December 9, 2011.
Source: FreeStockCharts.com, by permission.

In 2004, approximately 80 percent of UTSI's revenues came from China, and it sought to diversify, with a goal of 50 percent from outside China by 2006. The company noted its successful contracts with emerging markets in India, Vietnam, and Latin America as movement in the right direction.

But shareholders had no way to judge a large amount of the non-China revenue. At the time, 15 out of that 20 percent foreign revenue—that is, three quarters of it—was generated in Japan. The majority of that came from BB Technologies, a subsidiary of the Masayoshi Son-controlled investment bank, SoftBank. Masayoshi Son was chairman of the board of UTSI beginning in 1995. This alone doesn't moot the astounding growth in UTSI revenues from BB Technologies from zero dollars in 2000 to $13.9 million in 2001 and $123 million in 2002—but surely Masayoshi Son's connections were of some value in Japan's interwoven corporate universe. And even a question about the quality of these revenues would discredit the vast majority of UTSI's non-China income and its goal of achieving 50 percent from outside of China in a mere two years.

When the company set the goal in 2004 to diversity its revenue, UTSI was trading around $26. Within two months it had dropped 35 percent to $16.84, and two years later—the year it said it would reach the goal of having non-China revenues at 50 percent of total—it closed off 71 percent, at $7.50. And this was all during the roaring bull market. By July 14, 2011, shares had collapsed to $1.43. Investors alert to related-party income avoided this devastating loss or profited through shorting.

Investors had to be willing to comb the footnotes for questionable related-party transactions at Quest Software in 2005. John issued a report to clients warning that the notes disclosed major management and director conflicts of interests with shareholders. Quest acquired two companies. Quest's Chairman and CEO and two other board members invested in a venture-capital fund that owned preferred stock in the two companies, entitling fund partners to cash payments of $95.6 million when the companies were acquired. Moreover, one of the board members was managing director of the fund. The clear conflict is that the fund's interest was in selling at the highest possible price, while Quest shareholders' interest was in paying the lowest.

While companies often have all sorts of cozy relationships among management, board members, and outside entities, rarely are they as blatant as at Quest. But they were blatant only to those who read the footnotes. And there management ended its discussion, concluding that its own interests were "not material." Management is unlikely to call its own conflict "material."[4] It was an earnings quality analyst's red flag.

The seemingly innocent "deferred revenue" line can also offer management all sorts of ways to make revenue appear better, but as in most of this chapter's cases, it's unsustainable.

Monitor Changes in Deferred Revenue

Some companies, such as software firms, receive cash in advance of performing services for their customers. As a result, they defer this revenue—which means they delay recognizing it as revenue—until the services are performed. It's crucial to watch the deferred revenue line.

Deferred revenue can be an indicator that revenue is rising or falling, especially when it is boosting reported revenue and may not be sustainable. The pressure to meet Wall Street's quarterly expectations can push management to defer revenue. Of course, there is no bottomless well of deferred revenue from which to draw, so this practice just puts off, rather than eliminates, the inevitable quarterly earnings disappointment.

For example, if revenue grew $40 million sequentially, but deferred revenue declined by $20 million, management may have accelerated recognizing some or all of that $20 million to keep the growth rate up. Wall Street penalizes stocks when growth expectations aren't met. But management can't put off the real revenue picture forever. Without new deferred revenue recognition, which could be suspect as well, or new growth, it's only a matter of time before a quarter brings real pain.

The next six places to look for trouble are not as predictive individually but together can further create a witches' brew of a company's aggressive revenue recognition.

Nonmonetary Transactions

Management can use nonmonetary transactions to boost reported revenue. For example, a company may provide products and services to a customer and in return receive stock, which may decline in value. It may also be illiquid, therefore tough to sell at any price. This was popular during the Internet boom as a way to show ever-increasing growth and fuel the stock price when companies paid each other in stock at inflated, unsustainable valuations.

John's 2005 report flagged Helen of Troy's non-monetary transactions in which the company exchanged its goods for advertising credits. The 10-Q filing describes the transactions:

> During the fiscal year ended February 28, 2003, we entered into nonmonetary transactions in which we exchanged inventory with a net book value of approximately $3,100,000 for advertising credits. As a result of these transactions, we recorded both sales and cost of goods sold equal to the inventory's book value. We had used approximately $2,000,000 of the credits through

the fiscal year ending February 29, 2004. In addition, during the quarters ended August 31, 2004 and November 30, 2004, we entered into additional non-monetary transactions in which we exchanged inventory with a book value of approximately $952,000 and $59,000 respectively, for additional advertising credits. As a result of these transactions, we recorded both sales and cost of goods sold equal to the inventory's book value, which approximated their fair value.

During the three months ended November 30, 2004, we used $368,000 of credits against these transactions and expect to use most of the remaining advertising credits acquired by the end of fiscal year 2005. All remaining credits are included in the line item entitled "Prepaid expenses" on our consolidated condensed balance sheets and "are valued at $1,743,000 and $1,100,000 at November 30, 2004 and February 29, 2004, respectively."

These transactions do not appear to have any favorable impact on earnings because the book values of the products were recorded both as sales and cost of goods sold. However, we regard nonmonetary revenue to be of low quality, and it should be factored out of the analysis when assessing the true demand for a firm's products.

While the "barter" here exchanged items of value, Helen of Troy could not use advertising credits to pay suppliers or employees. Those credits were only worth real sales if the advertising produced them. Such real sales from advertising were far from certain and the revenues, and therefore earnings, of low quality.

Bill-and-Hold Revenue

In this sleight of hand, the vendor invoices the customer and recognizes the transaction as revenue, but the products aren't shipped until later. If this is a company's practice, it should note the policies in its SEC filings.

Tom encountered this at an absurd level as a junior high–age investor. There actually was a company that recognized revenue of a finished product when it rolled off the assembly line and into storage. No customer, no invoice. This is the kind of fraud that shareholders simply can't see. Tom invested $100 in the company because his best friend's father served as general counsel. A go-go IPO during the late 1960s boom, the company said it had a modular housing construction technique that was going to answer the country's affordable-housing problems. But when a housing unit came off the assembly line and left as inventory, the company didn't even invoice a customer—it booked revenue immediately. The only way to know this was to suspect the rapidly rising revenue combined with equally fast-rising deferred revenue. Not only did the company eventually fail, because the revenue wasn't real, it did so spectacularly enough to become a Harvard business school case study.[5]

One-Time Gains, or Interest Income in Revenue

A company may include in revenue an item that should be reported below the operating line. For example, from the 1990s to early 2000s, consulting firm Computer Associates included interest income as revenue. Although disclosed in footnotes, this would escape all but the most careful observer, who would see interest income in gross and operating margins and—ironically and misleadingly—in EBITDA. But interest income is not revenue because Computer Associates was not a bank, so the inflated sales figures made everything on down the income statement questionable at best. In November 2006, CEO Sanjay Kumar was sentenced to twelve years in prison for inflating sales figures in 1999 and 2000 and for other accounting misdeeds.[6]

Growth in Sales-Type Leases

A company can lease a product but treat it as a sale, a sales-type lease. Consider a copier company that leases to a business for a certain term. The company is allowed to recognize revenue up front by discounting future lease revenues to present value, but it's aggressive. If using the operating lease method, the company is required to recognize revenue ratably over the term of the lease.

There is nothing inherently wrong with sales-type leases, but rapid growth in them can be a problem if accrual earnings outpace the growth in cash flows. All this does is bring future revenues forward, which can boost short-term results, but just puts off the day of reckoning.

Purchasing a Distributor

When a company (buyer) purchases a distributor, it can slip by some double counting. The buyer has already sold items to the distributor and booked revenue. What the distributor hasn't sold remains in inventory, which the buyer can sell and count again. Not only that, but the buyer can sell at retail the same inventory for which the distributor paid wholesale prices. An example is luxury accessory maker Coach's 2005 purchase of the remaining 50 percent of its Japanese distributor, allowing Coach to post Japanese sales at the higher retail margin (what the Japanese distributor earned) than at wholesale (what the distributor paid Coach).

Changes in Revenue Recognition Policy

Change in revenue recognition policy should raise eyebrows, if the policy is changed to an earlier one of more aggressive revenue recognition. But a change to a more *conservative* policy can also boost results by double counting revenue. Management will take a charge to write off all prior revenue that would not have been recognized under the new revenue recognition policy. Instead, that revenue is deferred and re-recognized at a later date. The investor should compare revenue recognition policies over the past several periods and pay attention to changes in the policy language.

The investor has to get up pretty early in the morning—and wear magnifying glasses—to catch the true revenue effect of some changes in revenue policy. In June 2003, John notified clients that wireless intellectual property company InterDigital Communications had changed its policy to one that appeared to be more conservative—and would have been in many cases—but allowed the company to aggressively recognize revenue in this circumstance.

InterDigital made its money by licensing its patented technology to wireless companies, and that revenue stream was volatile and unpredictable. Figure 2.4 shows that license revenue declined in 1999 and

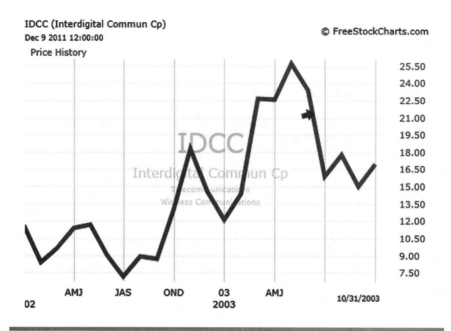

IDCC (Interdigital Commun Cp)
Dec 9 2011 12:00:00   © FreeStockCharts.com
Price History

Figure 2.4 InterDigital: 2002–October 31, 2003.
Source: FreeStockCharts.com, by permission.

again when the telecom bubble burst in 2000. After an almost flat 2001, revenue jumped 67 percent. But John advised skepticism about whether that growth could continue. This was in large part because InterDigital recognized revenue under one policy and then wrote it off when it changed to an allegedly more conservative policy. But Wall Street sees write-offs as one-time events and forgets about them. When the company recognized revenue under the new, allegedly more conservative policy, it appeared that revenues had risen. Of course, that too presented a problem, because the new recognition was one-time and the apparent growth was unsustainable.

Indeed, things did not play out well for InterDigital. During the wireless communications industry expansion in the early 2000s, companies such as InterDigital and Qualcomm held patents that they believed covered emerging technologies used in phones. Investors expected large paydays, believing that wireless phone companies would begin paying license fees and royalties.

InterDigital shareholders thought they saw the pot of gold when Nokia, which had fought like many phone makers against the patent holders, took a large reserve against potential liability for these license fees—and then raised that reserve. When the Finnish then-giant later changed its tack on paying the license fees to InterDigital, the latter's stock tanked, as Figure 2.4 shows. The arrow indicates the June 13, 2003 issuance of John's report.

A decade later, the FASB issued published revenue recognition rules for multi-deliverable contracts.[7] The rules gave companies such as networking infrastructure maker Juniper Networks the opportunity to massage contracts for its benefit. In January 2011, John stated on CNBC that networking-equipment maker Juniper "may cough up a hairball in future quarters." Indeed it did. John wrote at the time[8]:

> Juniper Networks benefits from the Accounting Standards update at the beginning of fiscal 2010 that changed revenue recognition for multi-deliverable contracts, which Juniper adopted for all transactions after January 1, 2010.
>
> Juniper sells software, hardware, and services to the communications industry, so contracts typically have multiple deliverables. Rather than defer the value of a contract and recognize the associated revenue ratably, the change allows companies like Juniper to break up the components of the contract and assign values to those components, recognizing some up-front, higher-margin components such as software. This gives the company enormous discretion on what to recognize and when, and the potential to front-load revenue. Year-over-year comparisons become meaningless.
>
> Because of this change, effective January 1, 2010, the company recognized $237 million in revenue for the year. During the first three quarters after the change, it recognized $128 million, with the lowest amount—$23 million—in the quarter ending March 2010. The change's anniversary comes in the first quarter of 2011, and the headwind to growth escalates as the year wears on. The revenue recognized in the fourth quarter of 2010 ($109 million) was more than double any prior quarter.
>
> As a result, 26 percent reported growth drops to approximately 15 percent, when accounting for the change. This is approximately 5 percentage points (500 bps) below management's forward guidance. To further grasp the magnitude for Juniper,

the accounting change impacts competitor Cisco's revenues by less than 1 percent.

The company also would have missed earnings estimates by approximately 10 percent a quarter over the last few quarters.

Since Juniper made the change, three metrics show the trouble. First, days in deferred revenue (DDR) have dropped each successive quarter to the lowest level since December 2008. The spread between the EBITDA Margin LTM and Operating Cash Flow margin LTM expanded to 300 bps from −400 bps in the year-ago quarter, suggesting that earnings quality has deteriorated progressively throughout 2010. [Chapter 5, "Cash Flow Warnings," explains how to calculate and use these metrics.] An expanding spread indicated declining earnings quality. Finally, days sales outstanding have increased year-over-year the prior two quarters, acting as a drag on cash flow.

Juniper traded around $39 on the anniversary of the accounting change in April 2011 (see Figure 2.5). Six days later, the company reduced guidance and began to underperform the S&P 500. Investors

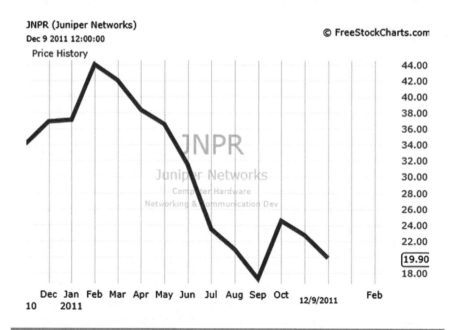

Figure 2.5   Juniper Networks: November 1, 2010–December 9, 2011.
Source: FreeStockCharts.com, by permission.

may not have seen a one-time guidance reduction to be serious if they were in love with the stock, but when Juniper guided lower again on July 26, the affair ended. Shares on August 4 were $23, off 40 percent. Figure 2.5 shows the damage.

Organic Revenue Growth Substantially Below Reported Levels

John alerted clients in 2005 that one-time events obscured real revenue growth at Helen of Troy. Due to recent acquisitions and foreign currency gains, Helen of Troy's revenue growth was much weaker than reported. On a reported basis, revenue grew 24.4 percent, or $41.3 million, in November 2004, compared with the prior year period. However, new product acquisitions accounted for 21.1 percent or $34.9 million of that growth. Because of purchase acquisitions accounting, growth rates are inflated, simply because prior year periods are not restated to reflect the impact of the acquisition on historical results.

With respect to foreign currency, the strengthening of the British Pound, Canadian Dollar, and the Euro relative to the U.S. Dollar positively affected reported revenue. According to the company's 10–Q filing for the November 2004 quarter, the net impact of foreign currency changes was to provide approximately $2.5 million of additional revenue relative to the year-ago period. While we will not speculate on the value of the dollar relative to foreign currencies, we do believe this to be a low quality source of revenue, due to its unsustainable nature.

Table 2.6 illustrates adjusted revenue to account for both the impact of acquisitions and foreign currency gains. An adjustment to reflect the

Table 2.6   Helen of Troy's New-Product Acquisitions and Currency Gains Overstate Revenues*

Quarter Ending	Nov. 2004	Feb. 2004	Growth
Revenue	$205,682	$165,386	24.4%
Less:			
Acquired Revenue	$34,857	—	—
Currency Gains	$2,461	—	—
Result: Adjusted Revenue	$168,364	$165,386	1.8%

*Dollar amounts are in millions of dollars.
Source: SEC filings.

impact of these other items on revenue lowers the company's growth rate from the 24.4 percent reported amount to just 1.8 percent for the November 2004 quarter.

John's report concluded:

In our opinion, Helen of Troy's earnings quality is low. Extended payment terms combined with a roll-up strategy, a weak U.S. dollar, and nonmonetary transactions pose several revenue-related concerns. Furthermore, the company's cash flow performance has been underwhelming, as free cash is negative and operating cash flows are weak relative to reported net income. Finally, financial leverage has increased substantially due to recent acquisitions; however, its return on equity has barely budged.

The black arrow in Figure 2.6 shows the price on the date of the report. Helen of Troy was the face that launched a thousand slips.

Figure 2.6 Helen of Troy: 1996–April 30, 2009.
Source: FreeStockCharts.com.

Conclusion

Of all the financial statement red flags for companies, revenue recognition is the most serious and least studied. Aggressive revenue recognition is at the heart of trouble across all the financials. Next in importance is aggressive inventory management, which also flows through all the statements and offers companies many ways to obscure true earnings quality.

Chapter 3

Aggressive Inventory Management

After revenue recognition, inventory is the second most important factor for earnings quality analysis.

When a company creates product inventory, it invests cash. Management spends the Benjamins well or poorly, depending on its skill at judging business trends. The risk is that, the longer inventory ages, the greater the possibility that the company is misallocating cash, misjudging the market and may have to write down inventory. Therefore, inventory affects profitability via gross margin on the income statement and shows demand for a company's products.

We analyze inventory numerous ways on the balance sheet to get a better sense of the impact it may have on the company's product demand. Similarly to DSO, we track inventory on a days sales basis and look for both year-over-year and sequential changes:

$$Days\ Sales\ in\ Inventory = (91.25 \times Inventory/Quarterly\ Cost\ of\ Goods\ Sold)$$

Let's turn to John's notification to clients about semiconductor maker Silicon Laboratories. In the quarter in which he flagged the issue, days sales in inventory (DSI) jumped dramatically.

Silicon Laboratories experienced a spike in its inventory levels in the June 2004 quarter when inventory grew 155 percent year-over-year compared with sales growth of 83 percent. Table 3.1 shows the result, that days sales in inventory (DSI) jumped 14 days year-over-year to 55 days. On a sequential basis, DSI increased five days.

During the June 2004 quarter conference call, Russ Brennan, Silicon's CFO, put the inventory situation in a positive light. According to Brennan, inventory at the finished-goods levels was depleted and "inventory distribution also went up consistent with our plan to increase MCU [microcontroller unit] sales and distribution infrastructure to support this ramping business and to support projected growth in our other broad-based, mixed-signal businesses." Despite this explanation, the next speaker, CEO Dan Artusi provided an outlook for the third quarter with revenue in the range of $120–$123.6 million and EPS of $0.36–$0.38, below Street expectations of $129 million and $0.40, respectively. Economic issues related to China during the quarter were in part to blame, but we think China is a longer-term probem that extends beyond one quarter.

The inventory analysis extends beyond the amount reported on the balance sheet. In general, management is quick to point out conservative revenue recognition policies, whereby revenue is not recognized until goods are sold through to the end user. In addition to inventory on the balance sheet, the company also records deferred income to distributors, to whom it affords rights of return and price

Table 3.1 Silicon Laboratories' Increasing DSI

Quarter Ending	July 2004	April 2004	Jan. 2004	Sep. 2003	June 2003
Inventories	$34,655	$28,606	$34,064	$18,572	$13,375
Cost of Goods Sold	$57,544	$51,866	$50,267	$38,061	$30,267
DSI	55	50	62	45	41

*Dollar amounts are in millions of dollars. DSI are in days.
Source: SEC filings.

protection for products they don't sell. This revenue recognition is deferred until the product is sold to the distributor's end customer. While deferred income represents some future revenue, in Silicon's case it also represents inventory sitting in the sales channel that has yet to be sold and is at risk. Table 3.2 illustrates the change in deferred income and in adjusted DSI at Silicon.

Viewed this way—with deferred income showing potential inventory at risk—the inventory situation is worse. While this revenue may be recognized if and when the distributor sells through to the end customer, DSI reflecting this inventory still in the channel jumped seven days sequentially and nineteen days year-over-year. Distributors may slow purchases from Silicon Laboratories until demand picks up and the goods are sold through, or the company may have to cut prices to move the goods through the channel, slicing profit margins.

Management admitted to excess supply in the sales channel with respect to demand for mobile handsets that use the company's chips. If the situation, in China in particular, does not turn around quickly and results in a protracted slowdown for the mobile market—which we think is a possibility—then the inventory situation will worsen before it gets better.

Table 3.2 Silicon Laboratories' Deferred Income to Distributors Worsens DSI*

Quarter Ending	July 2004	April 2004	Jan. 2004	Sep. 2003	June 2003
Deferred Income to Distributors	$14,582	$11,716	$11,526	$5,389	$5,901
Adjusted DSI	78 [+7 days sequential; +19 days year-over-year]	71	83	57	59

*Dollar amounts are in millions of dollars. DSI are in days.
Source: SEC filings.

To be sure, investors are aware that inventory spiked in the recent quarter. The question is whether this is a one-quarter blip or a major issue. Negatively, technology research firms have consistently overestimated cell-phone demand. . . . Given that the market researchers have consistently been wrong with respect to consumer demand, there is a risk that the inventory build-up situation across all of these companies—including Silicon—is a significant long-term risk.

We can dig deeper for information on whether inventory issues are a blip or persistent. Inventory is not one undifferentiated blob. For example, with a soft-drink company, it can start with the sugar or high fructose corn syrup (horrors) and other raw materials, then treating these with the secret-formula mixing process (work in process) and then canning or bottling the concoction as finished goods ready for distribution. It doesn't matter that, in today's world, parts of this process are performed in dozens of facilities at different times throughout the world. Management still has to control the process in a manner beneficial and transparent to shareholders. Not all companies do. So, while it's important to look at inventory as a whole, companies show their management expertise and earnings quality in all stages of the inventory production process, sometimes revealing important trends to the alert investor.

Inventory Components

We now mine the raw inventory number on the balance sheet because it may be insufficient to detect earnings quality issues for companies that sell physical products requiring inventory production stages (even the often-used example of the lemonade stand has these definable stages). Companies typically, though not always, report raw materials, work in process, and finished goods. The best list them under inventory on the balance sheet, but for the rest we find the information in the notes to the financials. And some, unfortunately, do not break out the components at all.

We then can calculate the DSI for each component and compare it to sales growth:

$$Days\ Sales\ in\ Raw\ Materials = 91.25 \times (Raw\ Materials/\\ Quarterly\ Cost\ of\ Goods\ Sold)$$

$$Days\ Sales\ in\ Work\ in\ Process = 91.25 \times (Work\ in\ Process/$$
$$Quarterly\ Cost\ of\ Goods\ Sold\,)$$

$$Days\ Sales\ in\ Finished\ Goods = 91.25 \times (Finished\ Goods/$$
$$Quarterly\ Cost\ of\ Goods\ Sold\,)$$

In Table 3.3, we use component information found in the footnotes for semiconductor vendor Intel to calculate DSI for each component and find excellent inventory management.

From Q4 2009 through Q2 2010, Intel's DSI rose well in excess of revenue, suggesting poor inventory management. The next two quarters' difference was unremarkable, but from there the company ran like an atomic clock. Revenues rose while inventories shrank. The efficiency came almost entirely from managing work in process from DSI of 43 to 26. Raw materials and finished goods remained the same, despite rising sales, but work in process moved faster.

Tracking the components here shows nothing but good at nimble Intel. During these two years, it was briefly caught off guard before it righted the chip—in an uncertain economic environment to boot. So be alert. More dramatic divergence from a company's normal inventory component pattern may be good or bad. It alerts the investor to look more closely to determine whether there are earnings quality issues and to see both good things or bad things coming down the road before others do. Next we'll explain that in more detail.

Positive and Negative Inventory Component Divergence

As with Intel, a well-run company's inventory components are consistent with a company's need to manage the ups and downs of revenue. They can diverge from a seasonal pattern or usual business conditions for either positive or negative reasons. A company receiving new orders knows to build inventory components to fulfill them, and the first positive sign may be a rise in raw materials followed by work-in-process: they diverge *positively*. Conversely, inventory components may bulge through poor management and poor demand, diverging *negatively*.

Table 3.3 Intel's Efficient Management of Work-in-Process Inventory Drives DSI Improvement: December Quarter 2009–October Quarter 2011* DSI for Inventory Components

Quarter Ending	Oct. 2011	July 2011	Apr. 2011	Dec. 2010	Sep. 2010	June 2010	March 2010	Dec. 2009
Raw Inventory and Total Inventory Evaluations (in Millions of Dollars)								
Raw Materials	$614	$546	$585	$471	$380	$407	$464	$437
Work in Process	$1,494	$1,450	$1,783	$1,887	$1,634	$1,637	$1,473	$1,469
Finished Goods	$1,851	$2,034	$1,731	$1,399	$1,409	$1,301	$1,049	$1,029
Total Inventory	$3,959	$4,030	$4,099	$3,757	$3,423	$3,345	$2,986	$2,935
Total Inventory DSI								
DSI	69	72	75	85	83	86	72	72
Revenues	$14,233	$13,023	$12,847	$11,457	$11,102	$10,765	$10,299	$10,569
DSI Sequential Change	(3%)	(5%)	(11%)	2%	4%	20%	1%	(26%)
Revenues Sequential Change	9%	1%	12%	3%	3%	5%	(3%)	13%
Inventory Component DSI								
Raw Materials	11	10	11	11	9	11	11	11
Work in Process	26	26	33	43	39	42	36	36
Finished Goods	32	36	32	32	34	34	25	25
Inventory Component Percentage of Revenues								
Raw Materials	4%	4%	5%	4%	3%	4%	5%	4%
Work in Process	10%	11%	14%	16%	15%	15%	14%	14%
Finished Goods	13%	16%	13%	12%	13%	12%	10%	10%

Source: SEC filings.

Consider the snake. It's good digestive inventory management when it snares its rodent dinner. The bulge nearer the head—raw material—promises good things to come along the digestive track through work-in-process and finished goods. Yum. It's efficient and only eats what it needs, and when it does, it's positive food inventory divergence.

Now consider a person at Thanksgiving, eating a meal many multiples more calories and sheer volume than usual. It takes far, far longer to digest (aging inventory), and, turkey's sleep-inducing tryptophan aside, there is the risk of inability to digest many nutrients and perhaps much of the meal at all (wasted inventory—call it a buildup of finished goods). Heartburn ensues.

Tracking inventory component divergence gives the investor advance notice of good or bad performance. Yet, few investors monitor these components, even though they can be the difference between investment profit and pain. We owe this subtle and very profitable concept to quality-of-earnings pioneer Thornton (Ted) O'glove, who presents positive and negative inventory component divergence in his path-breaking *Quality of Earnings*.[1] We will leave out "component" to call this simply positive or negative divergence.

At its root, positive divergence occurs when a company knows that business ahead is good, so its raw material inventory picks up while work in process and finished goods either lag or do not increase at the same rate. This can be useful to identify an investment opportunity in many places, but especially in a cyclical business or a turnaround situation. With positive divergence, companies in these situations likely see better cash flow, earnings, and stock price ahead.

The investor wants to avoid the opposite: when finished goods pile up in excess of sales while raw material inventories and work in process are flat or declining absolutely or relative to sales. This negative divergence is a good predictor of potential inventory write-downs and *poor* earnings, cash flow, and stock price.

Inventory component divergence is less amenable to analysis than many other indicators because some companies provide components annually, not quarterly, in the footnotes and not on the balance sheet, or not at all. To focus initial research, O'glove in 1987 emphasized that the investor should concentrate on "industries subject to rapid changes in products and taste" such as "high fashion, seasonal goods, and high tech."[2] This is sound advice, though the investor with expertise in other industries can do inventory component analysis there. The bottom line: Focus on negative divergences wherever you find them and understand the business.

Negative Divergence: Crocs and Maxim Integrated Products

While high fashion can certainly be a fertile hunting ground, any retailer subject to fashion tastes and trends can experience ballooning inventory through the slightest error in estimating demand. Even the best management can have trouble predicting fickle public taste for established, let alone new, apparel.

A useful example of misjudging retail demand is shoe company Crocs, whose stock plummeted in late 2007 into 2008, ahead of the broad market crash. DSI for finished goods and in relation to sales gave plenty of warning. Table 3.4 shows that raw materials and work in process were flat while finished goods soared.

Dramatic negative divergence of finished goods to sales sequentially is evident from the third quarter of 2007 to the first quarter of 2008. DSI exploded versus revenues from the second quarter to third and fourth of 2007. DSI still rose in the first quarter of 2008, and then the company slammed on the inventory brakes, with DSI dropping by 67 percent in two quarters. People were—and are—buying the shoes, but the company got demand wrong, overinvested in inventory, and brought investors great pain. Warehouses were chock-a-block with crocks of Crocs.

This is a reminder that avoiding a blowup is one thing, but to profit from it does not require perfect timing. Short sellers often mistakenly anchor to the highest recent price and think they "missed it" (just as longs can anchor to the recent lower prices and rue their timing). Remember that on the short side you make as much on the downside if a stock goes from 100 to 50 as from 50 to 25, 10 to 5—you get the idea. All those still provide 50 percent gains. For Crocs, it's the third quarter of 2007 when exploding DSI appeared in the 10-Q filed November 14, 2007, and the fourth quarter DSI jump in the 10-K filed February 29, 2008. There was money to be made, not only shorting on the first DSI in the 10-Q, but also acting on the second, the 10-K information over three months later. (See Figure 1.3 in Chapter 1.)

Crocs offers an unusually clear case where inventory component analysis could have led an investor to avoid, sell, or short Crocs at appropriate times. There are equally important cases where the analysis is subtler.

For so-called "tech" companies that make physical products, the longer their inventory collects dust, the sooner the company or competitors incorporate advances so that aging inventory either becomes obsolete and unsellable at any price or brings declining average selling prices that quickly eliminate profit margins. This competition risk is so intense that some investors avoid altogether so-called "physical tech" product companies, where price deflation is the norm and volume has to be growing for revenues and profits to stay in place. (They heed Berkshire Hathaway Vice Chairman Charlie Munger's advice to investors that technological advances bring products and favorable declining prices that benefit consumers and not shareholders of the producers.)

John's June 27, 2005 report on analog circuit maker Maxim Integrated Products shows negative inventory divergence predicting poor earnings quality and trouble ahead. Maxim buys silicon-wafer raw materials or

Table 3.4 Crocs' Negative Inventory Divergence: June Quarter 2007–September Quarter 2008*

Quarter Ending	Sep. 2008	June 2008	March 2008	Dec. 2007	Sep. 2007	June 2007
Raw Materials	$20.1	$22.4	$23.8	$20.4	$22.3	N/A
Work in Process	$0.3	$0.2	$3.3	$3.3	$2.5	N/A
Finished Goods	$120.6	$197.6	$238.4	$224.7	$170.5	$118.6[†] (total)
DSI	64	136	192	207	177 [154 finished goods versus total]	117
Revenues	$174.2	$222.8	$198.5	$224.8	$256.3	$224.3
Change in DSI	(53%)	(29%)	(7%)	34% [17% FG versus total inventory]	51% [32% FG versus total inventory]	—
Change in Revenues	(22%)	12%	(12%)	(12%)	14%	—

*Dollar amounts are in millions of dollars.
[†]Company filings did not provide inventory components for the June quarter 2007.
Source: SEC filings.

manufactures wafers itself. Work in process consists of manufacturing the chips on the wafers (also called die) and determining how many of them form the "die bank" inventory—the good die that can be parts of more product or shipped to customers for their use.[4] John advised clients that raw materials DSI did not keep pace with the rise in DSI for work in process and finished goods.

Inventories on the Rise

We are concerned with Maxim's recent high level of manufacturing output, which has not only kept gross margin elevated, but has increased inventory levels substantially. In fact, inventory levels, mostly in die-bank inventory, have increased significantly and are expected to rise in the near future. In the March 2005 quarter, inventory, as measured by days sales in inventory (DSI) increased to its highest level in the past eight quarters. As illustrated in Table 3.5, *DSI increased 18 days sequentially and 46 days year-over-year to 130 days in March.*

We also note the negative inventory divergence in the March 2005 quarter with an increase of 59 percent, and 31 percent year-over-year, in both finished goods and die bank respectively, compared to an increase of only 12 percent in raw materials. In our opinion, manufacturing continues well beyond necessary to satisfy future demand. Should demand not grow as expected, we can expect a future decline in margins.

Table 3.5 shows that finished-goods DSI increased 6 days sequentially and 18 days year-over-year, compared to flat sequentially and a 4-day year-over-year increase for raw materials DSI. However, the company attributes the majority of the DSI increase to higher die-bank or work-in-process inventory, which has risen 12 days sequentially and 23 days year-over-year.

According to Maxim, the buildup in die bank has been necessary to manage lower lead times as well as anticipated increased demand. But as Table 3.6 reveals, Linear Technology, Maxim's most direct competitor, maintains DSI of only 53 compared to Maxim's 130 days with equivalent lead times of 6 weeks, strongly suggesting Maxim's die bank expansion may be unnecessary. In fact, Maxim's lead times have contracted significantly from

Table 3.5 Maxim Integrated Products Negative Inventory Divergence, from Fourth Quarter of 2003 through Third Quarter of 2005*

Quarter Ending	March 2005	Dec. 2004	Sep. 2004	June 2004	March 2004	Dec. 2003	Sep. 2003	June 2003
Raw Materials	$16,407	$16,674	$17,025	$14,713	$10,757	$10,027	$10,995	$10,249
Work in Process (Die Bank)	$96,414	$87,654	$80,025	$73,833	$68,153	$70,137	$72,591	$79,687
Finished Goods	$46,642	$42,254	$38,588	$29,239	$24,456	$28,111	$31,503	$31,256
Raw Materials DSI	13 [flat seq.; +4 YoY]	13	13	11	9	9	11	11
Work in Process (Die Bank) DSI	79 [+12 seq.; +23 YoY]	67	61	54	56	62	72	82
Finished Goods DSI	38 [+6 seq.; +18 YoY]	32	29	21	20	25	31	32

*Dollar amounts are in millions of dollars.
Source: SEC filings.

12 weeks six months ago to 6 weeks today, but that improvement isn't expected to last. Management believes "lead times of six weeks [are] likely a bottom." Should lead times return to normal levels, the excess die-bank inventory would be unjustified at best.

Because they think that die-bank inventory does not generally become obsolete, Street analysts aren't concerned about this particular inventory growth. Lost on them is that there is quite a distance between obsolete (zero value) and full value, and the company has a tendency to write off inventory, dragging down margin levels. In fact, inventory write-downs of $5.0 million and $11.9 million in 2004 and 2003 respectively reduced gross margins both years, and those write-downs included both work-in-process and finished-goods inventory. This indicates that excess die-bank inventory poses some risk of obsolescence.

We also believe that these high inventories threaten continued production at current rates. Given that depreciation is nearly half of the cost of goods sold for Maxim, spreading that high fixed cost over lower output would dramatically reduce gross margin. As a result, we think the high gross margins and inventory levels augur Maxim's future earnings disappointment.

Table 3.6 Maxim Integrated Products' Worsening DSI, from Fourth Quarter 2003–Third Quarter 2005*

Quarter Ending	March 2005	Dec. 2004	Sep. 2004	June 2004	March 2004	Dec. 2003	Sep. 2003	June 2003
Inventory	$159	$147	$136	$118	$103	$108	$115	$121
Cost of Goods Sold	$112	$119	$120	$126	$112	$103	$93	$88
DSI	130	112	103	86	84	96	113	125
DSI for Competitor: Linear Technologies	53							

*Dollar amounts are in millions of dollars. DSI numbers are in days.
Source: SEC filings.

Figure 3.1 shows the story's sad end. When John issued this report on June 25, 2005, Maxim shares stood at $38.83. In six months, they dropped 20 percent to around $30 while the broad market advanced. Avoiding that loss was good because shares haven't traded above $30 since, but there's more. Paying attention to these warning signals also avoided a devastating loss when, in late 2007, the company reported a restatement and went onto the pink sheets on October 2 at $28.26. When the stock returned to the Nasdaq a year later, the first-day close was $13.73. Investors aware of the issues avoided or profited from losses.

Analyzing inventory components offers positive and negative information. Overall, though, rising inventory by itself is no indicator of problems. What matters is inventory buildup *relative* to other factors.

Inventory Buildup

Investors should watch closely the rate of buildup versus sales. Inventories may rise for good or bad reasons, but rarely do analysts consider that

Figure 3.1 Maxim Integrated Products: 2004–December 9, 2011.
Source: FreeStockCharts.com.

lower inventory buildup—shown also in decreasing accounts payable— may mean that existing inventory ages while the lower percentage of new, presumably more market-responsive inventory is most likely to sell. If aging inventory is a greater percentage of total inventory, then mark- downs, write-downs, and obsolescence have a more severe impact. This is especially troubling with consumer products—companies from whom customers demand today's products in new packaging.

Inventory buildup also can be a problem for newly acquired com- panies. When one public company acquires another public company, examining the target's inventory buildup can show trouble ahead for the acquirer. In November 2006, John issued a report to clients that, among other things, noted VeriFone's risk from substantial inven- tory buildup at its acquisition of Lipman Electronic Engineering. As Table 3.7 shows, in each of the four quarters prior to the report, inventories surged on a year-over-year basis, and DSI grew 81 per- cent from 90 days in the June 2005 quarter to 163 days in the June 2006 quarter.

While inventories ballooned, Lipman's gross profit margin remained relatively stable. This masked underlying weakness in Lipman's profitability, because the margin benefited from increased production spreading fixed costs across more product units. The company stated in the footnotes to the

Table 3.7 Inventory Buildup at VeriFone's Lipman Acquisition: September Quarter 2004–June Quarter 2006*

Quarter Ending	June 2006	March 2006	Dec. 2005	Sep. 2005
Cost of Goods Sold	$35.7	$33.1	$40.8	$29.7
Inventory	$63.8	$57.4	$53.9	$48.5
DSI	163	158	121	149
Quarter Ending	June 2005	March 2005	Dec. 2004	Sep. 2004
Cost of Goods Sold	$33.1	$31.1	$39.0	$23.4
Inventory	$32.6	$32.0	$31.9	$34.1
DSI	90	94	75	133

*Dollar amounts are in millions of dollars. DSI numbers are in days. Source: SEC filings.

financial statements that it experienced a loss of pricing power and that it built up inventory in expectation of sales that—particularly in one subsidiary—never materialized. However, despite the disappointing sales, the company had not written off the inventory. That risk to future quarterly margins remained.

VeriFone shares closed at $32.15 on November 13, 2006. Shorting took some patience: The shares rose during the next year, but the company could avoid the inevitable only so long. On December 3, 2007, the company announced that it would restate quarterly financial statements for the nine months before July 31, 2007. The stock price dropped 46 percent that day and extended the loss to 58 percent in three days.[3] Seeing the inventory buildup gave alert investors ample time to sell the stock or short for profit.

LIFO Reserve Change

In a system where revenue is recorded when a sale is made, the company must figure out the cost of goods sold by taking a physical inventory. There are three methods: LIFO (last-in first-out), FIFO (first-in first-out), and WAC (weighted average unit cost). FIFO bases costs chronologically, LIFO reverse chronologically, and WAC on the weighted averaged for the period. An investor wants consistent treatment, so that comparisons are meaningful. Changes from one method to another for any purpose, such as valuing reserves, are cause for concern.

The LIFO reserve is the difference between the FIFO and LIFO cost of inventory for accounting purposes. The LIFO reserve is an account used to bridge the gap between FIFO and LIFO costs when a company is using FIFO but would like to report LIFO in its financial statement, which it is allowed to do. When input prices decline ("first in"), the reserve is reduced and the cost of goods sold (COGS) declines. But management can also dip into the reserve by reducing LIFO inventory and use it as a source of earnings. When a reserve is reversed, it's a credit to the income statement. Essentially, it's 100 percent margin, so the EPS boost is significant. A reduction in the reserve for no apparent reason is a red flag.

If a company reverses or lowers its LIFO reserve, it may cause an unusual change in gross profit margin. Without a plausible explanation, management may be boosting EPS stealthily.

While LIFO accounting is probably the best understood of the inventory accounting concerns, consider the situation of impaired inventory. Generally accepted accounting principles (GAAP) require that inventory be written down to fair market value when the impairment is realized. If the company later sells that reduced-value inventory, it can see a jump in gross margin, because much of the cost of goods sold related to that merchandise was booked in the inventory charge. So Wall Street analysts add back a one-time impairment charge, but they do not note that future profits are generated as a direct result. When they "forget" to adjust future reports accordingly, results look better, but they're one-time only.

Here's another about-face on inventory: writing it off today only to sell it down the road.

Sale of Written-Off Inventory

It seems impossible, but a company can write off inventory now, yet still sell it later. This is among the most aggressive inventory actions management can take. When a company writes off inventory in one quarter as obsolete and then sells it in another quarter, it artificially overstates margins. As with all write-offs, if a company has more than one it may well "kitchen sink" them, taking a big hit all at once rather than dying the death of 1,000 cuts. If so, the overstated benefits when then-written-down inventory is subsequently sold appear even more dramatically but unsustainably "good."

This happened frequently during the 2000–2002 crash, when many companies that made physical technology products built up inventory, expecting skyrocketing demand to continue. Sometimes, they wrote it off and sold it later. In 2001, for example, networking equipment maker Cisco Systems recorded an excess inventory charge of $2.25 billion (a write-off) based on future sales forecasts, caught by the recession with declining demand in an industry where technology changes rapidly.

In the dramatic explosion of telecommunications networking equipment for Internet network buildout, Cisco's inventory zoomed from $655 million at October 30, 1999, to $2 billion a year later, reaching an all-time high of $2.5 billion a quarter after that. No wonder Cisco took a startling $2.25 billion write-down all at once to take a one-time hit that allowed it to "get it all behind." The company stated: "This additional excess inventory charge was calculated based on the inventory levels in excess of 12-month demand for each specific product. We do not currently anticipate that the excess inventory subject to this provision will be used at a later date, based on our current 12-month demand forecast." Yowza!

But it didn't take long to partially revise that forecast. In subsequent quarters, Cisco used and sold some of the inventory, reversing the charge and benefitting the income statement, as Table 3.8 shows.

Of the $2.25 billion reserve recorded in FY 2001, 32 percent—*$712 million*—was in effect later sold. The company actually sold $23 million to outside customers, used inventory internally for a gain of $457 million in operating cash flow, and settled for $252 million with customers who probably cancelled orders.

The reversal of reserves through sale, utilization, and settlement appears to boost revenues, but only because of the prior severe write-down. This creates the appearance of improvement where there would have been none. Moreover, the magnitude of the "inventory utilized" and the uncertainty over valuation for internal use makes it hard to have any confidence in these numbers, operating cash flow, margins, or EPS. The best advice is to avoid—not even short—such a stock.

Change in Inventory Valuation Method

Here, a company may change from average cost to retail method to value inventory. The retail method recognizes markdowns as the products are sold, while the average cost measures markdowns when made.

Table 3.8 Cisco Systems' Sale of Written-Off Inventory: 2001–2002*

	Total	FY 2002	FY 2001
Initial inventory write-off			($2,249)
Use of written-off inventory:			
Sale of inventory	$32	$23	$9
Inventory utilized internally	$457	$408	$49
Settlement of purchase commitments	$232	$103	$129
Total benefit from previously written-off inventory	**$721**	**$534**	**$187**

*Dollar amounts are in millions of dollars.
Source: SEC filings.

Consider mythical Teenybopper Inc. that sells tops. It realizes it's ordered far more of its St. Swithin's day tops than it can sell in that short holiday season. It puts a clearance sign on the display for the tops announcing a markdown from $15 to $10. The conservative and preferred method is average cost, which recognizes the markdown, therefore reducing inventory valuation, when made—when the sign is put on the display and tops, if sold, would be rung up at the register at $10. The aggressive practice is the retail method, where the store puts up the sign, but only recognizes the markdown and reduces inventory value retrospectively, when the top is rung up at the register at the marked-down price.

The change from average cost to retail method stretches out the period between markdown and actual reduction in inventory value. The average cost method is more accurate. The inventory is worth less the moment it's marked down; the top isn't worth $15 anymore. In fact, it may actually be worth even less than $10, because in retail, the first markdown is rarely the last, until the last stop for the hapless St. Swithin's day tops is the discount outlet mall (Tom's favorite shopping destination).

Inventory Step-Up

An inventory step-up is when a company makes an acquisition and increases—"steps up"—the value of the acquired company's inventory on the balance sheet. When the inventory is sold, the stepped-up cost is expensed as a special, nonrecurring item. A March 2008 Assay Research report showed these problems at Jarden, a diversified consumer products company:

> We question the quality of Jarden's reported gross margin improvement over the past two years, given that the Company excluded manufacturer's profit in inventory—the purchase accounting fair value adjustment to acquired inventory—from the calculation. When a company makes an acquisition, it records the acquired assets, including inventory, at fair market value, which can be above book value. In those cases where inventory is "stepped-up," future cost of sales would be higher, since the carrying value of the acquired inventory was adjusted upwards at the time of the deal when the acquired inventory is sold. During nine out of the

Table 3.9 Jarden's Gross Margin "Improvement": March Quarter
2006–December Quarter 2007

Quarter Ending	Dec. 2007	Dec. 2006	Sep. 2007	Sep. 2006	June 2007	June 2006	March 2007	March 2006
Gross Margin	27.3%	25.1%	28.2%	26.0%	27.6%	24.1%	24.5%	23.5%
Year-over-Year Change (bps)	220		220		350		100	

past twelve periods, *Jarden has adjusted its gross margin upwards by excluding the portion of reported cost of sales attributable to this inventory step-up* [emphasis added]. Jarden reported that its adjusted gross margin increased year-over-year by 220 basis points in the December and September quarters, and by 350 and 100 basis points during the June and March periods, respectively [see Table 3.9]. Because of the frequency and recent significance of the charges [see Table 3.10], we are concerned that Jarden's gross margin may not have improved as much as reported. [4]

Table 3.10 Jarden's Quarterly Adjustments to Costs of Goods Sold for Manufacturer's Profit in Inventory, 2005–2007*

Year	Quarter			
	Q4	Q3	Q2	Q1
2007	$50.5	$45.3	$27.1	None
2006	$6.5	$3.9	None	0.3[†]
2005	$4.3[†]	$4.2	None	16.4

*Dollar amounts are in millions of dollars.
[†]Includes inventory write-offs of $0.3 million in Q1 2006 and $2.5 million in Q4 2005.
Source: SEC filings.

These adjustments suggested that Jarden's gross margin improvement in 2007 was unsustainable. While 2008 was harsh to all stocks, Jarden nevertheless dropped 60 percent from March 1, 2008, to its March 9, 2009 bottom, 12 percentage points more than the S&P 500's fall.

Conclusion

Inventory management is not easy, so when a company does it well—knows its customers, seasonality, and product risks—it shows high earnings quality. When management gets it wrong, inventory analysis can show trouble ahead. But when they're not just "getting it wrong"—when a company hides the deteriorating situation and poor earnings quality—that's the ticking bomb this chapter's tools will help you avoid.

Aggressive revenue recognition and inventory management are the top two predictors of poor earnings quality, but others compete for the title. We move now to other ways companies unsustainably boost earnings.

Chapter 4

More Unsustainable Boosts to Earnings

Revenue recognition and inventory management are key predictors of poor earnings quality, but the balance sheet and income statement offer more playgrounds for management manipulation. This chapter combines these important balance sheet and income statement concerns organized by the balance sheet's categories of assets, liabilities, and owners' (shareholders') equity. It's important to know this most basic of all relationships: assets = liabilities + shareholder equity. In these three categories you'll find a number of line items to analyze to better assess, whether revenues are overstated, expenses understated, or cash flow unsustainable. (We covered the all-important inventory line in the last chapter.)

Proceeding from line to line, our guide is always that laws, regulations, and pronouncements from the Financial Accounting Standards Board (FASB) and others are rarely black and white. They leave management with discretion. Given the importance of choices among accounting treatments, look first for any accounting changes. Management can hide behind them to manipulate earnings quality. Even legitimate, required, and defensible changes may make it difficult or impossible to compare the current period with another in order to see company trends. Changes in accounting principles, estimates, and reporting entities raise serious concerns.

Accounting Changes

Accounting treatment changes almost always change comparisons of apples to apples to comparisons of apples to kiwis, obscuring reality and earnings quality. Three types of changes are key: changes in accounting principles, estimates, and reporting entities.

Changes in Accounting Principles

Nondiscretionary accounting principle changes are those issued by a standard-setting body such as the FASB. The company restates prior years to conform to the change—the dreaded "restatement" that, no matter how benign, frightens investors—or shows the cumulative effect of the change in the current-period financials. For the latter, investors have to consult the notes to find the effect for the year of the change.

Frequent changes in principle include changes in inventory method (last-in-first-out, LIFO, or first-in-first-out, FIFO), the method to value pension assets, type of depreciation, and choice of percentage-of-completion or completed contract method. On the surface, these may seem unobjectionable, but a company cannot change a discretionary practice willy-nilly. The change must be to a practice that's in some way better than the prior treatment. Of course, this is not always the case— "better" is hardly a black and white standard. If a company wants to change principles to achieve a certain result, it will do so. Investors must be on guard that when a company chooses a new method, it may not be for best practices, but rather to obscure poor results by making comparisons difficult.

Changes in Estimates

Financial statements are chock full of places where management must estimate, and those estimates are opportunities for manipulation. For example, if management lengthens the depreciation and amortization (D&A) period, it reduces operating expenses, boosting EPS. In 2005, VeriFone Holdings reduced its amortization expense 43 percent from 1.4 percent to 0.8 percent, artificially boosting EPS. Lengthening a depreciation period boosts EPS in the short term and hurts it in the long term, because the depreciation, although smaller on a yearly basis, lasts longer. So after the accounting change, a company will still be taking depreciation expenses in years when it wouldn't have been under the previous depreciation term. The resulting change in EPS signals that management may be doing other things as well to meet nearer-term Wall Street expectations.

The place to start is to track D&A as a percentage of fixed assets. If the percentage declines, the company may have extended the D&A period. Then check further. Management estimates warranty obligations, collections on accounts receivable, returns, use of tax-loss carryforwards, the useful life of a car, truck, or airplane, and much more. Investors must exhume the changes in estimates from the footnotes.

Changes in Reporting Entities

In *mergers*, the reporting entity changes. This offers management a way to consign all sorts of expenses and charges to the past, making the newly formed company's first reports look better. *Acquisitions* are tougher, because the reporting entity doesn't change, but comparisons are cloudy or meaningless.

It's not impossible to get to earnings quality roots with mergers and acquisitions, but often it's better to just avoid the stock.

Throughout this chapter you will see these three areas of accounting changes crop up in different ways.

Assets

We start with two key earnings quality indicators from the balance sheet accounts receivable and allowance for doubtful accounts, and then move to goodwill, intangibles, and other assets. Each allows you to spy aggressive accounting and deteriorating fundamentals.

Reported accounts receivable have two components. You will see "accounts receivable, net of doubtful accounts," offering another chance to fiddle with the accounts receivable number. "Doubtful" isn't exactly scientific. This allowance offers its own set of possible concerns.

Allowance for Doubtful Accounts

First, it's a *good* thing that a company reports accounts receivable "net of allowance for doubtful accounts," because even the very best business is going to have deadbeat or failing customers now and then. But there is extraordinary room for judgment in how likely a customer is to pay, so this is another opportunity to uncover earnings manipulation. Manipulating this allowance affects receivables, and it carries across the financial statements. This can be where management finds that penny or two the company needs to please the Street at earnings time and keep its stock price out of trouble.

Reducing doubtful accounts may be an unsustainable source of income. No ongoing business has zero doubtful accounts. Reducing the allowance can then be an earnings quality red flag.

Finding where management manipulates the allowance is complicated. Not all companies disclose the reserve on a quarterly basis, making it difficult to track. Some firms disclose reserves annually, but then it can be too late for investors to identify a trend. But where the quarterly information is available, compare the quarterly allowance for doubtful accounts as a percent of gross accounts receivable. Do this by adding the allowance back to accounts receivable and calculating the percentage relationship between the two amounts:

Allowance for doubtful accounts/(Allowance for doubtful accounts + Net accounts receivable)

If the percentage of allowance for doubtful accounts drops sharply relative to gross accounts receivable, it may indicate an artificial boost to revenues and, therefore, earnings. The company likely did not record enough bad debt expense to maintain previous reserve levels. As a result, the lower expenses bring higher operating margins and higher net income.

What we want is that the allowance tracks gross receivables, rising and falling in tandem and showing that customer-credit quality is consistent as revenue grows. Declines (using the allowance as a cookie jar) and increases (customer-credit quality is worsening) alike are suspect, pointing to poor earnings quality and likely a deteriorating business.

In September 2004, John advised clients that the allowance for doubtful accounts at Silicon Laboratories and Synaptics was a probable source of EPS manipulation:

During the June quarter, Silicon Laboratories failed to increase its allowance for doubtful accounts to keep pace with the year-ago quarter. Given that DSO jumped in the quarter due to back-end-loaded revenue in the period, we believe the company's receivables carry *more* risk, *not less*. Had the company maintained the allowance percentage comparable to receivables growth, reported EPS would have been $0.01 lower.

Table 4.1 shows that despite an over 100 percent year-over-year *increase* in receivables from $33 million to $69 million in Q2 2004, the allowance *decreased* from 2.8 percent to 1.9 percent of receivables. It is highly doubtful that a *doubling* of receivables—even if for good reasons, such as revenue gains—are of such a substantially high quality as to merit about a 33 percent *decrease* in the allowance. Business just doesn't work that way.

When the company contorts but can eke out only another penny of EPS, there is no clearer signal of manipulation done to please the Street.

John turned to Synaptics:

Similarly, in 2004, Synaptics also obtained an earnings boost by reducing its level of allowance for doubtful accounts in the quarter relative to gross accounts receivable. We think the large ramp

Table 4.1 Silicon Laboratories' Questionable Allowance for Doubtful Accounts: June Quarter 2003 through June Quarter 2004*

Quarter Ending	July 2004	April 2004	Jan. 2004	Sep. 2003	June 2003
Gross Receivables	$69	$57	$49	$50	$33
Allowance for Doubtful Accounts	$1.3	$1.3	$1.1	$0.9	$0.9
Allowance for Doubtful Accounts as Percentage of Gross Receivables	1.9%	2.3%	2.2%	1.8%	2.8%

*Dollar amounts are in millions of dollars.
Source: SEC filings.

in receivables increased the risk of collection and the company should have increased the allowance level. In the September quarter, the allowance was just 0.6 percent of gross receivables, which is down from 1 percent a year ago—a 40 percent drop. We also maintain that the absolute level appears to be low as well. Table 4.2 shows accounts receivables have more than doubled in the past six quarters, while the allowance hasn't budged.

John's June 2005 report alerted clients that Maxim Integrated Products increased accounts receivable while reducing its allowance for doubtful accounts:

Despite the increase in accounts receivable, the company reduced its allowance for doubtful accounts and may have achieved a boost to reported earnings. Table 4.3 shows that the allowance as a percentage of gross receivables fell in 2004 to 2.4 percent from 3.9 percent in the year-ago period.

Gross accounts receivable *jumped* 53 percent while the allowance as a percentage *dropped* 38 percent—from 3.9 percent to 2.4 percent. Because a certain portion of receivables represented extended payment terms to international customers—business that is growing for Maxim—we might expect to see the allowance *increase* rather than *decrease*. We note that the company reports its allowance for doubtful accounts on an annual basis. Assuming no changes in recent quarters, reported earnings per share would have been significantly less in 2004 than in 2003.

Table 4.2 Synaptics's Questionable Allowance for Doubtful Accounts: June Quarter 2003–September Quarter 2004*

Quarter Ending	Sep. 2004	June 2004	March 2004	Dec. 2003	Sep. 2003	June 2003
Gross Receivables	$29.6	$22.0	$18.9	$17.8	$16.1	$13.3
Allowance	$164	$130	$130	$130	$160	$160
Allowance Percentage	0.6%	0.6%	0.7%	0.7%	1.0%	1.2%

*Dollar amounts are in millions of dollars.

Table 4.3 Maxim Integrated Products Questionable Allowance for Doubtful Accounts: June Quarters 2002, 2003, and 2004*

Quarter Ending	June 2004	June 2003	June 2002
Allowance for Doubtful Accounts	$4,920	$5,118	$3,176
Net Accounts Receivable,	$197,508	$126,760	$129,812
Gross Accounts Receivable	$202,078	$131,878	$132,988
Allowance for Doubtful Accounts as Percentage of Gross Accounts Receivable	2.4%	3.9%	2.4%

*Dollar amounts in millions of dollars.

Businesses just don't see their customers' payment quality increase *faster* than the rate of new receivables. The decreased allowance for doubtful accounts was a bright red waving flag. Trouble came soon. In Maxim's 10-K filing for fiscal year 2005, ending in June, the 2004 allowance appeared as $13.4 million, not $4.9 million; 2005's was $14 million, while accounts receivable fell from $197 million to $192 million. Maxim borrowed income from the future. Chapter 3's Figure 3.1 shows the disaster for the stock.

Analyzing receivables and doubtful account reserves reveals whether the company is playing games with revenues on the income statement and is potentially papering over business deterioration. Further down the balance sheet's asset side, we find more possible warnings in goodwill and intangibles.

Goodwill and Intangibles

Management can manipulate goodwill and intangibles to inflate assets. If goodwill and intangibles are large as a percentage of total assets, it could mean that assets are overvalued due to acquisitions. If goodwill changes without an acquisition, it means the company adjusted a purchase price allocation. A popular momentum stock through 2011 illustrates this.

Customer-relations management software provider salesforce.com acquired three public companies and three private companies in 2010, for $403 million. It allocated the purchases almost entirely to acquired developed technology and goodwill and intangibles, at about 25 percent and 75 percent, respectively. There is no way to know whether the company's valuations for these are reasonable. Moreover, they accounted for 17 percent of FY 2011 total assets, and with the $277 million purchase of San Francisco Mission Bay real estate for a world headquarters, comprise the *entire* increase in total assets from FY 2010 to FY 2011. The latter is bad enough: one hardly thinks of San Francisco real estate in calendar 2010 as value-priced. This suggests a management capital decision based on something other than value pricing expected to bring good returns on investment. (Worse, after buying the building, reports are that costs zoomed out of control, management canceled the plan for the campus, and leased significant other space in the city.[1]) But previous decisions on allocating to goodwill, intangibles, and capitalized software gave management enormous latitude to manipulate asset values.

If salesforce.com were growing rapidly, perhaps none of this would matter. But its growth rates were only good—not great—and EBITDA, EBIT, net income, and free cash flow have fallen dramatically in the quarters prior to this writing. This puts the company in a bind. Because Silicon Valley "tech" companies pay heavily in stock options ("everyone else is doing it, so we have to"), this puts pressure on management to do what it can to keep the picture bright and the stock price aloft ("who really notices the option footnotes and potential dilution anyway?"). The ending is rarely a happy one.

Goodwill Increased in a Period When No Acquisition Occurred

If a company has increased goodwill when it hasn't acquired a company, it may have created an unsustainable boost on the income statement.

When a company makes an acquisition, it is allowed up to 12 months to adjust the purchase price for the acquired company's carrying value of assets and liabilities. A write-down in assets, or conversely a write-up in liabilities, reduces the equity of the transaction and goodwill. These purchase price adjustments do not have to flow through the income statement as expenses if done before the end of one year following the acquisition.

As a result of the purchase price reallocation within a year, expenses are kept off the income statement, artificially boosting earnings in the period of adjustment.

This treatment can also affect future periods, and investors' inattention to these adjustments allows management a vast opportunity for manipulation. If a company reallocates the purchase price by writing down the value of an asset and increasing the value of goodwill, it builds in a future gain. If the company sells that asset later for more than its carrying value, it recognizes a gain on the income statement.

The benefit does not end with built-in gains. If the asset written down is a depreciable asset, then the related depreciation expense will also be reduced, thereby increasing earnings. Keep in mind that, under accounting rules, goodwill is no longer amortized, so operating expenses are immediately reduced. Goodwill is subject to impairment testing, but the process of valuing a company is so gray and based so much on expectations, that a company can delay recognizing an impairment charge for years.

Goodrich Corp. provided a clear example of manipulating goodwill in 2004, when John's former firm Behind the Numbers notified clients of concerns at the company:

> According to Goodrich's June 2003 quarter 10-Q, [a purchase price] adjustment *lifted* goodwill by $43.4 million. But it was easy to miss on the balance sheet, because the sale of Goodrich's Avionics business *reduced* goodwill by $46.3 million. According to the filing, "of the $43.4 million increase to goodwill as a result of business combinations completed or finalized, $42.4 million related to revisions to the purchase price allocation for the Aeronautical Systems acquisition and $1.0 million related to the adjustment of the purchase price of an acquisition due to an earn-out agreement." The company did state in its 10-K that the purchase price was subject to potential upward or downward revision based on change to net assets between October 1, 2002 and May 31, 2003 as well as on the funded status of employee benefit plans. However, this was a fairly sizeable adjustment. To put the size of this increase in goodwill in perspective, the company booked $500 million in goodwill at the time of the acquisition, almost a 10 percent increase in the goodwill balance.
>
> In addition, the company recorded a non-cash increase to the restructuring reserve of $18.4 million in the first quarter, which, again, did not flow through the income statement. This was to adjust upwards the expected cost of integrating the acquisition.

A material increase in goodwill from a purchase price adjustment requires scrutiny. It means that either assets have been written down, or acquisition-related liabilities have been increased. In the case of the former, it leads to the possibility that assets will be sold later and artificially high gains could be booked. Normal operating expenses could be booked into the acquisition liability and never hit the income statement. In either case, profits can be artificially inflated.

Goodrich's goodwill manipulation shows one more way management can inflate profits unsustainably. Moving from goodwill and intangibles down the balance sheet to other current assets, capitalization offers management another chance to manipulate the numbers as well.

Other Current Assets: Capitalization

Another way companies can make the current picture brighter is through capitalizing assets. When "other current assets" divided by revenue increases, it may indicate that the company is treating an expense as an asset and overstating earnings. Track this relative to revenue—other current assets divided by revenue—and track as you do DSO. When this number is rising, it may indicate the company is increasing the practice of capitalizing expenses—treating expenses as assets that allegedly will be repaid out of future income. This treats an expense as an asset, overstating earnings now against an uncertain future when assets may or may not yield compensating earnings.

Mulford and Comiskey identify four analytical tools to detect aggressive capitalization[2]:

1. A review of the company's capitalization policies
2. A careful consideration of what the capitalized costs represent
3. A check to determine whether the company has been aggressive in its capitalization policies in the past
4. A check for costs capitalized in stealth

A simple way to cover these four points is to divide other current assets by revenue. Identifying where this increases then points the investor to SEC filings for further examination.

Mulford and Comiskey note that the most conservative treatment is to immediately expense acquired in-process research and development, patents and licenses, direct-response marketing, and other research and development.[3] If they yield future income, great, but until then, they shouldn't be assets that show a stronger balance sheet and greater shareholder equity than warranted.

Software companies *may* capitalize software development costs once technological feasibility is reached, but this is so subject to management judgment that Mulford and Comiskey note, "In fact, one could reasonably argue that managements can raise or lower amounts capitalized by choice, raising or lowering earnings in the process."[4]

Salesforce.com again exhibits a practice emblematic of many software companies.[5] Table 4.4 shows the company's capitalized software costs on the balance sheet for the past three years.

The bulk of the 2011 acquired developed technology came from three acquisitions. While GAAP allows the treatment, it gives the company great latitude. The decision to boost the balance sheet by FY 2011 acquisitions through allocation to acquired developed technology, goodwill, and intangibles allows management significant discretion to manage the asset side of the balance sheet. It also raises questions that seem more pertinent when salesforce.com's *revenue* is *growing* with consistent gross margins, but EBITDA and EBIT margins, EPS, and levered and unlevered free cash flow are *declining* dramatically from FY 2010 highs.

Mere questionable capitalization by itself is not the determining factor in earnings quality analysis—it's one of many. America Online, for example, may have capitalized member acquisition expenses in 1995 and 1996 in order to show a profit. But after that and until it paid a $3.5 million fine in 2000,[6] the company grew at a red-hot rate, overwhelming any earnings

Table 4.4 Salesforce.com's Capitalized Software: 2009–2011

Year	2011	2010	2009
Other Current Assets:			
Total Capitalized Software	$128.0	$34.8	$30.0
Capitalized software, net	$29.2	$22.7	$17.5
Acquired developed technology, net	$98.8	$12.1	$12.5
Revenues	$1,657	$1,307	$1,079

*Dollar amounts are in millions of dollars.
Source: SEC filings.

quality effect from that practice. That lasted until the Time Warner merger and the bottom fell out of the online advertising market and the stock. Salesforce.com is not growing anywhere near red-hot. Currently, it's merely warm, and in recent quarters, the company is pulling out all the stops—including multiyear invoicing—to put off the day when revenue growth declines and the stock price goes with it. At this writing and based on these and other earnings quality issues, Tom has shorted via puts profitably.

Therefore the frequency of capitalization, the items capitalized, and the relative size of those items tells the investor whether capitalization is a serious concern or not.

Now we leave assets to turn to the other side of the balance sheet, liabilities, which presents its own set of potential earnings quality concerns.

Liabilities

Deferred revenue represents an easy opportunity for management to manipulate earnings quality. This is revenue a company receives before it delivers the product or service. Until it delivers, that revenue is at risk—it's not yet an asset.

Deferred Revenue

Days in deferred revenue are calculated as:

$$Days\ in\ Deferred\ Revenue\ (DDR) = (91.25 \times deferred\ revenue)/ \\ quarterly\ revenue$$

Track DDR relative to DSO (DSO minus DDR) for 8 to 12 quarters. If it is declining, the company is generating less deferred revenue relative to the terms it is offering customers. This may generate more upfront revenue, but it only borrows from the future.

John started shorting Medidata Solutions in September 2011, when adoption of a new accounting standard showed significant, but unsustainable, revenue growth. The accounting change formed an estimated 70 percent of Medidata's total $10 million year-over-year revenue growth. Without the change, the growth rate would have been 7.5 percent. The huge increase was not new revenue—only revenue pulled forward—so deferred revenue trends deteriorated after the one-time boost. DDR fell sharply year-over-year (see Table 4.5).

Table 4.5 Medidata's declining DDR: June Quarter 2010–June Quarter 2011*

Quarter Ending	June 2011	March 2011	Dec. 2010	Sep. 2010	June 2010
Days Deferred Revenue (DDR)	132	189	161	201	217
Deferred Revenue	$72.48	$84.47	$83.77	$90.40	$95.78
Sequential Change	(30%)	17%	(20%)	(7%)	(11%)
Year-over-Year Change	(24%)	(16%)	(14%)	(13%)	(7%)

*Dollar amounts are in millions of dollars. DDR numbers are in days.

Declining deferred revenue suggests that Medidata probably booked more revenue up front due to the change.[7] This is a strong sign to avoid, sell, or short a stock.

So far, this chapter has shown the items most predictive of earnings quality problems. The next concerns are less predictive, but when they appear together with others, the investor should investigate further.

Noncash Deferred Revenue

When the company credits deferred revenue but debits accounts receivables, balance sheet analysis becomes more opaque. The company is not receiving cash for its deferred revenue, which should make investors skeptical.

Changes in Other and Accrued Liabilities

Reserves are often lumped into the "accrued liabilities," "other current liabilities," or "other liabilities" accounts on a company's balance sheet, and it is difficult to determine what these accounts contain. It's typically fruitless to contact the company for information. Therefore, the investor must infer what is driving the change in these accounts on a quarterly basis. This is another balance sheet issue that is also very important to the income statement.

As with all of our important metrics, you should track accrued liabilities (we'll stick with "accrued liabilities" to cover those "other liabilities," and "other current liabilities"; the detection of warning signs is the same) relative to revenue for 8 to 12 quarters. If the company takes serial charges, it may indicate that it is building up reserves. If these liabilities relative to revenue drop sharply, it could indicate the company reversed a previously established reserve. This would then be a credit to the income statement at a 100 percent margin, boosting profits and overstating EPS.

Companies maintain reserves for many reasons, usually against a contingent liability. For example, will they have to pay out on warranties or protect against customer non-payment? The key question, though, is whether the company is using reserves to smooth income—often called cookie jar reserves, because you can fill the jar and take from it as you need—resulting in questionable earnings quality. Some warning signs for reserves are balance sheet concerns, but they also affect the income statement.

Both the balance sheet and the income statement can be used to confirm suspicious behavior. For example, if accrued liabilities typically amount to 10 percent of quarterly sales, and in the current quarter they represent 5 percent of sales while operating profit margin jumps 400 basis points for no apparent reason, a reserve may have been reversed and net income artificially bolstered.

Reductions in Warranties

Reducing reserves for warranties boosts EPS. Management can manipulate this reserve at will. Returning to Synaptics, John's 2004 report revealed an earnings boost from a reduction in accrued warranty liability:

> In recent quarters, we believe Synaptics obtained an earnings boost through the reduction of its accrued warranty liability. This account has been reduced both in absolute dollars and relative to revenue. The cost of the warranty is estimated at the time of revenue recognition, and the obligation is affected by failure rates, material usage, and service delivery costs incurred by the company in order to correct the problem.
>
> As Table 4.6 shows, while revenue was $38.1 million in September 2004, the accrued warranty was just $596,000, or 1.6 percent of revenue. Conversely, in the year-ago period, revenue was $29.6 million, while the reserve was nearly $1 million, or 3.3 percent of revenue. We also note that the reserve in both absolute terms and on a percentage basis has fallen in each of the past five quarters. Further detail provided in the quarterly 10-Q report shows that the cost of warranty claims and settlements nearly doubled versus the year-ago period to $535,000 from $288,000 in September 2003.

Table 4.6 Synaptics Rrevenue versus Accrued Warranty: September Quarter 2003—September Quarter 2004*

Quarter Ending	Sep. 2004	June 2004	March 2004	Dec. 2003	Sep. 2003	June 2003
Total Revenue	$38,091	$35,147	$34,284	$34,274	$16,110	$13,341
Accrued Warranty	$596	$704	$891	$937	$969	$1,002
Accrued Warranty as Percentage of Total Revenue	1.6%	2.0%	2.6%	2.7%	3.0%	3.6%

*All dollar amounts are in thousands of dollars.
Source: SEC filings.

Were investors to believe that revenues steadily increased sequentially for quarters, while the company's potential warrant liability declined each quarter? This suggests that management may be reducing the warranty reserve to boost EPS. Had the company maintained a 3.3 percent warranty/revenue ratio, earnings per share in the September quarter would have been $0.015 lower.

A penny here, a penny there, and you're likely seeing desperation and manipulation. But it's far more than a penny at issue where pension liabilities overwhelm many long-lived companies. Real fear can drive management to actions that can make you laugh out loud, and then avoid trouble or profit.

Boosts from Pension Plans

A huge issue for companies with traditional defined-benefit pension plans is the assumption for returns. Many have used a number like 8 percent annualized during a decade with flat to no returns overall from the market and negative or close to negative inflation-adjusted returns from fixed-income investments. This has meant huge increases in the number of underfunded pension plans. The change of even one percentage point in expectations can change hundreds of millions of dollars. Eight percentage points in a flat period is unethical at best.

Companies like General Motors declared bankruptcy, not the least from the burden of retiree benefits. The same pressure hurt Eastman Kodak, which also went belly-up. Both were for a long time considered widow and orphan stocks, but they may have created instead of supported them. Still alive at writing, Sears Holdings also has large pension liabilities and is struggling to meet them.

No wonder management waves a wand to magically raise return assumptions in lower-return environments. Increasing expected investment return and reducing pension liability also increases tangible book value. The company puts off funding pensions at the level it should if return assumptions were sensible, in effect raiding the pension account. It just borrows from the future until it can no longer do so.

Debt

Debt is less easy to manipulate, but the ways companies use debt matters. Most investors begin with one of two viewpoints. One camp believes that debt is always and everywhere bad. The other group holds that debt-free companies should take on debt, because the deductibility of interest expense reduces the cost of capital and may lower the hurdle for management to invest that capital for greater return, boosting earnings and free cash flow. It's not this black and white.

Of course debt represents risk, and it can indicate trouble. It is axiomatic that unsustainable debt—where the company most simply states it can't make payments—leads to an unsustainable company. "Unsustainable" can mean, at best, acquisition at a fire-sale price by a stronger company, a recapitalization that almost always leaves common stockholders with a fraction of their former ownership share, or, of course, bankruptcy.

But there is therefore no substitute for the detailed and necessary task of identifying all debt terms, including fixed or floating interest rate, maturity, recourse or non-recourse, convertibility, lender ability to call or convert the debt to equity, company repayment restrictions or options, coverage ratios, and dependability of cash flows.

Financial Companies, Leverage, and a Checklist

The typical analysts' emphasis on the ratio of cash to debt is superficial and a first step only. They may even go farther than one step for companies in the business of selling nonfinancial products. But their eyelids grow heavy with the complexity of debt at financial companies that depend on leverage to increase profits and offer increased risk. Those who require securitizations to maintain their business—timeshare vendors, credit card issuers, and, at various times, mortgage issuers, for example—have with alarming frequency entered bankruptcy or

been reduced to a fraction of their former values when credit spontane-
ously combusts. *Know your company's debt intimately.* An investor will
encounter at least several credit crises in an investing lifetime.

Adhere to these guidelines when considering companies with debt:

1. Avoid all companies whose business models depend on securitizations or consistent access to credit markets. Prudent risk management would eliminate almost all such financial companies.
   Instead, consider them strong short candidates at various times in
   the credit cycle.[8]
2. Only buy companies with large debt to assets where you can model
   interest coverage, maturity dates, and other terms, such as convertibility and covenants, with confidence, through at least one business cycle with a serious downside. Refinancing may be required at
   the worst times—uncertain and unknown in advance, of course—
   on arduous or no terms.
3. Carefully monitor the uses of debt to determine adequate returns
   on capital raised. Debt becomes a quality of management and
   quality of earnings problem when the benefits on earnings from
   debt interest rate deductions are outweighed by all the ways
   management can misuse the cash to destroy value and hurt
   earnings.
4. Debt used to fund dividends and/or stock buybacks must pass the
   most stringent of tests—and usually fails. If value-minded management finds its shares at a significant discount to intrinsic value and
   to opportunity costs, debt for repurchases might be a proper use
   of capital (and using lower-interest debt to repurchase stock and to
   retire the obligation to pay those shares' future dividend streams
   can be a positive allocation and very good for cash flow). But management rarely has the financial training to allocate capital this
   properly and subtly. Some companies, such as General Electric,
   can steadily increase debt while paying dividends and buying back
   shares, but few can do so indefinitely. And GE's mind-numbing
   financial complexity should tell investors only one thing: stay away.

Because there is such a large class of income-hungry investors who
choose dividend-paying stocks as a rule, debt for dividends deserves
further discussion.

Increasing Debt to Maintain or Increase Dividends

A company with a history of dividends eventually attracts a long-term shareholder base because of that dependability, and a history of rising dividends only locks in the shareholders more tightly. A dividend-paying company's management therefore will sell its first-born rather than cut—let alone eliminate—its dividend. Income-loving investors would sell en masse and destroy the stock price. Therefore, a company may build up debt to pay dividends and put off the day of dividend-cut reckoning.

So when is a dividend good or bad for a company with debt? Value investors like to get paid somehow, through dividends, buybacks at opportunistic prices, buyouts, spinoffs, and other value-creating events. But growth investors view dividends as a signal that a business has no better uses for the capital and that, somehow, growth is over. What *should* matter is that:

- The dividends are paid out of excess capital—capital not needed to run the business.
- Management cannot find other investments that offer higher returns on the excess capital.
- The debt is not increased to pay or maintain a dividend—unless, for example, at a negative real interest rate, such as large credit-solid companies, including Microsoft, were able to obtain in the post-2008 credit bubble low-interest environment.

Eventually, in almost every case, debt for dividends is unsustainable. What begins as a way to maintain a shareholder base ends when the dividend, at best, remains flat or worse is cut or eliminated. Like so many accounting manipulations, debt for dividends just borrows from the future—putting off a day of reckoning when dividends are cut or eliminated and dividend-hungry shareholders will bolt.

Debt Caveat

Lost in the past decades of subdued inflation has been the truism that inflation favors debtors and disfavors creditors. Debt with fixed and manageable interest is just as positive for a company as it is for the homeowner with a 30-year, 4 percent fixed-rate mortgage when inflation rises. The flip side, of course, is that a deflationary environment makes the debt more onerous. If you know which environment we are in at any time, you can make a lot of money betting on it (good luck!). In the long term, paper currency inflates, and that's that, but in the short term, anything can happen.

Shareholders' Equity: Book Value and Tangible Book Value

All balance sheet items play roles in shareholder equity. The value investor on the long side, like Tom, focuses, not on how much can be *gained*, but, rather, on how much could be *lost*. One metric is to evaluate hard assets, or tangible book value (TBV) per share.

$$TBV/share = [shareholder's\ equity - (goodwill + intangibles)]$$
$$/diluted\ shares$$

John's 2005 report to clients on Helen of Troy included a reminder of why intangible assets and goodwill aren't protection for the investor. He noted:

> The balance sheet is bloated with intangible assets. Acquisitions are often less synergistic than management's tend to believe, thus creating less shareholder value than perceived. Furthermore, in recent years it has been apparent that there is a tendency to overpay for acquired entities. With respect to Helen of Troy, intangible assets accounted for 46.8 percent of total assets at November 2004 compared with 26.5 percent in the year-ago period. *As a result, tangible book value is just $1.1 million.* [emphasis added] The breakdown in intangibles includes $201.5 million in goodwill, $157.7 million in trademarks, $29.6 million in license agreements, and $17.4 million in other intangibles.

So let's stick with the tangible. But even then, in the world of investing some tangible book value is better than others. When it's made up of a lot of cash, that's good—except in an inflationary environment. A formula is only as good as its inputs, so all TBV's material components must be checked—not just cash and debt. TBV is least valuable when accounts receivable and/or inventory are manipulated, in which case the investor should examine the *trend* and *nature* of both. They could increase for the right reasons, such as growing business and more customers, or for the wrong reasons, such as poor business trends, poor customer financial strength, or getting the marketplace wrong and yet showing higher TBV. Assuming too high returns on pension investments understates pension liabilities and overstates TBV. And so on. Therefore, TBV is extremely useful but can't be taken for granted.

Footwear company Skechers provides a great example of TBV that is static while varying dramatically in quality, due to volatile accounts receivable and inventory. It introduced a new product line in 2009, and when customers avoided it in droves, inventory ballooned. Table 4.7 shows that the company's tangible book value remained flat for four quarters, though its accounts receivables and inventory trended worse than revenues.

Skechers' new Shape-Ups shoes were initially successful. Then demand for the shoe, which offered a rolling, convex sole, fell off. Skechers misjudged demand, inventory swelled, and DSO and DSI trended dangerously upward. The effect became most visible with year-over-year comparisons beginning in the December quarter of 2010.

From the December quarter of 2009 to the Sepember quarter of 2010, inventory percentage gains dwarfed revenue increases, until the September quarter of 2011. Accounts receivable rose faster and dropped more slowly than revenues. Gross margins slid and partially recovered recently. EPS, EBITDA, and free cash flow (OCF minus capex) collapsed. Valuation multiples went sky high. The lesson and caveat: *And yet, somehow, TBV was basically flat for six quarters, because it didn't show the worsening quality of the inventory or lengthening receivables.*

While certain negative accounting indicators are more important than others, no one of them alone is sufficient. Take them as a whole. The long investor can truly profit by understanding the quality of balance sheet items and their relation to long-side metrics, such as TBV. John profitably shorted Skechers. (Tom notes that at this writing Skechers has corrected the inventory issue and has brought gains to long investors who saw it in process. Today's short may be tomorrow's long, when management successfully addresses accounting and business concerns.)

Quest Software provides yet another example of when not to put all your chips on TBV. In October 2005, John advised clients that the company's acquisition strategy did not create value. TBV raised a red flag. Where Quest's acquisiting led to increased revenues, earnings, and operating cash flow, TBV increased by a mere penny. At Skechers other

Table 4.7 Skechers' Tangible Book Value versus Working Capital and Other Trends: December Quarter 2009–September Quarter 2011*

Quarter Ending	Sep. 2011	June 2011	March 2011	Dec. 2010	Sep. 2010	June 2010	March 2010	Dec. 2009
Inventory	$238	$326	$376	$399	$327	$219	$189	$224
Revenues	$414	$436	$478	$456	$556	$506	$493	$389
Accounts Receivable	$245	$276	$320	$266	$286	$305	$292	$220
Gross Margin	43%	33%	41%	40%	46%	47%	48%	49%
Inventory Change Year-over-Year	(27%)	49%	99%	78%	—	—	—	—
Revenues Change Year-over-Year	(26%)	(14%)	(3%)	17%	—	—	—	—
A/R Change Year-over-Year	(14%)	(10%)	10%	21%	—	—	—	—
DSO	68	62	55	58	49	54	47	50
DSI	110	110	123	123	83	70	73	96
OCF Minus Capex	N/A	$5	($45)	($63)	($29)	($55)	$18	$21
EBITDA	$10	($40)	$23	$9	$63	$65	$87	$48
Diluted EPS	$0.17	($0.62)	$0.24	$0.07	$0.74	$0.82	$1.15	$0.58
Tangible Book Value per Share	$18.55	$18.62	$19.08	$18.69	$18.90	$17.81	$17.02	$15.82

*Inventory, revenues, and accounts receivable dollar amounts are in millions of dollars. DSO and DSI are in days.
Source: SEC filings.

issues led to questioning TBV, but at Quest came the reverse: TBV signaled trouble elsewhere. John wrote then that:

> We question whether Quest management's acquisition strategy has created value for its shareholders. Our thesis is based on three observations:
>
> - While the company has turned profitable subsequent to the tech-related downturn, those earnings have not flowed through to the balance sheet, which has become bloated with intangibles.
> - While acquisitions benefit revenue and net income, and thus operating cash flow, the expense is an investing cash outflow. Adjustments to reflect the cash payments result in plummeting free cash flow.
> - Several acquisitions were the result of related-party transactions or occurred at prices substantially higher than Quest's own valuation.

Like most technology companies, Quest suffered a downturn in 2000–2001 but has returned to profitability over the past three fiscal years, generating diluted earnings per share of $0.82. In contrast, Table 4.8 shows tangible book value increasing from $1.309 to $1.313 per share from 2002 through 2004, while nearly *all* of the earnings disappeared, likely the

Table 4.8 Quest's Tangible Book Value versus Pricey Acquisitions and Stock Options

Year Ending	Dec. 2004	Dec. 2002
Assets	$843,351	$591,281
Goodwill and Intangibles	$365,307	$234,833
Tangible Assets	$478,044	$356,448
Shareholder's Equity	$606,912	$477,982
Tangible Book Value	$128,868	$121,534
No. Shares (increase shows effect of stock options)	98,158	92,820
Tangible Book Value per Shares	$1.313	$1.309

*All dollar amount are in millions of dollars.
Source: SEC filings.

result of pricey acquisitions, and to a certain extent, massive stock option plans as well.

Thus, while the acquisitions have led to increases in revenue, earnings, and operating cash flow, they've created virtually no value for shareholders. We are concerned that they have led only to the enrichment of Quest's management.

Tangible book value is a useful investing tool when it signals problems elsewhere, as at Quest. The investor must analyze the entire balance sheet to know how reliable a measure of true asset value TBV is.

Items Special to the Income Statement

Profit Margins

Profit margins hypnotize most investors. As margins rise and fall, it becomes easier not to delve into them. But it's essential not to take gross profit or operating margins at face value. Companies can control some but not all costs, and fluctuations can be spun all sorts of ways. Sequential changes will impress or depress the quarter-driven Street, only to have the reverse effect next quarter. The Street's focus encourages management to play along.

Gross Profit and Input Costs

Most investors watch the trend in gross profit margin and stop there, yet the components matter. Management may or may not have control over inventory input costs, but their treatment is important. Remember, it is normal for gross profit margins to vary—we'd be suspicious of any that were unchanging. We know they will move. We're concerned with unusual changes.

"Inputs" are the components of products, from cotton for jeans to silicon for semiconductors. To detect problems in input costs requires industry and company-specific knowledge. Sometimes the company will reveal when an input's higher cost negatively affected gross profits, sometimes not. When an input rises in price and the company can't increase product prices commensurately, gross margins decline. But when the input's price falls and boosts gross margins, management may, like the rooster, take credit for the sunrise, though the price benefits to gross margins and profit are unsustainable.

Teen and tween clothing retailer Aeropostale is an example of a business for which the chief input is cotton, a commodity whose price is volatile, but should be well known to management of a clothing retailer whose main products are jeans and T-shirts. In 2011, clothing retailers, including Aeropostale, faced, not only consumer headwinds, leading to markdowns, but an almost parabolic spike in cotton prices—their single largest product input (see Figure 4.1). This squeezed gross profit.

Aeropostale reported plummeting EPS for the quarter ending July 30, 2011—$0.04 versus prior year's $0.46. It cited product mix leading to higher inventory and markdowns, and cotton prices for the decline in gross margins. The stock collapsed.

On November 3, 2011, the company provided that rare animal, a pre-earnings "update"—not a warning, but rather an increased earnings estimate for the quarter ending three days before and for which it would report at the end of the month. And not just any old penny estimate hike, but 85 to 200 percent above prior guidance. Though the prior earnings report and conference call emphasized cotton prices—which had declined at least for the time being towards pre-spike levels—this press release did not mention them, but instead attributed the improvement to

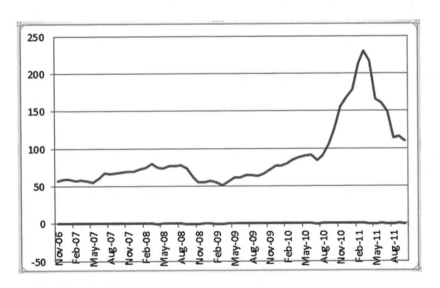

Figure 4.1 Monthly cotton prices in cents per pound: November 2006–September 2011.
Source: www.indexmundi.com.

"better than expected gross margins for the quarter." The same sales a year earlier produced EPS of $0.63—more than twice as much as the November 3 update on far better gross margins. But the Street saw only an 85–200 percent jump in estimates. Gross margins or operating margins or both would likely still lag the year-ago period. Table 4.9 shows they did. "Better than expected" still wasn't great.

In fairness, the company didn't spin this in the press release, and the CEO said, "We remain cautious, given industry-wide costing pressures and the current retail environment." This may imply that the margin boost was actually due to cotton input price improvement and that product pricing remained at risk. But why did management release an earnings anti-warning, unless it intended to promote the gross margin improvement to obscure its year-over-year and sequential failure to improve margins to normalized levels? The pre-announcement showed management blatantly attempting to manage the stock price.

It worked. The stock jumped 19 percent. Those who bought before, as Tom recommended (see the arrow in Figure 4.2), benefitted from this rise, but Aeropostale's future earnings power was still unclear. The rise in gross profit, while welcome, would likely still lag. After all, sales still fell a small 1 percent year-over-year and same-store-sales a larger 9 percent, with EPS less than half of what it was a year ago on the same sales. There was no indication of improving trends, and margins and profits were still at risk. When the actual results came at the end of the month, diluted EPS came

Table 4.9 Aeropostale Flat Revenues, Declining Gross Margins and EPS: July Quarter 2010–October Quarter 2011

Quarter Ending	Oct. 2011	July 2011	April 2011	Jan. 2011	Oct. 2010	July 2010
Revenues (in Millions of Dollars)	$597	$468	$469	$839	$603	$495
Gross Margin	27.1%	24.4%	29.1%	52.8%	36.6%	37.3%
Diluted EPS	$0.30 (actual) (original estimate $0.09–$0.15; revised Nov. 3 to $0.27–$0.28;	$0.04	$0.20	$0.94	$0.63	$0.46

Source: SEC filings.

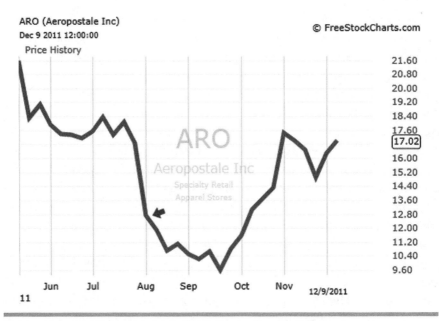

Figure 4.2 Aeropostale: May 2011–December 9, 2011.
Source: FreeStockCharts.com, by permission.

in at $0.30—two to three cents higher than the early November update and substantially higher than the prior estimate. The stock stayed firm.

It's possible to argue that Aeropostale couldn't be expected to plan for such a dramatic rise in cotton prices, but we don't buy it. They should know what business they are in—jeans and T-shirts are made of cotton, their largest input—especially given their lengthy tenure in the business. While the 2010–early 2011 spike was especially dramatic, cotton prices have varied considerably. The company could hedge but didn't.

The takeaway here is to know your industry and its inputs for cost of goods sold. Where you can, watch market pricing. Most commodity prices are easy to find. Note whether management fully discloses any effect the inputs have on gross margins and whether execs use subsequent improvement to trumpet growing revenues and margins. Price changes in cost of goods sold inputs are not sustainable as sources of earnings quality, but a dramatic increase in consumer demand and increased volume could make up for it. It is impossible to know Aeropostale's earning power ahead because of the input costs, so any investor must be sure to obtain a cheap-enough valuation that offers a very large margin of safety.

The next item special to overstating EPS on the income statement is serial charges.

Recurring "One-Time" Charges

Some companies take numerous "one-time" charges, quarter after quarter, showing that, while a particular charge may be indeed one-time only, the company's habit is to take one-timers all the time. This is a bright red flag with respect to earnings quality. Investors and professional analysts tend to overlook one-time charges, because, by definition, they are not expected to continue. But serial one-time charges may allow a company to establish reserves or bundle normal operating costs, making future results look better than they are.

Another example is lowering asset values of ongoing equipment via a write-off, which effectively lowers future depreciation expense for an asset still in use, and therefore increases net income. Lower-than-expected selling, general, and administrative (SG&A) expenses may indicate use of previously established reserves, indicating low earnings quality.

It's relatively easy to spot an income statement littered with charges, but as a guideline, the long investor should run from those companies with serial restructuring charges. They are not worth the effort to figure out. Table 4.10 teaches this, showing Hewlett-Packard's restructuring charges and merger and related restructuring charges for the 12 quarters—*three years!*—to the quarter ending in July 2011.

Hewlett-Packard's recurring charges are a material percentage of EPS. The danger for this company—and all other serial restructurers and acquirers—is that they can bundle whatever normal expenses they want into the charges, and these numbers will significantly affect operating margins and EPS. In any quarter, management could adjust these numbers a little or a lot, creating unreliable results for the quarter and any comparisons. When the charges someday end, as they must, the effect will be so dramatic for this company with flat revenues that the Street will undoubtedly trumpet that things have "turned around." But an apparent turnaround based on the end of recurring charges is unsustainable.

Because there is zero confidence in HP's earnings power, a long investor should simply pass. It would also be a dangerous short, because the Street will see a positive catalyst of unexpected and sudden year-over-year increases in this previously negative EPS despite flat revenues.

Another way for management to manipulate earnings unsustainably is through taxes.

Table 4.10 Effects of Hewlett-Packard's "One-Time" Restructuring Charges on EPS: October Quarter 2008–July Quarter 2011*

Quarter Ending	July 2011	April 2011	Jan. 2011	Oct. 2010	July 2010	April 2010
Restructuring Charges	($150)	($158)	($158)	($235)	($598)	($180)
Merger and Related Restructuring Charges	($18)	($21)	($29)	($51)	($127)	($77)
Total	($168)	($179)	($187)	($286)	($725)	($257)
Operating Income	$2,668	$3,147	$3,633	$3,454	$3,048	$3,115
Weighted Avg. Diluted Shares	2,054	2,150	2,182	2,249	2,322	2,345
Effect on Operating Margin (bps)	(54)	(57)	(58)	(86)	(237)	(84)
Effect on EPS	($0.08)	($0.08)	($0.09)	($0.13)	($0.31)	($0.11)
Diluted EPS	$0.93	$1.05	$1.17	$1.10	$0.75	$0.91
Percentage Effect of Charges	8.6%	7.6%	7.7%	11.8%	41.3%	12.1%
Quarter Ending	**Jan. 2010**	**Oct. 2009**	**July 2009**	**Apr. 2009**	**Jan. 2009**	**Oct. 2008**
Restructuring Charges	($131)	($38)	($362)	($94)	($146)	($19)
Merger and Related Restructuring Charges	($38)	($60)	($59)	($75)	($48)	($311)
Total	($169)	($98)	($421)	($169)	($194)	($292)
Operating Income	$3,213	$3,036	$2,634	$2,462	$2,780	$3,065
Weighted Avg. Diluted Shares	2,358	2,366	2,382	2,349	2,410	2,440
Effect on Operating Margin (bps)	(54)	(32)	(153)	(62)	(68)	(86)
Effect on EPS	($0.07)	($0.04)	($0.18)	($0.07)	($0.08)	($0.12)
Diluted EPS	$0.93	$0.99	$0.69	$0.71	$0.75	$0.84
Percentage Effect of Changes	7.5%	4.0%	6.1%	9.9%	10.7%	14.3%

*Dollar ($) amounts are in millions of dollars except for EPS and bps numbers.
Source: SEC filings.

Tax Valuation Allowances

In the start-up phase, many businesses do not generate profits. Tax accounting allows the company to carry forward some losses and use them to reduce future taxable income. Because that's an obvious future benefit, income reduced by the loss carryforward would reduce taxes. Net operating loss carryforwards (NOLs) are a deferred tax asset.

But the value of that asset depends on what profits and tax rates the company estimates it will have. If the company believes that it may not be able to realize fully the NOL benefits, it must record a tax valuation allowance. The tax valuation allowance is a reserve against the possibility that the company may not obtain the full value of its deferred tax asset.

Because it is impossible to know what the future holds, companies may change their assumptions about the value of the deferred tax asset and therefore change the tax valuation allowance. If companies need a few million here or there to meet Wall Street expectations, they may switch their expectations about future income and use of the NOLs to lower—reverse—the allowance, improving current EPS. This may get the company past the quarter to please the Street, but eventually the allowance has nowhere lower to go.

Footnotes on taxes will show if the company reversed the allowance. To know whether to dig deeper to find it, the investor should compare the expected tax rate indicated by management (in the earnings press release or conference call, if at all) and forecast by Wall Street with what is actually reported in the quarter. An artificially low tax rate may indicate that the tax allowance was reversed, benefitting current EPS. Investors should then review the tax notes in the financial statements to find whether the allowance was reversed and whether management had its hand in the tax-allowance cookie jar.

Foreign Tax Rates and Foreign Profits

Today, a major tax rate issue concerns companies' foreign versus domestic tax incentives. Because the United States has the world's second highest corporate tax rate, after Japan,[9] U.S. company managements rationally attempts to maximize earnings in lower-tax foreign jurisdictions. The problem is that this restricts companies' ability to move capital to where it can best be used.

Financial media frequently mention the huge amounts of cash that U.S. corporations earn and maintain abroad in lower-tax nations. But this isn't a moral, ethical, or legal issue. It is the law. Therefore, it's not only entirely rational but is required for a company to defer U.S. taxation indefinitely by keeping the money abroad, especially when the deferral isn't deducted from net income. Repatriation of the cash can incur taxes up to 30 percent. But the tax situation distorts rational capital allocation. It may make sense not to pay higher taxes or to defer them, but companies might need the cash for domestic acquisitions. Hewlett-Packard, for example, incurred huge debt to acquire EDS in 2009, but couldn't repatriate the 80 percent of its earnings that provide cash flow overseas. Cash also might be needed to shore up domestic operations, pay down debt, or maintain dividends and stock repurchases. A company that cannot meet these obligations will eventually have no choice but to repatriate cash and incur the tax, giving it a higher effective rate and lowering earnings.

When Behind the Numbers issued its July 2009 report on the offshore profits tax, it identified potential government action to raise revenue from foreign profits and, regardless of that action, risks to tax rates facing seven companies with huge operations, profits, and cash abroad. At the time, Behind the Numbers noted several key points—and at writing the tax distortion persists:

The Government Is Focusing on Foreign Profits as a Source of Tax Revenue

- Proposals call for intercompany transactions to be recognized as taxable events.
- Limiting expense deductions for companies that utilize laws to defer taxes on foreign profits are being examined.
- The [then current] Administration wants to impose sanctions on countries that do not disclose information about tax haven situations.
- Rep. Charles Rangel has already floated proposals to limit tax deductions for U.S. multinationals with operations overseas.

Repeating the 2004 Tax Holiday on Repatriated Cash is Unlikely

- Companies with large amounts of cash overseas, but high debt and falling operating cash flow in the U.S. could use a tax holiday to bring cash back cheaply to shore up the situation.
- The 2004 act was designed to repatriate cash to the U.S. to spur capex and job growth.

- In reality, little monitoring was done and many companies launched large share repurchases in 2005.
- Another holiday seems unlikely, as the administration has never addressed it, the government needs cash too, and terms of a new holiday would likely be onerous.

Tax Rules and Proposals May Hurt Shareholder Value by Preventing Domestic Acquisitions

- Investors would think that the [2008–2009] stock market sell-off would lead to more mergers, given lower stock values.
- U.S. multinationals appear unwilling to pay the taxes to use foreign cash and are therefore passing on domestic deals that may be better bargains.
- Companies are fearful that offshore cash may be taxed and appear to be favoring complex foreign deals to spend it.

In fact, many large and familiar companies with the widest share ownership are strongly affected. Shareholders of Cisco Systems, Motorola (before its spinoff), Google, Merck, Hewlett-Packard, General Electric, and Coca-Cola are unaware of most of these concerns:

Cisco Systems Shows a High Cash Balance It Cannot Access

Because 81 percent of its $33.6 billion in cash is overseas, Cisco is forced to issue debt in the United States, cash flows are falling, and Cisco is cutting capex and stock repurchases.

Motorola Is an Example of a Company That Needs to Repatriate Cash to Shore-Up U.S. Operations

The company's domestic tax rate jumped from 26 percent to 67 percent last year, as tax provisions on foreign earnings were changed and non-deductible foreign exchange and translation adjustments were incurred. Nearly all of its debt is U.S.-based, domestic operations are posting huge losses, and cash flow has been negative for three years. Dealing with these issues is hampered because Motorola cannot access $5.4 billion of its $7.0 billion in cash without incurring taxes.

Google Is in Strong Shape, Both Domestically and Internationally, but May Still Have Issues

Google's tax rate is rising, but there is still a huge tax savings in its earnings, due to foreign tax differentials. The strong operations and cash hoard could make it a poster-child target for new tax law changes. Google lists tax treatment of foreign cash as two of its risk factors.

Merck Also In Strong Shape, but Some Risks *Are* Still Worth Noting

Merck carries no provision for taxes on cash that may need to be repatriated. But it may need the cash—taxes or not. Vioxx litigation shows that Merck is at risk of large contingent cash needs. Driving shareholder value via repurchases may be tough without some foreign cash.

Hewlett-Packard Shows that a Domestic Acquisition Can Be Tricky

Hewlett-Packard had about 80 percent of its earnings overseas when it bought Electronic Data Systems. The huge debt for that deal will need to be paid with domestic cash flow, but cash flow is down so far in 2009. The company has already had to reduce share repurchases.

General Electric—Here's Another Risk for GE

Income was boosted in 2008 by increasing the prior-year foreign earnings classified as indefinitely reinvested overseas. GE continues to raise significant capital and has considerable exposure to commercial real estate. More weakness could force repatriation of cash and large earnings hit.

Coca-Cola U.S. Risks Rising

A tax on high-fructose corn syrup sodas is being proposed in the Senate. That could hurt case volume, and Coke already has seen huge drops in volume domestically. Coca-Cola Enterprises has enormous debt to deal with, and weak volumes will hurt more. We still expect that situation to force more margin to Coca-Cola Enterprises and less to Coca-Cola. Declining U.S. cash flow could make it tough to maintain the dividend and stock repurchases.

In December 2010, Behind the Numbers observed that tax rates were already rising for some companies whose sales increased in higher tax foreign countries, such as Japan, that tax rates rose in the United States, and that companies incurred higher taxes in some foreign jurisdictions where tax credits expired. This means that investors—absent another repatriation holiday similar to that of 2004—must look behind reported tax rates to the potential rate, possibly originating from closing the gap between foreign and domestic taxation and/or the necessity to repatriate foreign cash and incur the taxes.

In the years since the 2008 stock market crash, investors have been fond of saying that, with all the cash on their balance sheets, large-cap stalwarts can pay huge dividends and make massive stock buybacks, giving investors safety in volatile times. But as we've seen, these billions are often abroad, unavailable for these salubrious purposes. The cash may prove cold comfort.

Now we can pull together this chapter's interrelated balance sheet and income statement concerns all in one place. It rarely gets this good for earnings quality junkies.

Combining Key Balance Sheet and Income Statement Concerns: Akamai Technologies

John's March 2, 2007 report to clients about Internet content delivery company Akamai Technologies, showed practices covered by most of the earnings quality warnings identified in this chapter. Here, focus on how unbilled accounts receivable help the company beat estimates, reserves boost EPS, and margins may be overestimated. These signal that, when such serious concerns appear together in one company, it's definitely time to avoid, sell, or short the stock.

Surge in Unbilled A/R Aids in Beating Estimates

Given the high expectations embedded in Akamai's stock price, management is increasingly under pressure to exceed consensus estimates. In the September quarter, the company relied heavily on unbilled accounts receivable to meet, and exceed, consensus revenue estimates. This was the first instance of suspect revenue quality.

For Akamai, unbilled receivables are generally billed within a month after revenue recognition. This form of revenue can be highly subjective, as can the assumptions for profit margin earned on the revenue. As a result, a sharp increase in unbilled accounts receivable could indicate more aggressive revenue recognition.

The Street's consensus revenue estimate for the September quarter was $108.8 million compared with reported revenue of $111.5 million. Had the unbilled receivables remained at the same proportion of revenue as in the year-ago period, reported revenue would have been $6.4 million less, resulting in a $2.7 million miss—likely to hurt the stock—instead of a nearly $3 million positive surprise.

In Table 4.11, Akamai's unbilled accounts receivable surged in the September quarter to 16.6 percent of revenue from 10.8

Table 4.11 Akamai's Unbilled Receivables as a Percentage of Rrevenues: September Quarter 2005–September Quarter 2006*

Quarter Ending	Sep. 2006	June 2006	March 2006	Dec. 2005	Sep. 2005
Revenue	$111.5	$100.7	$90.8	$82.7	$75.7
Accounts Receivable	$56.4	$61.0	$56.9	$51.0	$42.6
Unbilled A/R	$18.5	$12.1	$8.7	$9.1	$8.2
Gross A/R	$74.9	$73.1	$65.6	$60.1	$50.8
Unbilled A/R as Percentage of Revenue	16.6%	12.0%	9.6%	11.0%	10.8%

*All dollar amounts are in millions of dollars.
Source: SEC filings.

percent in the year-ago period and 12.0 percent sequentially. Previously, the company had exceeded expectations without regard to its unbilled revenue, so our concern is heightened. The information for December is not yet available, but we note that subsequent to the September quarter, the company made new acquisitions, which will further obscure its revenue growth rate. In the December quarter, the company beat revenue expectations by less than $3 million, with $800,000 coming from acquisitions.

The combination of recognizing a greater proportion of unbilled revenue and subsequently making new acquisitions could indicate a slowdown more marked than what's evident in the reported financials.

Reduction in Reserve Levels Boosts EPS

In addition to the increase in unbilled accounts receivable, the company has reduced reserve levels, which have boosted EPS in the short term and accounted for a large portion of the EPS surprise. Table 4.12 shows that the reserve levels reported for the September quarter were the lowest of the last five quarters at 10.0 percent and declined by 360 bps year-over-year.

In the September quarter, the reduction in reserve levels added $0.01 to EPS in a quarter where the company beat

Table 4.12 Akamai's Receivables Up, Reserves Ratio Down: September Quarter 2005—September Quarter 2006*

Quarter Ending	Sep. 2006	June 2006	March 2006	Dec. 2005	Sep. 2005
Revenue	$111.5	$100.7	$90.8	$82.7	$75.7
Gross A/R	$74.9	$73.1	$65.6	$60.1	$50.8
Total Reserves	$7.5	$9.2	$9.9	$8.0	$6.9
Reserves as Percentage of Gross A/R	10.0%	12.6%	15.1%	13.3%	13.6%

*Dollar amounts are in millions of dollars.
Source: SEC filings.

expectations by $0.02. The reduction also added $0.01 in June, accounting for half of the earnings surprise. For the December period, information on the reserves is not yet available; however we note the company beat EPS expectations by only $0.01. We're pounding the table: A penny here or there is a red flag that management is manipulating to boost earnings.

While December data are unknown at this time, the first sign of weakness occurred in the September quarter, with unbilled receivables. The combination of the potential for more aggressive revenue and expense management raises our concerns with respect to Akamai's earnings quality ahead.

Wall Street Too Bullish on Margins

Akamai's gross profit margin has eroded by 200–300 basis points in recent periods, and the slide is expected to continue. Table 4.13 illustrates that gross profit margin in December was 77.8 percent, a reduction of 300 basis points from the year-ago period.

In each of the last four quarters, there has been a downward trend in gross profit margin. Analysts further expect that the trend will continue with margins falling 120 basis points in 2007 and approximately another 100 basis points in 2008. We believe margins could fall further.

Table 4.13 Akamai Gross Margins

By Quarter and Year	Dec. 2006	Sep. 2006	June 2006	March 2006
Gross Margin	77.8%	78.1%	79.5%	82.7%
Quarter Ending	Dec. 2005	Sep. 2005	June 2005	March 2005
Gross Margin	80.8%	80.3%	79.8%	80.5%
Fiscal Year	2008e	2007e	2006	2005
Gross Margin	75.9%	76.8%	78.0%	80.3%

Source: SEC filings.

The reduction in gross profits is attributable to renewed depreciation from increased infrastructure spending. The company had been generating revenue and profit from fully depreciated infrastructure, which boosted the previous gross profit margin relative to the current period.

While gross profit margin has trended down, operating margins have expanded (see Table 4.14). For the December period, the operating profit margin expanded 420 basis points year-over-year to 34.4 percent, a trend continuing over the past several quarters. Conveniently, Wall Street is estimating that operating profit margins will expand at a rate that offsets the decline in gross profit. Operating profit is expected to expand nearly 200 basis points in 2007 and another 120 basis points in 2008. The EBITDA margin is expected to be 41 percent.

There are several reasons we believed that these estimates may be too aggressive:

- The increase in video content will result in more price concessions to price-sensitive customers.
- Competition will drive down pricing.
- New distribution methods threaten Akamai's competitive advantage.
- The monetization of content is not Akamai's core competency.
- Akamai's infrastructure expenses could be larger than anticipated.

Table 4.14 Akamai Operating Margins

	Dec. 2006	Sep. 2006	June 2006	March 2006	Dec. 2005	Sep. 2005
Operating Margin by Quarter and Year	34.4%	34.3%	32.5%	29.8%	30.2%	29.7%
	June 2005	March 2005	FY 2008e	FY 2007e	FY 2006	FY 2005
	27.4%	27.2%	36.0%	34.8%	32.9%	28.8%

Source: SEC filings.

Margins Will Further Be Pressured by Increases in Capex and Lower than Anticipated Operating Leverage

Akamai's network operates at 20–30 percent capacity so as to ensure it fulfills performance guarantees to customers. The increase in video consumption will further strain the networks, in our view. In the past, management has managed cash flow by underinvesting in capital expenditures, and we believe reinvestment could accelerate faster than earnings models assume. Therefore, the company will generate less revenue off of a fully depreciated base of servers (depreciated over three years), which further pressures gross profit margins.

Table 4.15 next shows capital expenditures and capitalized software in relation to total revenue over the past five years. Capital expenditures have increased to 16 percent of revenue from around 10 percent in prior years.

If video consumption continues to grow at triple digits rates as some expect, then Akamai's infrastructure will have to keep pace in order to fulfill service guarantees. However, given the development of new technologies that will compete with Akamai, either the company will have to make more acquisitions or reinvest more aggressively in infrastructure than it has, either of which will increase depreciation and weigh on gross profit margins.

Table 4.15 Akamai's Rising Capital Expenditures and Capitalized Software Costs as Percentage of Revenue: 2002–2006*

Year	2006	2005	2004	2003	2002
Revenue	$428.7	$283.7	$210.0	$161.3	$144.9
Capital Expenditures	$69.3	$27.0	$12.3	$1.4	$7.3
Capitalization of Internal-Use Software Costs	—	$9.2	$9.9	$8.0	$6.9
Total Capex	$69.3	$36.2	$20.1	$8.9	$14.2
Total Capex as Percentage of Revenue	16.2%	12.8%	9.6%	5.5%	9.8%

*Dollar amounts are in millions of dollars.
Source: SEC filings.

Table 4.16 Akamai Declining to Flat R&D versus Revenues: 2002–2006*

Year	2006	2005	2004	2003	2002
Revenue	$428.7	$283.7	$210.0	$161.3	$144.9
R&D	$33.1	$18.1	$12.1	$13.0	$21.8
R&D as Percentage of Revenue	7.7%	6.4%	5.8%	8.1%	15.0%

*Dollar amounts are in millions of dollars.

As the market shifts toward video, which opens the door to new technologies and pricing models, we feel that the operating leverage embedded into Akamai's financial expectations is aggressive. First, increased competition from companies such as LimeLight, with lower pricing points, could slow revenue growth more than expected. The pricing further pressures gross margins. If new delivery methods gain traction as some suggest, this will require greater investment in R&D and other operating expenses.

Table 4.16 shows that the company has invested approximately 6–8 percent in R&D over the past three years and had cut it significantly from prior periods. If the advent of video downloads is a "massive disruption" as many suggest, then the company risks being woefully underinvested in new technology. But even a small increase in R&D spending would blow a hole in the operating leverage assumptions current in Wall Street's models.

This also does not consider increased expenses on the sales and marketing side. Reductions in headcount led to a decrease in spending on S&M relative to revenue in prior periods; however it has begun to accelerate, as shown in Table 4.17.

Table 4.17 Akamai Increasing Sales and Marketing to Revenue: 2002–2006*

Year	2006	2005	2004	2003	2002
Revenue	$428.7	$283.7	$210.0	$161.3	$144.9
Sales and Marketing	$119.7	$77.9	$55.7	$47.6	$64.8
Sales and Marketing as Percentage of Revenue	27.9%	27.5%	26.5%	29.5%	44.7%

*All dollar amounts are in millions of dollars.

Figure 4.3 Akamai: Mid-2004–October 16, 2009.
Source: FreeStockCharts.com, by permission.

These proved more than enough predictors of trouble. At the second following quarterly earnings release, the stock dropped 30 percent in a few days while the best market was positive. Figure 4.3 shows Akamai's shares losing 78 percent from the issuance of John's report—the black arrow—to their bottom in the following year.

Conclusion

Our goal here and throughout the book is to find the key items—the *best* predictors for discerning earnings quality—and view them together. Revenue recognition, which affects the income statement's top line and all the financial statements, may be the king of the earnings quality mountain, but other lines on the income statement may raise concerns too. Similarly, inventory management is the key balance sheet earnings quality concern, but the investor must closely analyze the other crucial balance sheet lines: accounts receivables, doubtful accounts, goodwill and intangibles, deferred revenues, pension obligations, and debt.

Chapter 5

Cash Flow Warnings

The cash flow statement may come last in the statements, but it is not least. Experienced investors understand the cash flow statement's crucial presentation of a company's cash reality, but most management's public communications suggest that they couldn't care less. They focus squarely on the Street's quarterly EPS estimates and strive to meet or exceed them. This short-term orientation may avoid the ruthless downgrades and selloffs when the company "misses by a penny." But just as *beating* by a penny may imply aggressive accounting or manipulating levers to squeak by Street estimates, *missing* by a penny may suggest that the company aggressively tried to find every last shekel between the couch cushions and still couldn't get there.

Every financial statement offers the opportunity for manipulation, because they all interrelate. Decisions regarding revenue, inventory, receivables, acquisitions, and share repurchases flow through all three. We focus so strongly on revenue recognition, because the income statement's top line affects all statements most seriously. But every line of the income statement affects the premise of cash flow, because the income statement's bottom line, net income, is the top line of the cash flow statement. If management uses aggressive accounting or manipulates numbers in the income statement, it calls into question the reliability of the cash flow statement.

The investor must look at all three statements to determine whether the cash flow statement properly adds back noncash items, accurately reflects working capital changes, and shows serial acquisitions, as well as whether management issues stock options or repurchases shares to mask their effects. All three statements come together in the cash flow statement and can manipulate this statement's job of presenting cash reality.

Overview of the Cash Flow Statement

The cash flow statement has three parts. From top to bottom, they are cash from operations (operating cash flow), cash from investing activities, and cash from financing activities. Each section is important.

Cash from Operations

Net income heads cash from operations, which ends with net cash from operations, more commonly known as operating cash flow (OCF). OCF is the actual cash change from the comparison period, based on the business alone without any spending on or selling of property, plant, or equipment, acquisitions (enumerated in the next section, cash from investing), or buying back shares, paying dividends, or issuing debt (in the cash from financing section). There are many numbers between net income and OCF. Most investors gloss over them and concentrate on a few. That's a mistake, because each line offers potential for mischief. There can be many a slip between the net income cup and the OCF lip.

Add Back Noncash Items, but Carefully

Noncash items appear on the *income* statement, because they affect how accountants evaluate them for tax purposes. So to reflect cash and not accounting reality, the first lines of the *cash flow* statement adds them back in to reflect cash reality.

Depreciation and Amortization

First up, the statement adds back depreciation and amortization (D&A). Chapter 4 showed how changes in measures of estimating D&A could benefit net income. D&A have another important role in determining the way that accurate cash flow measures are important for understanding a company's current and future cash needs. Manipulating D&A by changing estimates can affect the quality of the cash flows.

Consider when a property such as a building is fully depreciated and owners have reaped the D&A tax benefits. They may spend hardly anything for years and harvest the cash flows. Judging from Dairy Queens in rural areas, Berkshire Hathaway spends little unless absolutely necessary on these fully depreciated restaurants. Warren Buffett took all the earnings and tax benefits years ago, and now the properties are enormous cash flow generators. Investors might look at the lack of D&A for these properties and worry that the company is starving maintenance capex and will eventually have to pay for deferred maintenance. But these are among the simplest, cheapest properties in the industry, and Berkshire determines that the cash flows earn greater returns when invested elsewhere.

In Chapter 4, we saw Akamai Technologies spend more than a billion dollars and fully depreciate its servers over only three years, benefiting the income statement. This inflated cash flow for a few years, until eventually it would be time to upgrade the systems. Then the expense would go back on the income statement, hurting net income and therefore cash flow. Management was underinvesting and giving the impression of earnings power, but they couldn't do it forever.

Fully depreciated equipment doesn't signal trouble ahead for Dairy Queen. But for Akamai, it did. Server technology and Akamai's business demand regular change—unlike the technology for soft-serve ice cream or quick burgers. Sooner or later, as happened, Akamai would have to replace the assets to maintain earnings on assets.

Depreciation and amortization is neutral. The investor needs to understand both a business and its equipment to determine if the D&A is more like that of a Dairy Queen or an Akamai.

Stock-Based Compensation and Excess Tax Benefits from Stock Options

This is where opportunities for investors to uncover true cash and potential manipulation begin. Despite massive company opposition, in 2004 FASB[1] issued the requirement for a company to include stock-based compensation as an operating expense. Yet, because it is noncash, it is added back to operating cash flow. Because so many companies grant stock options as compensation, the investor must review the underlying numbers in the notes to determine the true effect on current and future cash flows.

Large option and warrant grants to employees and other parties can mean massive future dilution of existing shareholder's ownership shares. Companies report diluted share numbers that include in-the-money options and warrants, but you don't see what *might* happen if out-of-the-money options were to come into the money. An investor buying long has to at least eyeball the magnitude of potential dilution, because sharecount affects valuation, risk and potential return.

To focus those eyeballs, the investor must look at the notes, where the company discloses the numbers of warrants and options as well as their strike prices and expirations. Compare the strike prices to the current stock quote. How many options at what strike prices are close to or far from today's quote? In how many years to do they expire? The idea is to see the timing and magnitude, if any, of potential sharecount growth to gauge what it could do, for example, to earnings, OCF, and free cash flow per share.

Adding back stock-based compensation can end up boosting operating cash flow. But that's not the only place where the financial waters are muddied. Another cash flow statement line common with West Coast tech companies is "excess tax benefit from stock options." This is a cash benefit—taxes were reduced—but no company can say that its normalized operating cash flows include the business of generating excess benefits from stock options. This became mostly moot when, in 2006, FASB stated that excess tax benefits from stock options should appear in the financing-cash flow section, not the operating section.[2] Today it's common to see companies subtract this number in net cash from operations and add it back in the financing section.

Treatment of tax benefits from stock options still matters and will for a while. Investors who review many years of data need to know whether a drop-off in operating cash flow is due to company performance or to the change in treatment of excess tax benefits from stock options. A few examples show both the effect of stock-based compensation on operating cash flow and the excess tax benefit.

We start with Rambus, which, like InterDigital, is an intellectual property (IP) company that licenses its technology to companies. But as Table 5.1 shows, for a number of years Rambus's OCF primarily came from generating tax benefits from stock options and adding back stock-based compensation—not from royalties from licensing advanced computer IP. The bottom lines of Table 5.1 show how much lower OCF would be without these items.

Table 5.1 Contribution of Stock-Based Compensation and Tax Benefit from Stock Options to Rambus Operating Cash Flow: 2003–2008

Amounts in Millions of Dollars for the Fiscal Period Ending	12 months Dec. 31, 2003	Restated 12 months Dec. 31, 2004	Restated 12 months Dec. 31, 2005	Restated 12 months Dec. 31, 2006	Restated 12 months Dec. 31, 2007	Restated 12 months Dec. 31, 2008
Net Income	23.2	22.4	28.9	(13.8)	(34.2)	(199.1)
Depreciation and Amortization	5.6	5.6	9.1	11.2	11.2	11.3
Amortization. of Goodwill and Intangibles	0.0	2.5	4.3	5.2	5.3	4.3
Depreciation and Amortization, Total	5.6	8.1	13.4	16.5	16.5	15.7
Other Amortization	–	–	1.1	3.2	–	–
(Gain) Loss from Sale of Assets	–	–	0.2	0.3	0.4	0.1
(Gain) Loss on Sale of Invest.	(1.8)	(3.6)	–	0.2	–	–
Asset Write-Down and Restructuring Costs	–	–	–	–	–	2.7
Stock-Based Compensation	–	18.8	20.5	40.5	44.8	37.2
Tax Benefit from Stock Options	19.2	23.2	0.7	–	–	–
Other Operating Activities	–	–	(17.5)	(11.2)	(15.3)	123.1
Change in Accounts Receivable	(9.2)	8.8	0.5	(1.6)	0.7	0.4
Change in Accounts Payable	0.4	6.6	(2.5)	(0.2)	3.8	(3.6)
Change in Unearned Revenue	4.4	(18.4)	(14.5)	(1.7)	(4.8)	–
Change in Inc. Taxes	–	–	(0.5)	0.1	0.8	(1.8)
Change in Other Net Operating Assets	(18.6)	(22.3)	3.5	25.0	(7.4)	(13.2)
Cash from Ops. (OCF)	23.4	43.7	33.8	57.2	5.3	(38.5)
OCF – tax benefit from stock options	4.2	20.5	33.1	57.2	5.3	(38.5)
OCF – stock-based compensation and tax benefit	4.2	1.7	12.6	16.7	(39.5)	(75.7)

Source: S&P Capital IQ.

Rambus shareholders believed they owned two things: a cash flow generator from IP royalties and a call option on the potential for back royalties if Rambus was successful suing companies it alleged used its IP without paying license fees and royalties.

But no. The company's actual business of earning royalties from licenses produced little operating cash flow for these five years. Shareholders owned only a company with cash flows almost exclusively from tax benefits and adding back share-based compensation. In fact, they were paying absurd OCF multiples solely to speculate on whether Rambus would earn future royalties on its technology and win back royalties through expensive and hard-fought litigation—litigation that in large part has been ongoing since the early 2000s with mixed results.

A better, simpler, and more conservative view of operating cash flow is not to add back stock-based compensation, maintaining the income statement's treatment of it as an operating expense only. Then, determine whether what may be real cash effects of excess tax benefits from stock options are providing an illusion of operating cash flow growth. Investors who ignore either of these can get clobbered.

Many investors stop now, after reviewing the lines adding back noncash charges and skip the next section of the cash flow statement: changes in working capital. This is a mistake. It shows where the company is borrowing and spending from operating cash flow.

Changes in Working Capital (Changes in Assets and Liabilities)

The cash from operation section ends with changes in working capital, also called changes in assets and liabilities. These include changes from period to period in accounts receivable, accounts payable, and inventory—all three reported on the balance sheet, relevant to the income statement, and crucial to the cash flow statement.

Trends in working capital are critical. Companies can manage working capital to increase cash from operations, and therefore free cash flow. That can work in one quarter or a year to improve the asset side of the balance sheet and mollify the minority of the Street that glances at operating cash flow, but the benefits are unsustainable.

Think of working capital as a pot that the company uses to even out the variations in customer payments, managing products between manufacture and delivery, and paying vendors. A certain amount of variation is normal, but poor trends should concern the investor.

Reducing *accounts receivable* boosts operating cash flow, but only so much. A company can theoretically only narrow days receivables outstanding to zero—it can't collect more than it's owed. It's good if a company becomes an efficient collections machine, because then it's not in effect lending to customers. But as accounts receivable improvements slow, so too do their benefits to operating cash flow.

Expanding *accounts payable* may improve operating cash flow today, but cannot boost it indefinitely. Only the most powerful companies, such as Wal-Mart or Apple, can dictate payment terms to vendors, and even those big dogs have to pay their vendors someday. The rest of the world's merely mortal companies must pay vendors within a reasonable time. Therefore, any benefit from stretching out payables eventually stops. Accounts payable are really just short-term financing from suppliers, so it's equivalent to debt. The supplier "lenders" consider them accounts receivable and will want to collect them, too. That's why exploding accounts payable may indicate a company, not with power, but rather in deep trouble—just as any company with unsustainable debt.

Expansion of inventory can be an investment in inventory customers want, or it can be a sign that no one wants it, it's building up, and write-downs loom. On the flip side, reduction of inventory may benefit working capital and operating cash flow, but it could mean working down excess inventory (good), writing off inventory (bad), or waning customer demand (worse).

One way to measure the impact of these working capital items is to calculate the cash conversion cycle (CCC):

$$\textit{Cash Conversion Cycle} = DSO + DSI \text{ minus } DPO \textit{ (days payables outstanding)}$$

Track this over 8 to 12 quarters to see if working capital affects the cash flow for a company. This will be an important indicator for Jacobs Engineering, an example we'll explore later in the chapter, because it pulls so many of the operating cash flow section warnings together.

Now, let's examine how working capital changes operate in a straight-forward case. Later we'll look at how highly acquisitive companies can manipulate working capital and operating cash flow by playing three-card monte—moving the ball around so much that you have no idea where cash really lies.

Table 5.2 illustrates that the eight quarters through September 30, 2011, for paper company Domtar Corp. showed a normal fluctuation in accounts receivable, inventories, and accounts payable. Accounts receivable are higher in the December quarter and lower in the March quarter. Inventories expand in the June quarter and decline in September's. And accounts payable vary a bit, but decline in the March quarter. That makes sense, because if your collections are good in that quarter, you're more likely to be paying vendors.

For these three working capital items the net over 8 quarters is $59 million, only 3 percent of Domtar's more than $2 billion in operating cash flow for the period, and the rolling last 12 months' (LTM) numbers show a similarly small effect. There is no material trend in any of the three categories. The company borrows from and repays steadily to each category, reflecting that the company managed its seasonal working capital needs well. No red flags here.

In contrast, consumer fashion accessory company Fossil's working capital management of inventories raises questions. Examining Table 5.3, you see that Fossil's inventories increase in three of four quarters (with the exception of 2009, the fallout from 2008 to 2009) and then decline for the quarter ending in January, normal for most retailers dependent on the all-important holiday shopping season. However, anticipated demand ultimately did not materialize. After the holiday season results showed the continued inventory deterioration, John in April shorted the stock, which fell 38 percent on its earnings release in May 2012.

Fossil's accounts receivable increased in the quarters ending in early October and January. Accounts payable increased in the quarter ending in April. But in the six quarters ending in April 2010, with the expected seasonal exception, working capital improvements boosted operating cash flow. And then they trended poorly, with rolling 12-month working capital changes turning negative from the quarter ending July 2010 to October 2011, reducing operating cash flow.

Where, as with Fossil, working capital changes are negative and the company survives, it is dipping into cash and/or using debt to stay afloat and eventually must pay the piper, as we'll see next with Under Armour. There are rare exceptions, such as companies that have negative working capital, but Fossil isn't one of them. The point is that there is a limit to how much and how long working capital improvements can boost operating cash flow, while there is no limit to how badly working capital mismanagement can lead to operating cash flow and company ruin.

Table 5.2 Good Working Capital Management at Domtar: December Quarter 2009–September Quarter 2011*

Quarter Ending	Sep. 2011	June 2011	March 2011	Dec. 2010	Sep. 2010	June 2010	March 2010	Dec. 2009
Sequential Change in Accounts Receivable	$5	$50	($111)	$61	$13	($57)	($90)	$86
Sequential Change in Inventories	($14)	$33	$1	($1)	($39)	$69	$10	$27
Sequential Change in Accounts Payable	$36	$7	($29)	($7)	($9)	$30	($25)	$13
Total	$27	$90	($139)	$53	($35)	$42	($105)	$126
Operating Cash Flow	$257	$306	$148	$166	$267	$610	$123	$185
Rolling LTM Working Capital Changes	$31	($31)	($79)	($45)	$28	–	–	–
Rolling LTM Operating Cash Flow	$877	$887	$1,191	$1,166	$1,185	–	–	–

*Dollar amounts in millions of dollars.
Source: SEC filings.

Table 5.3 Fossil's Working Capital Changes: January Quarter 2009–
October Quarter 2011*

Quarter Ending	Oct. 2011	July 2011	April 2011	Jan. 2011	Oct. 2010	July 2010
Sequential Change in Accounts Receivable	($61)	($1)	$51	($19)	($111)	$1
Sequential Change in Inventories	($77)	($44)	($23)	$24	($90)	($47)
Sequential Change in Accounts Payable	$1	$24	($15)	$10	$24	($1)
Total	$136	$21	$12	$15	$177	$45
Rolling LTM Working Capital Changes	$130	$171	$195	$184	$195	$60

Quarter Ending	April 2010	Jan. 2010	Oct. 2009	July 2009	April 2009	Jan. 2009
Sequential Change in Accounts Receivable	$43	($30)	($49)	$22	$53	($17)
Sequential Change in Inventories	($3)	$36	($29)	$34	$4	$42
Sequential Change in Accounts Payable	($16)	($2)	$35	($2)	($25)	$20
Total	$24	$3	($42)	$54	$32	$38
Rolling LTM Working Capital Changes	$38	$46	$81	$44	$1	($47)

*Dollar amounts are in millions of dollars.
Source: SEC filings.

Table 5.4 reveals that sports clothing retailer Under Armour's inventory grew faster than revenues year-over-year and as a percentage of LTM revenues grew for eight quarters through September 30, 2011. This is a great example and common to apparel retailers, so stick with us on this one.

Inventories as a percentage of sales (A) grew year-over-year, as did LTM DSI (B) sequentially for the five quarters to September 30, 2011, while LTM operating cash flow (C) declined for six of the last seven quarters and net cash dropped off a cliff from the quarter ending December 31, 2010, to

Table 5.4 Under Armour's Expanding Inventories and Declining Operating Cash Flow, December Quarter 2009–September Quarter 2011*

Quarter Ending	Sep. 2011	June 2011	March 2011	Dec. 2010	Sep. 2010	June 2010	March 2010	Dec. 2009
Revenues Change Year-over-Year	42%	42%	36%	36%	22%	24%	15%	–
Inventories Change Year-over-Year (A)	63%	74%	68%	45%	28%	(1%)	(10)	–
Inventories as Percentage of Revenues	69%	107%	80%	72%	60%	87%	64%	67%
Change Year-over-Year	15%	22%	23%	7%	5%	(21%)	(22%)	–
LTM Average DSI (B)	14	141	134	128	126	124	130	136
Sequential Change	2%	5%	5%	2%	2%	(5%)	(5%)	–
LTM Operating Cash Flow Sequential Change (C)	(108%)	10%	(147%)	(18%)	(38%)	(9%)	(8%)	–
Cash and Equivalents	$68	$120	$111	$204	$134	$156	$166	$187
ST and LT Debt	($110)	(37)	($14)	($16)	($19)	($16)	($18)	($20)
Net Cash	$42	$83	$97	$188	$115	$140	$148	$167

*Dollar amounts are in millions of dollars.
Source: SEC filings.

Table 5.5 WMS Industries' Expanding Receivables, 2010 by Quarter

Quarter Ending	Dec. 2010	Sep. 2010	June 2010	March 2010
Accounts Receivable Year-over-Year Change	37%	37%	25%	22%
4-Quarter Average A/R Sequential Change Year-over-Year	7%	8%	6%	6%
4- Quarter Average DSO Sequential Change Year-over-Year	6%	5%	4%	3%

Source: SEC filings.

September 30, 2011. In line with the Street's focus, investors apparently were mesmerized by the revenue growth, bidding up the stock from $27.83 on September 30, 2009, to $86 two days after the September 30, 2011, earnings release. But growing revenue was turning into less operating cash flow and more and more inventory. The company could only keep it up until the quarter ending in March 2011, when it spent cash and increased debt. This can't go on forever.

Figure 5.1 WMS Industries: September 2010–December 2, 2011.
Source: FreeStockCharts.com, by permission.

In 2011, John profitably shorted gaming company WMS Industries and Green Mountain Coffee Roasters, due to their working capital red flags. Table 5.5 shows WMS's expanding receivables through Dec. 31, 2010. They presaged a plummeting stock. Figure 5.1 shows the stock from September 2010 through December 2, 2011.

Last of all, highly acquisitive companies can turn working capital inside out, making it nearly impossible to determine the quality of operating cash flow. For example, Green Mountain Coffee Roasters grew revenues at red-hot rates before and after acquiring Diedrich Coffee in May 2010 and Van Houtte in December 2010. Prior to the acquisitions, inventories had fluctuated within a reasonable range and then exploded. For the six quarters including and after the Diedrich acquisition, the company was free cash flow negative for four quarters, breakeven for one, and positive for one, with positive operating cash flow for only three of the six.

This shows a company whose acquisitions and revenue growth obscured weaker organic growth. Green Mountain should have focused on collecting receivables and liquidating inventory. But investors cared only for revenue growth, even though it did not increase value, and their buying drove the shares ever higher. They rose 238 percent for 2011 to the August 3 high, and then began a trend downward. They fell off a cliff in November, plummeting 39 percent on November 10 alone, when the quarterly report came out, reducing the year's gain by 90 percent.

These are dramatic examples of where working capital changes can show deteriorating earnings quality. Through analyzing these accounts on the cash flow statement, the investor can understand better the real nature of operating cash flow.

Net Cash from Operations (Operating Cash Flow)

Over time, operating cash flow (OCF) should track net income. The trend of OCF as a percentage of net income tells a lot both about earnings quality and OCF sustainability. A declining percentage calls into question the quality of EPS, OCF, or both. As with almost all indicators, it's best to track this for 8 to 12 quarters.

OCF declined as a percentage of net income at Maxim Integrated Products, whose balance sheet, revenue recognition, and income statement issues appeared in prior chapters. The percentage of decline warned of trouble. John's June 27, 2005, report to clients showed his concerns about Maxim's operating cash flow:

For the past seven quarters, Maxim has experienced a general decline in operating cash flow as a percentage of net income. Although the company saw a sequential increase in cash from operating activities for the March 2005 quarter, from 106 percent of net income to 136 percent, we note the substantial decline year-over-year. Table 5.6 shows that fall from 174 percent to 136 percent, attributable to increases in accounts receivable and inventory. This negative trend could lead to inventory write-downs and extended payment terms, increasing risk to future earnings.

We note that a tax benefit due to stock options comprises a significant proportion of Maxim's cash from operating activities, representing 17.3 percent and 23.6 percent of operating cash flow for the March 2005 and December 2004 quarters, respectively. Because Maxim relies heavily on employing stock options as means of compensation, the company reports this tax benefit as an operating activity, thus boosting its operating cash flow. We disagree with

Table 5.6 Declining OCF as Percentage of Net Income at Maxim: March Quarter 2003–March Quarter 2005*

Quarter Ending	March 2005	Dec. 2004	Sep. 2004	June 2004	March 2004
OCF	$170.2	$135.1	$208.0	$177.9	$189.7
Net Income	$125.5	$144.6	$144.5	$124.7	$109.2
OCF as Percentage of Net Income	136%	106%	144%	143%	174%
OCF – Net Income	$44.6	$8.5	$63.7	$53.2	$80.5

Quarter Ending	Dec. 2003	Sep. 2003	June 2003	March 2003
OCF	$172.4	$155.5	$169.3	$128.0
Net Income	$98.5	$87.4	$81.7	$77.6
OCF as Percentage of Net Income	175%	178%	207%	165%
OCF/ – Net Income	$73.9	$68.1	$87.5	$50.4

*Dollar amounts are in millions of dollars.
Source: SEC filings.

this accounting technique and regard the tax benefit as a financing activity instead. *The tax benefit is not a result of the company's operating activity nor is it sustainable.* (emphasis original)

Once the benefit is removed, Table 5.7 illustrates that Maxim's cash from operating activities as a percentage of net income falls substantially year-over-year from 140 percent to 112 percent. This highlights our concern over potentially inflated cash from operating activities. Under new stipulations by FASB, companies will be required to report the tax benefit as a financing activity, reducing operating cash flow beginning day one of Maxim's fiscal year following July 1, 2005. Because Maxim relies heavily on stock options

Table 5.7 Tax Benefits Boost Maxim's Operating Cash Flow: June Quarter 2003–March Quarter 2005*

Quarter Ending	March 2005	Dec. 2004	Sep. 2004	June 2004
OCF	$170.2	$153.1	$208.0	$177.9
Net Income	$125.5	$144.6	$144.5	$124.7
Tax Benefit from Stock Options	$29.4	$34.1	$23.8	$39.8
OCF Minus Tax Benefit	$140.8	$119.0	$184.5	$138.1
OCF Minus Tax Benefit as Percentage of Net Income	112%	82%	128%	111%
OCF – Tax Benefit – Net Income	$15.2	$25.7	$39.9	$13.4

Quarter Ending	March 2004	Dec. 2003	Sep. 2003	June 2003
OCF	$189.7	$172.4	$155.5	$169.3
Net Income	$109.2	$98.5	$87.4	$81.7
Tax Benefit from Stock Options	$36.5	$41.6	$34.6	$32.0
OCF Minus Tax Benefit	$153.2	$130.8	$120.9	$137.2
OCF Minus Tax Benefit as Percentage of Net Income	140%	133%	138%	168%
OCF – Tax Benefit – Net Income	$44.0	$32.3	$33.5	$55.5

*Dollar amounts are in millions of dollars.
Source: SEC filings.

as compensation, Its operating cash flow will be greatly affected, and—holding everything else constant—the company will experience declining OCF in the near future.

Maxim has experienced a great upsurge in its free cash flow over the past eight quarters, rising 16.6 percent as shown in Table 5.8. Street analysts commend the company for its particular strength, but we note that free cash flow will deteriorate in the near future when the tax benefit from operating cash flow disappears. Thus, investors who price the stock on a cash flow basis may witness multiple expansion without any underlying operating improvement. They would sell the stock.

Operating cash flow is therefore only as understandable as its components, just as net income on the income statement requires analysis of the line items. More investors do the latter than the former. Similarly, more

Table 5.8 Tax Benefits Boost Maxim's Free Cash Flow: June Quarter 2003–March Quarter 2005*

Quarter Ending	March 2005	Dec. 2004	Sep. 2004	June 2004
OCF	$170.2	$153.1	$208.0	$177.9
Tax Benefit from Stock Options	$29.4	$34.1	$23.8	$39.8
Capital Expenditures	($13.8)	($31.4)	($66.3)	($68.9)
Free Cash Flow with Tax Benefit	$156.4	$121.7	$141.7	$109.0
Free Cash Flow without Tax Benefit	$127.0	$87.5	$118.1	$69.2

Quarter Ending	March 2004	Dec. 2003	Sep. 2003	June 2003
OCF	$189.7	$172.4	$155.5	$169.3
Tax Benefit from Stock Options	$36.5	$41.6	$34.6	$32.0
Capital Expenditures	($69.8)	($70.0)	($23.0)	($28.4)
Free Cash Flow with Tax Benefit	$119.9	$102.4	$132.5	$140.9
Free Cash Flow without Tax Benefit	$83.4	$60.8	$97.9	$108.9

*Dollar amounts are in millions of dollars.
Source: SEC filings.

investors care more about net margin—how much revenue turns into net income—than they do about operating-cash flow margin, which is the percentage of revenues that turns into operating cash flow. Both matter.

Operating Cash Flow Margin

The operating cash flow margin helps determine how much of the revenue is translating into cash flow and is crucial, because it reflects business strength better than earnings. Measure it on a rolling 12-month basis to smooth it out. If it starts to drop off, find out whether it's short-term or persistent. Then you can see if there's trouble and know to avoid it.

The rarer and happier situation occurs with a company whose OCF margin is rising without any of the short-term ways to boost it. If the investor can buy that stock at an attractive valuation, it's an excellent chance to profit. Table 5.9 shows that Apple, in the three years to the quarter ending September 24, 2011, showed a steady increase in operating cash flow margin.

Apple's sequential change in LTM operating cash flow margins is simply superb. But let's say you are concerned that Apple's OCF is overly influenced by adding back stock-based compensation and changes in working capital. Using LTM (net income + D&A)/revenues produces equally dramatic and more consistent results.

Apple is a company that, throughout these three years, wrung more operating cash flow out of each dollar of revenue, no matter how you count it. No wonder investors have continued to profit from this efficient cash-generating machine.

Operating Cash Flow Minus Net Income

Another way to look at OCF and net income is to track the absolute numbers, not only percentages, to make sure you've got the picture. Ideally, we want to see operating cash flow consistently exceed net income. We need to compare this year-over-year to remove business seasonality. We are looking for trends. Is operating cash flow minus net income this year worse than last year? What has been the year-over-year trend for the last four to six quarters? If a company keeps stretching to make its numbers, it can often show up in year-over-year trends.

John's December 2004 report to clients expressed concern over the divergence between operating cash flow and net income at RAE Systems (now private):

Table 5.9 Apple's Tasty Operating Cash Flow Margin Core: December Quarter 2008–September Quarter 2011*

Quarter Ending	Sep. 2011	June 2011	March 20 11	Dec. 2010	Sep. 2010	June 2010	March 2010	Dec. 2009	Sep. 2009	June 2009	March 2009	Dec. 2008
Revenues	$28	$29	$25	$27	$20	$16	$13	$16	$12	$10	$9	$12
OCF	$10	$11	$6	$10	$6	$5	$2	$6	$3	$2	$1	$4
LTM OCF and Percentage of LTM Revenues (Operating Cash Flow Margin LTM)	34%	32%	30%	28%	28%	28%	26%	24%	23%	25%	23%	–
Sequential Change	7.0%	6.9%	7.1%	(0.3%)	2.2%	7.1%	8.4%	4.1%	7.9%	6%	–	–
LTM (Net Income Plus D&A) as Percentage of LTM Revenues	26%	25%	24%	23%	23%	23%	23%	21%	21%	20%	19%	–
Sequential Change	2.7%	5.1%	1.8%	1.0%	0.4%	2.0%	5.3%	3.0%	3.0%	6.2%	–	–

*Dollar amounts are in billions of dollars.
Source: SEC filings.

RAE's cash flow from operations dipped to negative in the September 2004 quarter, while the company's net income grew 15.5% sequentially and 45.4% year-over-year. Table 5.10 illustrates that for the past six quarters, operating cash flow has amounted to just negative $363,000 compared with net income of $4.2 million, resulting in an operating cash flow to net income deficit of $4.5 million.

When the company had negative operating cash flow before, net income also declined. In the September 2003 quarter and every other quarter for a year, net income jumped while cash flow dipped into negative territory, without balancing in other quarters. This raises earnings quality questions.

The operating cash flow deficits have largely been driven by working capital items such as inventory and accounts receivable. Future cash flow may also be negatively impacted—payables that RAE's stretches today will have to be paid. The company generated $616,000 in cash flow from payables this year (2004) and $224,000 in the most recent quarter, and $669,000 last year. But stretching out payables is just a form of short-term financing. It can't last forever and whatever benefit it provides today to cash flow will be reversed and adversely.

On December 15, 2004, RAE traded at $8.05. Six weeks later, shares stood at $6.55. Cash flow concerns formed one of several reasons for the report, and those negative catalysts came quickly.

Table 5.10 RAE Systems' Operating Cash Flow Lags Behind Net Income: June Quarter 2003–September Quarter 2004

Quarter Ending	Sep. 2004	June 2004	March 2004	Dec. 2003	Sep. 2003	June 2003
Operating Cash Flow	($1,216)	$1,475	($1,244)	$1,065	($494)	$51
Net Income	$1,051	$910	$185	$486	$723	$795
OCF Minus NI	($2,267)	$565	($1,429)	$579	($1,217)	($744)
NI as Percent of OCF	(86%)	62%	(15%)	46%	(146%)	1,559%

*Dollar amounts are in thousands of dollars.
Source: SEC filings.

In February 2005, John warned clients that operating cash flow lagged well behind net income at Openwave Systems:

> As Table 5.11 shows, in four out of the past six quarters, Openwave's quarterly operating cash flow has lagged behind its reported net income. In our opinion, this is a sign of poor earnings quality. In the most recent two quarters, to December 2004, the company turned the corner to profitability, generating a net income of $2.8 million. Meanwhile, operating cash flow during the same period was negative $19.2 million. The primary factor driving the poor operating cash flows in the December quarter was the substantial increase in accounts receivables.

Ultimately, Openwave shares fell more than 99 percent. ('Nuff said.)

Our last example here comes from John's February 2005 report on personal care products company Helen of Troy, whose lackluster operating cash flows showed poor earnings quality.

> Helen of Troy's operating cash flows have turned negative, even while net income has grown. This typically indicates periods of poor earnings quality. Net income grew to $31.1 million in November, up from $25.1 million in the year-ago period. Meanwhile, operating cash flow dropped to negative $1.1 million from $12.9 million over the same period. As a result, the operating cash flow/net income ratio was −3.5 percent in November 2004, down from 51.3 percent in the year-ago period.

Table 5.11 Openwave's Operating Cash Flow Lags Behind Net Income: June Quarter 2003–December Quarter 2004*

Quarter Ending	Dec. 2004	Sep. 2004	June 2004	March 2004	Dec. 2003	June 2003
Operating Cash Flow	($1,904)	($14,463)	($186)	($15,548)	($19,351)	($12,717)
Net Income	$1,866	$975	($737)	($5,738)	($9,387)	($13,989)
OCF Minus NI	($3,770)	($15,420)	$551	($9,810)	($9,964)	$1,272

*Dollar amounts are in thousands of dollars.
Source: SEC filings.

The results in Table 5.12 (see page 144) are presented on a year-over-year basis to account for seasonality. As the table shows, operating cash flow has weakened considerably in each of the last three quarters. The key drivers of this deterioration have been large increases in inventory and accounts receivables, as well as an increase in accrued expenses.

So Helen wasn't so beautiful after all.

While operating cash flow minus net income and OCF/NI are better-known formulas, we turn to indicators you haven't seen before. They are extra steps of analysis unique to this book.

About EBITDA

EBITDA—earnings before interest, taxes, depreciation, and amortization—appears constantly in the financial media and company press releases, and is sometimes loosely thrown around as "cash flow" or even (yowza) "free cash flow." EBITDA is operating income from the income statement (EBIT) with D&A added back and ignoring anything below it, such as interest and taxes. Adding back D&A makes sense, but taxes and interest are expenses. EBITDA, adjusted EBITDA, and other formulations are not real cash flow.

The cliché is that EBITDA is "earnings before bad stuff." It doesn't account for working capital changes, which are key to understanding the direction of the business and red flags. By adding D&A back in, EBITDA assumes the fixed assets will not be replaced. And by ignoring interest expense or income taxes, it doesn't take into account how the company is financed.

The latter points to the defensible use for EBITDA and variations such as EBIT capex and EBITDAR. Value investors like Tom routinely estimate a normalized enterprise-value-to-EBITDA multiple because buyers—usually private equity—use this multiple to determine what gains they could make if they purchased a company and added debt. Levering up usually means interest deductions and shifts in tax liability, which is good for buyers if the business cash flows can cover the payments. For these buyers, it is precisely because they know how they will adjust a target's capital structure that EBITDA is just fine for that purpose. An EV-to-EBITDA multiple can help the investor on the long side evaluate margin of safety and potential return for a buyout candidate.

Table 5.12 Helen of Troy's Operating Cash Flow Lags Net Income: Year-over-Year, Fourth Quarter 2003–Third Quarter 2005*

Quarter	Q3 2005	Q3 2004	Q2 2005	Q2 2004	Q1 2005	Q1 2004	Q4 2004	Q4 2003
Operating Cash Flow	($1,091)	$12,864	($19,277)	$1,617	$140	($13,031)	$75,763	$47,012
Net Income	$31,135	$25,062	$18,848	$13,098	$14,483	$14,844	$7,518	$6,458
OCF – NI	($32,226)	($12,198)	($38,125)	($11,481)	($14,343)	($27,875)	$67,245	$40,554
OCF as Percentage of NI	(3.5%)	51.3%	(102.3%)	12.3%	1.0%	(87.8%)	994.5%	728.0%

*Dollar amounts are in millions of dollars.
Source: SEC filings.

Another exception where EBITDA is useful comes with a company that is growing rapidly through acquisitions. In the rare case where you can have great confidence in the acquirer's disciplined track record paying value prices for excellent future returns, EBITDA is a reasonable measure until free cash flow grows and normalizes. These are two ways that EBITDA is useful to the long investor, but the short seller knows management can also use EBITDA to obscure or manipulate cash reality.

EBITDA Margin LTM Minus Operating Cash Flow Margin LTM

Tracking the spread between the EBITDA margin and the operating cash flow margin can show possible manipulation. This is a better tool than OCF minus net income because this calculation will pick up more clearly whether the company is pulling levers on the income statement to generate a lot of growth in EBITDA. Use rolling LTM from quarter to quarter to smooth out fluctuations. Then note, not the absolute value of the difference, but the trend—whether it's widening considerably. Companies usually, but not always, produce more EBITDA than OCF, because it doesn't account for working capital.

There is no absolute value at which the spread shows a problem. It might be 5 percent for one company and 10 percent for another one, even if in the same industry. It's the trend that matters. If the LTM EBITDA margin expands, but doesn't translate into cash flow, then the spread will widen—the result of the equation grows—and that's the concern. It is a tipoff that something is going on to make the income statement look pretty without cash coming in the door. Table 5.13 shows clothing retailer Under Armour's textbook widening LTM spread for 8 quarters through September 2011.

A number of things can cause it. It might be stuffing the channel. Maybe the company reversed a reserve or overstated its gross profit margin or managing operating expenses to make margins look more attractive. The reality is that the margin improvement is of low quality when the spread widens. We track this for the previous three years.

It doesn't get any clearer than with the well-known streaming and DVD delivery company Netflix for the two years to September 30, 2011. Table 5.14 shows that Netflix's LTM EBITDA margin was basically flat, while the LTM OCF margin dropped considerably. The spread widened—it used to be negative and turned to positive, as EBITDA became greater than operating cash flow. As with the next example of Jacobs Engineering,

Table 5.13 Under Armour Widening EBITDA Margin – OCF Margin Spread: December Quarter 2009–September Quarter 2011

Quarter Ending	Sep. 2011	June 2011	March 2011	Dec. 2010	Sep. 2010	June 2010	March 2010	Dec. 2009
LTM EBITDA Margin	12.9%	12.7%	13.3%	13.5%	13.7%	13.4%	13.5%	13.3%
LTM OCF Margin	(3.2%)	(1.7%)	(2.1%)	4.7%	6.2%	10.7%	12.3%	13.9%
LTM EBITDA Margin Minus LTM OCF Margin	16.1%	14.5%	15.3%	8.8%	7.4%	2.7%	1.2%	(0.6%)

Source: SEC filings.

this pointed to low-quality earnings, cash flow issues, and moderating demand, all of which appeared in the Netflix earnings report for the quarter ending September 30, 2011. Netflix shares had already plummeted, but we see in Figure 5.2 that they had farther to fall.

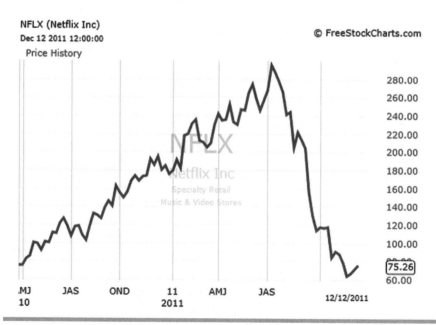

Figure 5.2 Netflix: April 2010–December 12, 2011.
Source: FreeStockCharts.com, by permission.

Table 5.14 Netflix's Widening EBITDA Margin–OCF Margin Spread: December Quarter 2009–September Quarter 2011

Quarter Ending	Sep. 2011	June 2011	March 2011	Dec. 2010	Sep. 2010	June 2010	March 2010	Dec. 2009
LTM EBITDA Margin	15%	15%	15%	15%	15%	15%	14%	14%
Sequential Change	(21%)	(1%)	3%	1%	1%	3%	4%	–
Year-over-Year Change	1%	3%	7%	9%	–	–	–	–
LTM Operating Cash Flow Margin	12%	13%	13%	13%	14%	17%	19%	19%
Sequential Change	(7%)	(3%)	3%	(10%)	(17%)	(10%)	(2%)	–
LTM EBITDA Margin Minus LTM OCF Margin	3%	2%	2%	2%	1%	2%	(5%)	(6%)

Source: SEC filings.

In 2011, John advised members of Motley Fool stock services about numerous operating cash flow concerns at Jacobs Engineering.[3] The company at the time combined all of the operating cash flow and net income items we've discussed in one big heaping bowl of short-seller soup. It begins with DSO and accounts receivable warnings, moves to OCF-minus-net income divergence, tap dances to the EBITDA-margin-minus-OCF-margin spread, and concludes where the working capital problems ensure a deteriorating cash conversion cycle. Beautiful to behold.

> Shares of Jacobs Engineering Group (JEC) score in the lowest quintile in our earnings quality model. Historically, companies with the lowest earnings quality have lagged behind companies with the highest earnings quality by 1,500 basis points annually over the past 10 years.

As shown in Table 5.15, the quarter ended April 2011 brought JEC its seventh consecutive year-over-year increase in days sales outstanding. Furthermore, the DSO reached at least a three-year high at 71 days.

Our concerns with respect to lengthening credit terms do not relate to the collectability of the receivables. Rather, the extension of credit terms often acts as a way to incentivize the customer and front-load revenue recognition. This creates a short-term boost to revenue at the expenses of long-term sustainability, because a revenue "gap" is created that must be filled by a new customer to offset the revenue pulled into the current period.

In addition, JEC witnessed an increase in its unbilled accounts receivable. Year-over-year, the unbilled accounts receivable (A/R) grew 14.3 percent compared with a revenue decline of 1.1 percent. An increase in unbilled revenue may signal aggressive revenue recognition, because the company's management has discretion in determining revenue recognition and profitability in percentage-of-completion accounting, as shown in Chapter 2.

In our view, managements engage in extended payment terms or accelerated revenue recognition when demand for a company's products is weakening. Otherwise, there is no incentive

Table 5.15 Growing DSO at Jacobs Engineering: April Quarter 2009–April Quarter 2011

Quarter Ending	Apr. 2011	Jan. 2011	Oct. 2010	July 2010	April 2010	Jan. 2010	Oct. 2009	July 2009	April 2009
DSO*	71	63	65	60	60	57	58	56	53
Sequential Change	13%	(3%)	7%	1%	5%	(1%)	4%	4%	3%
Year-over-Year Change	18%	10%	12%	9%	12%	10%	4%	–	–
Four-Quarter Average DSO*	65	62	61	59	58	56	55	54	–
Sequential Change	4%	2%	3%	2%	3%	2%	1%	NA	NA
A/R as a Percentage of Revenue	78%	69%	71%	66%	66%	63%	63%	61%	58%

*DSO numbers are in days.
Source: SEC filings.

to front-load revenue to boost short-term results. In fact, management reduced its guidance on the conference call, citing uncertainty in the market.

Prior to the April quarter, OCF minus net income had also fallen year-over-year for four consecutive periods. This is another sign of poor earnings quality, because it means the net income reported on the income statement is not resulting in a corresponding amount of cash flow. It remained weak in the most recent quarter with a cash flow shortfall to net income. While there is some seasonal effect in this quarter, cumulatively the company has had a shortfall over the past year.

Finally, Table 5.16 reveals that the spread between the LTM EBITDA margin and the LTM OCF margin has expanded to 5 percent, the highest in at least three years. As operating margins have held steady, OCF margins contracted. As a result, profits generated on the income statement have converted less and less into cash flow.

In our view, EBITDA does not represent an adequate measure of cash flow, primarily because it does not account for changes in working capital, which are often key indicators that management is stretching in a given quarter or over time.

Table 5.16 Jacobs Engineering Widening EBITDA Margin – OCF Margin Spread: April Quarter 2010–April Quarter 2011*

Quarter Ending	April 2011	Jan. 2011	Oct. 2010	July 2010	April 2010
EBITDA Margin LTM	6	6	6	6	6
EBITDA LTM (Millions)	$153	$150	$153	$140	$152
Quarter's EBITDA (Millions)	$155	$134	$204	$118	$144
OCF Margin LTM	2%	1%	2%	3%	4%
EBITDA Margin LTM Minus OCF Margin LTM	5%	5%	4%	3%	2%

*All dollar amounts in millions.
Source: SEC filings.

Based on the tone of the conference call, we could see a continued negative trend. CEO Craig Martin stated:

"We are big believers that as you take share, you position yourself best for the more robust cycle of the market. So we would certainly be willing and able to sacrifice margin in order to expand our market share. And in fact, that's part of our plan. One of the ways that our cost structure helps us to steal share in these down cycles is that we have that beneficial cost position."

This effort to steal share may compress margins in the future, and, given that the demand scenario is pessimistic, cash flows may continue to be weak.

Table 5.17 shows that, as a result of poor cash flow metrics, the company's cash conversion cycle has been on the rise, reaching at least an 11 quarter high at 58 days and well outside of the normalized band of prior quarters and years.

With this perfect confluence of earnings quality indicators, it was no wonder the company missed earnings the next quarter. JEC's stock price plummeted 38 percent from $50 a share to approximately $31 at the October 2011 lows.

With operating cash flow issues now wired into our brains, we see in front of us a mirage. That is, a "Cash" EPS mirage, unique to this book.

Table 5.17 Jacobs Engineering Rising Cash Conversion Cycle: April Quarter 2010–April Quarter 2011

Quarter Ending	April 2011	Jan. 2011	Oct. 2010	July 2010	April 2010
Cash Conversion Cycle	58	50	50	49	47
Sequential Change	16%	(1%)	4%	3%	10%
Year-over-Year Change	23%	17%	15%	16%	16%
Four-Quarter Average	52	49	47	45	44
Sequential Change	6%	4%	4%	4%	4%

Source: SEC filings.

Cash EPS Mirage

Cash EPS is net income minus accruals. The accruals are the changes in the following:

- Total current assets
- Total liabilities
- Cash
- Securities and investments
- Total current portion of long-term debt
- Depreciation and amortization

If net income is greater than Cash EPS, then management has created an earnings mirage. Many times companies report profits and earnings growth that are mirages, when all of them came from changes in accruals only.

Cash EPS should be greater or equal to the company's reported EPS. Watch the trend. A quarter or two doesn't necessarily mean much, but a clear negative trend calls into question whether management is estimating based on experience in order to manipulate the numbers.

Consider short-term liabilities (such as interest, taxes, utility charges, wages) that continually occur during an accounting period, but are not supported by an invoice or a written demand for payment. When preparing financial statements for that accounting period, such liabilities are estimated on the basis of experience (based on previous payments). Similar increases in the assets of the firm (which may also continually occur) are not taken into account, in order to comply with accrual basis accounting rules. Management can use its "experience," which it can determine to suit its needs.

Over a number of quarters, if cumulative reported EPS is greater than Cash EPS, it signals poor earnings quality. If Cash EPS is negative and reported EPS is positive, then the latter is all coming from accruals. This is a low-quality source of profits and may be a persistent problem.

Returning to Jacobs Engineering, Table 5.18 shows that the company's earnings driven by accruals as Cash EPS were cumulatively negative over the example period.

Table 5.18 Negative Cumulative Cash EPS at Jacobs Engineering: April Quarter 2010–April Quarter 2011

Quarter Ending	April 2011	Jan. 2011	Oct. 2010	July 2010	April 2010
Cash EPS	($0.85)	$0.49	($0.82)	$0.00	($1.96)
Sequential Change	(274%)	(160%)	132,334%	(100%)	(221%)
Year-over-Year Change	(57%)	(70%)	(1,219%)	(100%)	(10,761%)
OCF Minus Net Income in Millions of Dollars	($143.50)	$74.45	($116.21)	$99.98	($200.70)
Sequential Change	(293%)	(164%)	(216%)	(150%)	(220%)
Percent Year-over-Year Change	(29%)	(56%)	330%	(46%)	81%
Quarterly OCF / Quarterly Net Income	(79%)	213%	(51%)	625%	(159%)
Percent Sequential Change	(137%)	518%	(108%)	(493%)	(148%)
Percent Year-over-Year Change	(50%)	(36%)	(177%)	112%	9,029%

Source: SEC filings.

Jacobs wasn't producing "real" EPS, a strong negative earnings quality indicator.

In 2011, John notified clients of his Parabolix Research service that Cash EPS was also a negative indicator for earnings quality for Digital River, an e-commerce solution company:

> The company has persistently generated negative Cash EPS, which removes changes in accruals from reported EPS. Where accruals have historically been a larger driver of performance than net income, as at Digital River, they are a source of low earnings quality.

Cash EPS was negative coming out of the 2008 crisis that ended near the end of the first quarter of 2009, and its rebound was quite weak. Table 5.19 shows that cumulative EPS for the nine quarters exceeded Cash EPS substantially by $2.11 a share. This means Digital River's earnings quality is low. Reported earnings were generated more by accruals and were fiction rather than reality.

Table 5.19   Negative Cumulative Cash EPS at Digital River: June
Quarter 2009–June Quarter 2011

Quarter Ending	Cumulative	June 2011	March 2011	Dec. 20-10	Sep. 2010
EPS minus Cash EPS	$2.11	($0.55)	($0.29)	$1.30	$0.93
Sequential Change		92%	(122%)	40%	(201%)
Year-over-Year Change		(40%)	47%	138%	(37%)

Quarter Ending	June 2010	March 2010	Dec. 2009	Sep. 2009	June 2009
EPS Minus Cash EPS	($0.92)	($0.20)	$0.55	$1.49	($0.20)
Sequential Change	371%	(136%	(63%)	(828%)	(94)
Year-over-Year Change	349%	(104%)	–	–	–

Source: SEC filings.

Eventually, this and other factors caught up with Digital River. It warned on July 28, 2011, after which its stock dropped 39 percent through August 26 versus 12 percent for the S&P 500.

The investor can combine information from the cash from operations and cash from investing sections to calculate free cash flow, another path to warning signs of earnings quality problems.

Free Cash Flow: Intersection of Operating and Investing Cash Flows

The financial world defines "free cash flow" in different ways, including:

> · *owner earnings = net income plus D&A minus capex*

"Owner earnings" is Warren Buffett's formulation, also called "structural free cash flow." It omits all other adjustments to net income and omits working capital changes.

> · *true free cash flow = net cash from operations minus capex*

It's "true," because it's the actual cash reality, even though adjustments, working capital, and more may or may not be sustainable or desirable.

· free cash flow to the firm = net cash from operations minus (expenses, taxes, changes in working capital, and changes in investments)

Table 5.20 Growing Free Cash Flow Margin at Priceline: June Quarter 2010–March Quarter 2012

Quarter Ending	March 2012	Dec. 2011	Sep. 2011	June 2011	March 2011	Dec. 2010	Sept. 2010	June. 2010
LTM FCF Margin	87.4%	86.0%	95.0%	87.5%	82.0%	69.7%	54.9%	56.2%
Sequential Change	1.6%	(9.5%)	8.6%	6.7%	17.6%	26.9%	(2.2)	–

Source: SEC filings.

These are ways that investors use free cash flow for comparative purposes, and value investors in particular will use more than one to get at what matters for the particular company and industry. For the purpose of identifying ways to manipulate free cash flow, we use true free cash flow, which uses OCF from the cash from operations section and capital expenditures (capex) from the cash from investing section.

We calculate free cash flow as a percentage of the revenues to arrive at the free cash flow margin. We use LTM free cash flow margin for the same reasons as LTM operating cash flow above. Table 5.20 shows that just as Apple has experienced a healthy growing operating cash flow margin, so has Priceline with its free cash flow margin. It steadily climbed over each four-quarter period, wringing more out of its billions in growing revenues.

To see the other side, we return to John's report on Helen of Troy, where he identified its poor free cash flow quality.

Helen of Troy's free cash flow—using the simplest calculation of OCF minus capex—has also been dismal in recent periods. Poor operating cash flows act as a cash drain. However, the company's acquisition of OXO in particular had a significant cost. Typically, we adjust capital expenditures to reflect the cash outlay for an acquisition, because all of the benefits of acquisitions are clearly evident in higher sales and net income. However, the cash cost is not. Helen of Troy included the cash of the acquisitions into capital expenditures, which we believe presents a fair picture of the company's free cash flow—which has been persistently negative. For the nine months ended November 2004, free cash flow was negative $302.1 million. Table 5.21 shows the last four quarters each compared to the prior year quarter.

With a number of examples now of this company's significant issues, it's fair to say that this Helen was the face that launched a thousand slips.

And with that we leave the interaction of the cash from operations and cash from investing sections to find the fewer, but still important, opportunities for manipulation in the investing and financing cash flow sections.

Cash from Investing

The cash flow statement's next section contains investments bought and sold. Most commonly, it includes additions to and sales of property, plant, and equipment, capital expenditures or "capex," acquisitions and sales of businesses, and purchases and sales of securities and cash instruments.

Companies either break out additions to and sales of PP&E or specifies "net," which combines the two. Here too, the investor has to look at trends. A company is not in business to sell its PP&E. A restaurant chain might be selling company-owned stores to franchisees, hoping to earn higher-margin, but nominally smaller, franchise fees, but the boost to cash from selling stores can't continue. Worst, if the company faces a cash crunch, it might sell both well-performing and poorly-performing company stores at any prices to get the cash. (We'll look at this in a moment with restaurant chain Steak 'n Shake.) If the company nets purchases and sales, that's a clue to go to the footnotes to find out what's what.

Growth and Maintenance Capex

The cash from the investing section also doesn't distinguish between growth and maintenance capital expenditures, and this is essential to evaluating cash reality. In a well-run company, management invests in growth capex only where it yields a sufficient return on capital and

Table 5.21 Negative Free Cash Flow at Helen of Troy: Year-over-Year Fourth Quarter 2003–Third Quarter 2005*

Quarter	Q3 2005	Q3 2004	Q2 2005	Q2 2004	Q1 2005	Q1 2004	Q4 2004	Q4 2003
Operating Cash Flow	($1,091)	$12,864	($19,277)	$1,617	$140	($13,031)	$75,763	$47,012
Capital Expenditures	$13,822	$53,794	$266,339	$3,286	$2,408	$1,719	($44,994)	$5,246
Free Cash Flow	($14,913)	($40,930)	($285,616)	($1,669)	($2,268)	$11,312	$120,157	$41,766

*Dollar amounts are in millions of dollars.
Source: SEC filings.

manages maintenance capex to keep the existing business in good shape—not putting off maintenance or upgrades essential to current operations. One capex number doesn't tell investors how much or well management spends company money on growth or maintenance.

Companies rarely break out growth and maintenance capex. Investors often use depreciation and amortization as a proxy for maintenance capex, but whether that makes sense depends on the business and how D&A works for its equipment. (We explained how important this is with Akamai's questionable D&A in Chapter 4.) But even knowing maintenance capex doesn't reveal whether management is starving itself to look good to a buyer—which is fine for shareholders if a buyer appears and pays a premium, but could cause more trouble later if the company isn't sold. Most simply, if you maintain your car, it lasts longer. Put it off, and you may find yourself broken down on a highway.

There is no rule about good or bad growth, or about maintenance capex. Growth capex can be a poor investment and lead to low-quality cash flows, or it can be an intelligent use of capital and lead to higher returns. And low maintenance capex can be correct (the restaurants, like Dairy Queen, require little updating) or a poor decision (putting off maintenance capex, boosting current cash flows and net income, only to have to pay it later, reducing cash flows and net income) that distorts real cash flows for the company.

Let's see these concepts in action. In 2008, a shareholder group led by Sardar Biglari, then-CEO of Western Sizzlin', a small restaurant chain, gained control of the iconic Steak 'n Shake chain and became CEO. Table 5.22 shows that for the two years prior to that change in the control, the chain's rapid expansion—seen in growth capex—and negative free cash flow marched it towards the drive-up window of doom. The company would have been already blown up were it not sustained by cash from willy-nilly restaurant sale-leasebacks.

Management saw the writing on the Steakburger® wall in the spring of 2008, reducing growth capex to nothing in the second fiscal quarter of 2008. Table 5.23 shows that Biglari, as CEO starting in June 2008, continued the trend from excess growth capex spending to a maintenance capex deficit. This boosted free cash flow and cash dramatically.

At first investors thought this was temporary, to return the balance sheet from the brink. Investors at several annual shareholder meetings questioned management's capex decisions after it appeared to be no

Table 5.22 Declining Free Cash Flow and Cash at Steak 'n Shake: July Quarter 2006–April Quarter 2008*

Quarter Ending	April 2008	Dec. 2007	Sep. 2007	July 2007	April 2007	Dec. 2006	Sep. 2006	July 2006
Depreciation and Amortization	$10.4	$7.6	$5.5	$7.5	$9.8	$7.2	$5.7	$6.8
Capital Expenditures	$10.5	$13.4	$12.5	$14.8	$17.7	$23.7	$15.0	$17.9
Growth Capex	$0.1	$5.8	$7.0	$7.3	$7.9	$16.5	$9.3	$11.1
Free Cash Flow	($3.8)	($6.2)	($5.5)	$2.0	($15.1)	($6.6)	$2.2	($5.1)
Cash and Short-Term Investments	$1.6	$2.0	$1.5	$3.9	$2.3	$5.2	$4.8	$3.8

*Dollar amounts are in millions of dollars.
Source: SEC filings.

Table 5.23 Free Cash Flow and Cash Turnaround at Steak 'n Shake: July Quarter 2008–April Quarter 2010*

Quarter	April 2010	Dec. 2009	Sep. 2009	July 2009	April 2009	Dec. 2008	Sep. 2008	July 2008
Depreciation and Amortization	$8.9	$6.9	$7.3	$6.9	$9.5	$7.4	$8.9	$7.8
Capital Expenditures	$1.6	$3.1	$2.6	$0.5	$0.6	$2.0	$1.6	$4.7
Maintenance Capex Deficit	($7.3)	($3.8)	($4.7)	($6.4)	($8.9)	($5.4)	($7.3)	($3.1)
Free Cash Flow	$9.8	$16.6	$8.6	$14.8	$9.6	$13.6	($2.0)	$5.0
Cash and Short-Term Investments	$81.0	$71.4	$54.4	$37.8	$35.0	$25.6	$6.9	$1.6

*Dollar amounts are in millions of dollars.
Source: SEC filings.

longer necessary to save the company. Biglari named a higher, but still low, $10 million capex estimate for fiscal 2011, which he achieved. This ambitious CEO wasn't prettying up the cash flow for sale. He simply made the rational decision to spend no more on the Steak 'n Shake business than required to derive desired returns on capital. With the company change to a holding company structure, the newly named Biglari Holdings could invest excess cash from Steak 'n Shake wherever it could earn the highest return, whether in more restaurants or elsewhere.

There is no rule, then, about the magnitude or allocation of growth or maintenance capex. The important earnings quality issue is to make sure that the money isn't being wasted. Breaking capex into its parts is key to this process.

Acquisitions

Cash spent to acquire companies appears in the cash from investing section of the cash flow statement. It's easy to skim over it and analyze the acquisition separately, but highly acquisitive companies can manipulate free cash flow when they acquire inventories.

When a company makes an acquisition, it's an investing cash outflow, but the liquidation of acquired inventory and collection of receivables are operating cash inflows. These are one-time events, but the highly acquisitive company can keep this up repeatedly until it stops, and then suddenly the real, sustainable operating cash flow appears—and it's almost always painfully less. The company "buys" growth until it can't anymore. Serial acquirers can use acquisitions to obscure real earnings and cash flow power until they stop acquiring.

Investors routinely omit acquisitions from their calculation of free cash flow. True, the cash isn't spent on the ongoing business, but this begs the question of whether management is allocating capital for higher return. James Montier cites a 2008 KPMG study showing that 93 percent of managers *think* their merger and acquisition (M&A) activity adds shareholder value, but fewer than 30 percent of the transactions *actually* do.[4] This suggests that if management does not assure investors that the merger or acquisition will be "accretive"—if it can't manage even that standard cheerleading—we better *really* watch out. This is particularly true with non-software "tech" companies, which face not only declining average selling prices (ASPs) but also eventual limits to market growth.

Cisco Systems provides a useful example. Table 5.24 shows that Cisco has been a serial acquirer, especially from 2005 through the end of 2010.

Cisco spent $15.5 billion on acquisitions from 2005 through 2011, yet its net income increased a mere $741 million, only 4.8 percent of the acquisition expenditures. On that basis, we can safely say that the investments have not paid off. So why should the investor not deduct some or all of acquisitions from free cash flow, when *a priori* it's impossible to know what the future return will be?

Cisco's serial acquisitions make it nearly impossible for the investor to determine true earnings power. In the fiscal fourth quarter ending July 31, 2011, the company announced $770 million in restructuring charges, and, for only the second quarter since that ending January 25, 2003— over eight years—did the company not make an acquisition. However, it started up the acquisition machine again in the quarter following its first restructuring charges.

Cisco stock closed at $13.86 on January 24, 2003, and stood at $18.01, plus small dividends, almost 9 years later, on November 7, 2011. Where's the shareholder value from all those billions?

Acquisitions can mask declining growth. In Cisco's case, investors had ample warning before the tech crash that the company was running hard to keep in place—and failing to do so, even if the stock price was rising.

Quest Software offers an example here too. Part of John's 2005 report to clients concerned Quest's acquisition strategy and negative free cash flow. (This report also appears in part in Chapter 4 to show that Quest's acquisitions added nothing to tangible book value.) John observed that acquisitions led to increases in revenue, earnings, and operating cash flow, but added no value for shareholders and appeared to have led largely to the enrichment of Quest's management. He wrote:

> Our second concern regarding the acquisitions is the large drain on the company's free cash flow. While the benefits of the acquisition are factored into operating cash flow, there is no penalty for the price actually paid for the acquired entities. As a result, in Table 5.25, we have adjusted free cash flow to reflect not only capital expenditures, but also cash paid for acquisitions to obtain a truer picture of both the acquisitions' benefits and costs.

When factoring in cash paid for acquisitions, free cash flow plummeted in the June quarter. More important, on a 12-month

Table 5.24 Cisco Systems Squanders Cash on Acquisitions: 2005–2011*

For the Fiscal Period:	12 months to July 30, 2005	12 months to July 29, 2006	12 months to July 28, 2007	12 months to July 26, 2008	12 months to July 25, 2009	12 months to July 31, 2010	12 months to July 31, 2011
Net Income	5,741.0	5,580.0	7,333.0	8,052.0	6,134.0	7,767.0	6,490.0
Cash from Operations	7,568.0	7,899.0	10,104.0	12,089.0	9,897.0	10,173.0	10,079.0
Capital Expenditure	(692.0)	(772.0)	(1,251.0)	(1,268.0)	(1,005.0)	(1,008.0)	(1,174.0)
Cash Acquisitions	(945.0)	(5,424.0)	(3,684.0)	(398.0)	(426.0)	(5,279.0)	(266.0)
Investment in Marketable and Equity Securities	4,145.0	(3,438.0)	(3,256.0)	(2,510.0)	(8,489.0)	(5,772.0)	–
Other Investing Activities	106.0	(10.0)	(151.0)	(17.0)	(39.0)	128.0	22.0
Cash from Investing	2,614.0	(9,644.0)	(8,342.0)	(4,193.0)	(9,959.0)	(11,931.0)	(2,934.0)

*Dollar amounts are in millions of dollars.
Source: S&P CapitalIQ.

Table 5.25 Acquisitions Drain Free Cash Flow at Quest Software:
September Quarter 2003–June Quarter 2005*

Quarter Ending	June 2005	March 2005	Dec. 2004	Sep. 2004
Operating Cash Flow	$14.7	$27.6	$38.0	$23.0
Capital Expenditures	$23.9	$3.0	$3.9	$3.9
Cash for Acquisitions	$44.9	$12.8	$0.7	$0.4
Free Cash Flow	($54.1)	$11.8	$33.8	$18.7
12-Month Cumulative OCF	$103.3	$101.0	$96.1	$87.8
12-Month Cumulative FCF	$10.3	$67.4	($32.5)	($37.9)
Quarter Ending	June 2004	March 2004	Dec. 2003	Sep. 2003
Operating Cash Flow	$12.3	$22.8	$29.7	$15.0
Capital Expenditures	$7.5	$16.6	$1.3	$1.5
Cash for Acquisitions	$1.7	$94.3	$0.1	–
Free Cash Flow	$3.1	($88.1)	$28.4	$13.5
12-Month Cumulative OCF	$79.7	$77.5	$76.7	–
12-Month Cumulative FCF	($43.2)	($42.0)	$65.2	–

*Dollar amounts are in millions of dollars.
Source: SEC filings.

rolling basis, free cash flow has been negative in four of the last
seven 12-month periods. These acquisitions have taken a toll on
Quest's cash-generating capability, and the operating benefits
appear to be minimal; another acquisition always seems necessary to boost the company's growth rate. We expect further
deterioration in free cash flow due to the $57 million paid for [an
acquisition] subsequent to the June quarter.

Serial Acquirers: Investing Long and Short

From the long side, Tom is wary of highly acquisitive companies, but
favors jockeys—master capital allocators with histories of successfully
acquiring companies and earning high returns on capital. An investor is
lucky to invest in a few in a lifetime, though Warren Buffett and Charlie
Munger, while the most famous, are only two of the few to date (and
Biglari Holdings' Sardar Biglari is almost certainly one in progress). Tom
wants financing to be out of cash flows or at extremely low cost—whether

through debt or share issuance. And at any time, he wants to buy a highly acquisitive company so cheaply and with such a low debt burden to cash flows that a liquidity crisis doesn't kill the company and stock.

John is equally wary of highly acquisitive companies, but he doesn't short them in a bull market. While their earnings quality may be a disaster or difficult to decipher, they can keep that going for a long time where credit flows. But in a bear market, access to capital shuts off. The company suddenly can't issue equity and finds it harder to get debt financing. When a company's in liquidity crisis mode, its weak cash flow starts to collapse. So, for a company with questionable earnings quality, track it during a bull market and wait for the bear market to short.

Now we move to the last section of the cash flow statement, less prone to manipulation, but the place to find where management misuses capital for share repurchases and dividends.

Cash from Financing

The most important thing to watch in cash flows from financing is cash paid for stock buybacks and dividends.

Silicon Valley companies have long maintained that they cannot compete for scarce, highly trained technical personnel or top executives without offering options packages. We won't argue the point but instead focus on what we do know is wrong: their practice of repurchasing shares at any price to mask or "make up for" options grants.

The only defensible buybacks are those that purchase company stock at such a discount to intrinsic value that it offers a return on capital greater than any other use of the cash. They should be opportunistic—when the stock price represents this greater value. By definition, buybacks to keep the share count down due to increasing share count from options or other means are not opportunistic. (Well, they may provide "opportunity" for management and employees, but not for shareholders.) Table 5.26 shows this sketchy practice at Rambus.

Over the nine years from September 2001 to the end of 2010, Rambus spent $829 million—it diluted shareholders by $403 million and then used $426 million of shareholder cash to compound the offense through buybacks. The net to shareholders for this expenditure of their money was that diluted share count *increased* by 4.9 million. It may appear that the company gave

Table 5.26 Rambus Share Count Increases Despite Buybacks: 2001–2010*

Fiscal Year Ending	Sep. 2001	Sep. 2002	Fiscal Year Change Dec. 2002	Dec. 2003	Dec. 2004	Dec. 2005
Issuance of Common Stock	$10.8	$3.5	$3.2	$25.9	$45.1	$8.5
Repurchase of Common Stock	–	$23.9	($20.5)	($29.8)	($21.7)	($88.2)
Weighted Average Diluted Shares	106.0	102.1	101.0	106.5	108.5	103.5
Share Price at Fiscal Year End	$7.36	$4.34	$6.71	$30.70	$23.00	$16.19
Fiscal Year Ending	**Dec. 2006**	**Dec. 2007**	**Dec. 2008**	**Dec. 2009**	**Dec. 2010**	
Issuance of Common Stock	$57.6	$11.8	$21.7	$20.7	$208.5	
Repurchase of Common Stock	($21.0)	–	($49.2)	–	($195.1)	
Weighted Average Diluted Shares	103.0	104.1	104.6	105.0	115.9	
Share Price at Fiscal Year End (in Dollars per Share)	$18.93	$20.94	$15.92	$24.40	$20.48	
Value Issued						$403
Value Repurchased						$426
Change in Diluted Shares 2001–2010						+$9.9

*Except where specifically indicated in column 1 of this table, dollar amounts are in millions of dollars.
Source: SEC filings.

with one hand and took with the other, but it actually grabbed with both. And as you can see, it made no difference to the company what the stock price was at issuance or repurchase. This runs close to what some might call theft from shareholders.

If this is routine for Silicon Valley companies, then they are all gambles. There is no margin of safety, management allocates capital for the good of employees, and shareholders are ripped off.

The financing section also tells whether the company uses debt to fuel buybacks and dividends. The rational investor is indifferent to cash or debt; all that matters is that the investment returns more than an alternative and higher than the cost of capital. (Of course, debt loads have to be payable and with a margin of safety, should credit dry up.) So, if the stock is selling for a discount consistent with extreme bear market lows, and interest rates are low due to the deflationary nature of economic contractions, it may make sense to issue debt to buy back shares, rather than to invest anywhere else. This is very, very rare.

But it almost never makes sense to issue debt to pay dividends. We have only to turn again to Hewlett-Packard to see debt increased to pay for dividends and to repurchase stocks.

Hewlett-Packard shows all the ways to completely obscure true earnings. Chapter 4 showed the clouding effect of "recurring nonrecurring charges" for serial acquisitions and restructuring. As earnings power declined in the last six years, the company turned to debt to fuel buybacks and dividends. It is unsustainable. See Table 5.27.

The problem started in 2006, when net cash began its decline to $24 billion dollars in net debt. The 2009 one-year improvement in net debt was almost exclusively due to a decline in cash spent on share repurchases.

The change in net cash—$24 billion—is almost 40 percent of the $58 billion spent on share repurchases. But it gets worse. During the same period, the company issued $12.2 billion in stock—whether for options or acquisitions. The company could not fund with cash acquisitions, stock issuances (grants or acquisitions), repurchases, and dividends ("Lions and tigers and bears, oh my!"), so it simply reduced cash and increased debt to the tune of $24 billion.

What good did this do for shareholders? At first, it appears HP doubled its EPS, where revenue increased 41 percent, net income by 50 percent, and OCF by 18 percent. It *looks* more efficient—as though they must have cut costs. But then you factor in flat gross margins, net margins up slightly from 6.8 percent to 7.3 percent, and declining levered

Table 5.27 Hewlett-Packard Uses Debt for Dividends and Share Repurchases and Gets Nowhere: 2006–July 2011

	Total (except net debt)	LTM to July 2011	2010	2009	2008	2007	2006
Cash from Operations	$74.30	$13.4	$11.9	$13.4	$14.6	$9.6	$11.4
Capital Expenditures	($20.8)	$4.4	$4.1	$3.7	$3.0	$3.0	$2.5
Cash Acquisitions	($31.8)	$4.4	$8.1	$10.4	$11.2	$6.8	$0.9
Cash Spent on Repurchases	($58.0)	$13.6	$11.0	$5.1	$9.6	$10.9	$7.8
Cash Spent on Dividends	($4.8)	$0.8	$0.7	$0.8	$0.8	$0.8	$0.9
Stock Issued	($12.2)	$1.0	$2.6	$1.8	$3.1	$2.5	$1.2
OCF after Above	($53.3)	$18.8	$19.8	$6.3	$21.6	$18.5	$9.6
Change in Net Cash	($24.0)	$12.8	$11.4	$2.5	$7.6	($3.3)	($11.2)
Net Income		$9.4	$8.8	$7.7	$8.3	$7.3	$6.2
Diluted Shares		2.194	2.372	2.437	2.567	2.716	2.852
Diluted EPS		$4.26	$3.69	$3.14	$3.25	$2.68	$2.18
Diluted EPS without Buybacks		$3.30	$3.09	$2.70	$2.91	$2.56	–

*Except for earnings-per-share (EPS) stats, all dollar amounts are in billions of dollars.
Source: SEC filings.

and unlevered free cash flow margins. Take out the reduced share count and EPS tracks net income exactly. The buybacks are responsible for 40 percent of the change from cash to debt. Unless Hewlett-Packard miraculously transforms itself into a sensible capital allocator, not to mention a better business, the buybacks and/or dividends will have to slow or stop, and down goes the stock.

Conclusion

The investor needs to scrutinize the cash flow statement carefully. Working capital changes can make operating cash flow look better than it is. Serial acquisitions obscure working capital, operating cash flow, and true free cash flow. Options grants, options tax benefits, and share issuances and repurchases can be all part of a game to cloud the real share count and cash flows of the business. If cash is indeed king, then the investor must analyze the cash flow statement to determine if it's real royalty or merely a pretender to the throne.

PART 2

Avoid Huge Losses

Chapter 6

The Long Strategy That Works for Our Long-Short Portfolio

What is the best long strategy to pair with short exposure? Telling you that is my job (Tom here) in this book, which advocates a long-short portfolio combining John's and my ideas. The answer is to use the strategy with more data in support than any other: "small cap value."

Whether it goes by the name of "deep value," "opportunistic value," or "banana value," all value investors, including me, select stocks with one or more of the following five important attributes: low price-to-asset value, low price-to-earnings, a pattern of insider buying, a stock price that has declined, and small market capitalization. These are the five common attributes in Tweedy Browne's landmark analysis of 50 studies of stock market strategy performance, "What Has Worked in Investing."[1] This chapter explains these five attributes and adjusts them where experience has shown me that they more effectively work with our long-short portfolio management strategy.

But two things matter before delving into any of these attributes. Every company considered for the long book must first, above all, more than pass the quality of earnings tests in this book. Whether low price to assets, low price to cash flow—any of the common attributes the studies identify—the company must show that it does not use aggressive revenue recognition, aggressive inventory management, artificial boosts to earnings, and this book's other criteria for avoiding trouble. Even an ugly turnaround can be (and has been, for me and others) a good value long, if management isn't playing games with the numbers that show the turnaround potential. But our point throughout is that earnings quality analysis improves risk management portfolio-wide—whether to buy a stock long or short, or simply to avoid it.

Second, and more important than any data, is that every investing strategy requires a temperament. For me it begins with this advice from value investor Sir John Templeton: "If you buy the same securities as other people, you will have the same results as other people."[2] We all like to think we're contrarians and that, at crunch time, we'd stand up like all those we admire in history and do the thing other people aren't doing. But Templeton, Buffett, and every value investor knows that each person is the biggest obstacle to his or her own investing success before strategy comes into play. A value investor cannot succeed without patience and nerves of steel.

Patience today is in short supply, when investors think "long term" is a week, a month, or a year. But who wants to be a grownup? Most investors, like children, want the profit candy *now*. So in a world where everyone wants it yesterday, the value investor stands alone attending the school of deferred gratification.

It takes time and patience to build a consistent, repeatable value investing process. It will almost always, despite the most obvious of catalysts, take time for the market to come to our viewpoint, and sometimes it doesn't. We're always asking, "Is my process right, and am I right more often than I am wrong?" We're also always honing the process to make it better.

It takes nerves of titanium to stand alone—to follow Templeton's truism and not do what everyone else is doing. That means the investor must believe strongly enough in one's investment process to buy unemotionally from panicked sellers and sell unemotionally to manic buyers. It is hard work to fight confirmation bias, the human tendency to believe that what we are doing is right if others do it too, and to selectively filter information that confirms our position. It takes a special temperament to act without affirmation from others, to keep your head when all around are losing theirs, and to know your work is good when others don't agree. In short, the red-blooded value investor starts to become interested when others avoid a stock like spoiled meat and then applies process with unstinting rigor.

My long investing requires patience to last for the unknown time it takes for an investment's catalysts to materialize and an unlimited supply of plain ol' gumption. Without them, all the rest is just empty calories.

The Great Debate: Are Stocks Ever Mispriced?

It's surprising to many today, but until very recently, only a brave few believed that stocks could be mispriced to offer an assiduous investor the opportunity to lose less and gain more. Warren Buffett is today cited everywhere for this proposition (as well as for many things he never believed!), but what is more widely accepted today wasn't always so. Buffett didn't always attract the now-familiar stadium-size crowds at the Berkshire Hathaway annual meeting in Omaha. Once the gatherings were held in conference rooms, and before that Buffett toiled entirely alone in his home office.

Fewer still knew his teacher and employer, Benjamin Graham. Graham and Dodd's 1934 first edition of *Security Analysis* and Graham's 1949 *The Intelligent Investor* invented the value-investing field. His firm Graham-Newman produced annualized 20 percent returns over decades. For perspective, an investor or money manager who achieves, say, 10 percent to 15 percent annualized returns over anything more than five years today is considered at the pinnacle of the field.

Graham taught Buffett at the Columbia Business School, giving Buffett the only A+ grade.[3] Graham and his firm gave apprenticeships to Buffett and other value investors such as Tweedy Browne's Tom Knapp, who achieved extraordinary success later in other investing venues. During the next 60 or so years after Buffett worked for Graham-Newman, he produced mind-boggling returns at his own investment fund and its successor Berkshire Hathaway, making millionaires of his clients and shareholders in his Omaha hometown and beyond.

All the while, he stuck to basic Graham strategies, though by his own admission he was limited over time by the increasingly high mountains of cash to invest from employing the smaller cap value strategies of his earlier years. Yet despite that, when asked to name his investing style at the 2011 Berkshire Hathaway annual shareholder meeting press conference, he answered, "Benjamin Graham." I listened with goose bumps (and not a little confirmation bias). What works, works. My long investing strategy does not go in and out of fashion to respond to the impatient "now" investor of any period.

Research Begins to Back Experience

Beginning in the 1970s and later, with data and computing power more available, researchers started to test investing strategies and analyze the data.

The results then and today overwhelmingly support small cap value's long-term outperformance. At the top of the list of resulting analyses is investment firm Tweedy Browne's remarkable study. They collected all the research available on stock performance worldwide, over a span of 54 years, to determine if there were any common attributes of success. Tweedy Browne chose not simply to continue its work privately for more and more profit, but to share for free what must have taken an extraordinary commitment of time and money.

This took place against great odds. The investment world at large accepted efficient market theory (EMT: you can't beat the market, so just use a market index; Eugene Fama, who has partially recanted in recent decades) and modern portfolio theory (MPT: asset allocation, diversify your portfolio among defined asset classes and then mechanically rebalance; Nobels to Markowitz, Sharpe and Miller).[4] These figures' power controlled the academy not just through their own work but that of Ph.D. candidates seeking careers, for decades.

Yet with increasing support, value investors started to get some respect with rigorous examination of the *same* data. With records of his own and eight other investment managers including Tweedy Browne, Buffett in 1984 gave the breakthrough speech "The Superinvestors of Graham-and-Doddsville" at his alma mater Columbia Business School. He convincingly refutes the efficient pricing cabal, referring to them as the equivalent of the "Flat Earth Society." Yet only in recent years—impossible to imagine today—has he become a household name and his investment strategy more than a curiosity practiced by a small club.

Meanwhile, though he and only a few real-world practitioners had understood securities mispricing for decades, growing computing power and curiosity not limited by dominant views and conventional wisdom, created new and strong competition for the people who had built careers on and received Nobel Prizes for EMT and MPT.

Perhaps the most effective and seminal knights scaling the EMT and MPT barricades have been economist Richard Thaler and sociologists

Daniel Kahneman (an eventual Nobelist, not cursed) and Amos Tversky (who would surely have shared Kahneman's prize were he still alive). They saw their disciplines converge and caused an investment earthquake by founding the field of modern behavioral finance.

The Tweedy Browne study presents their work along with path-breaking papers by Josef Lakonishok and many others. The data support the idea that yes, Virginia, there is inefficient stock pricing, and you can take advantage of it. Tweedy Browne's data found the five attributes enumerated at the beginning of this chapter. They are not merely academic conclusions; they *do* work in the real world.

This brief discussion covers a crucial investing debate from the 1930s to today, now covered in its entirety like never before in Justin Fox's riveting *The Myth of the Rational Markets*.[5] The Tweedy Browne study and Fox's book are the two indispensable texts for the nonacademic investor to learn not only what works, but why and how value was freed from the closet. Fox's masterwork shows the Davids against all odds creating the work to overcome the Goliaths. Then the Tweedy Browne work focuses on the investing alone. With the virtues of rationality and a remarkable lack of apparent bias, it collects and analyzes studies including data for as long as 54 years; short and long periods of the best months and worst months alone; and many variations, all corrected for survivorship and other statistical distortions, across all sorts of strategies.

By now, after taking a breath, no reader doubts that I answer this section's question "Are stocks ever mispriced?" as I do the title of Thurber and White's book, *Is Sex Necessary?*

Yes!

But just as we know that sex is necessary, we also know that its success requires practice. So too does finding small cap values require a disciplined, repeatable process anyone can crack.

The Five Attributes Common to Investing That Work

Gathering and analyzing the 50 studies in its work, Tweedy Browne found these five common attributes of successful investing:

1. Low price-to-asset value (book value)
2. Low price-to-earnings (cash flow, high dividend yield with low payout ratio)

3. Pattern of insider buying (company share repurchases included)
4. A stock price that has declined (because of reversion to the mean)
5. Small market capitalization.

These attributes rarely appear alone, with selected stocks often exhibiting two or even all of them. And because my own experience and subsequent research make my own process unique, you'll see that I adapt each of the Tweedy Browne elements and add some of my own.

Low Price-to-Asset Value (Tangible Book Value)

This attribute selects stocks selling at a discount from book value, defined by Tweedy Browne as "what the company itself paid for its own assets," and stocks selling at discounts from what a common stockholder could receive if the business were liquidated.

These stocks are tougher to find today, because there's more competition. Plenty data are available, and all the information has made spotting and exploiting our favored types of inefficiencies much more difficult. The Internet is probably the worst enemy of investors: Information inefficiencies are far less common, and mispricing is harder to find. I say "worst enemy" because the information creates the illusion that deeper work isn't required and that obstacles don't remain, which isn't true. Once I see an idea that seems interesting, I'm unconcerned about the source and do my own work from the bottom up.

One thing hasn't changed. Stocks satisfying this criterion usually exhibit very low market capitalizations—from small to micro caps with market capitalizations under $1 billion, $250 million, or even lower. The smaller the market cap, almost always the fewer shares traded—less liquidity. This means that the more money there is to invest, the harder it is to buy these mispriced and outperforming stocks because it is difficult and sometimes impossible to accumulate enough of them relative to your total investable assets to make a difference to your returns, to "move the needle" for those whose cars lack digital mph guides today.

No wonder, then, that Buffett has pointed out that it's a huge advantage *not* to have a lot of money—he used $1 million—because you can take advantage of the universe of smaller and more illiquid stocks that offer greater mispricing. As his Berkshire Hathaway grew from a micro-cap stock to one of the highest market capitalizations today, churning out billions to invest each month, Buffett himself has warned that his company will achieve lower annualized returns. Yale's legendary endowment manager David Swenson—with his own successful long-term record— agrees that size is the enemy of performance.[6] The irony is that small cap value investing success raises the bar to continue those returns—the better you do, the more money you make, the less able you are to apply the strategy that made you money in the first place. Of course, for most of us "the more you make" is likely to be quite enough before "too much."

Yet fear not whether you are investing a little money or a lot. The principle remains: If you pay as deep a discount as possible to the value of a company's tangible assets, you will have a margin of safety, you stand to lose less if you are wrong. Mispricing may be better with small caps, but catalysts can work wonders with larger market capitalization stocks. As your assets grow, you can still gain from catalysts such as mergers, spinoffs, or emerging from bankruptcy, seeing an ugly turnaround's potential success while others don't. These can be large and small capitalization stocks. Catalysts can be just as hard for an investor to see in all sizes of stocks, not just small ones.

Margin of Safety

The phrase "margin of safety" is thrown around in the value world with abandon (even by me!). It means that at some point the assets are so cheap that just as you are about to buy them, another buyer will arrive to pay more to purchase the business and that because of how cheap it is, the assets would have to be sold for practically zilch for you to lose money. At some price, *someone* will pay more to take the shares off your hands, whether that someone is an activist investor (more on this later), private equity firm, or simply an enlightened hard-working investor alone in the home office, as Buffett was in the late 1950s and early 1960s. This is part of what's behind the value investor's guide that *almost any* stock is a buy at the right price, but *no* stock is a buy at any price.

But of course there is no guarantee. "Someone" might not buy your cleap stock. That's why it's a "margin" of safety but not absolute safety. What a company paid for its assets has nothing to do with their price today or their price in a liquidation fire sale. This is why, for example, Graham calculated liquidation value using a percentage of accounts receivable and inventory, not 100 percent of their value. Not only that, but although buying at a discount to the assets' apparent value *should* work, the reality is that asset value is something of a moving target. If a company comes on hard times, or the economy gets the rug pulled out from under it, buyers are often unwilling to pay anything more than a fraction of the asset value, and rightfully so. They, like the value investor, want to be compensated for taking risk. Here the investor's patience is tested: the company selected must have the balance sheet to survive and the investor must wait for the reversion to the mean, catalysts, and more.

Calculating Reward to Risk Odds

I prefer companies whose book value is tangible—touchable—based on "hard" assets, whether cash, commercial real estate, agricultural land and products, precious metals (and sometimes base ones), oil and gas in the ground, or the like. These are easier to value and less likely to lose all value, though that value may still change in a flash at any given time.

What I do is determine a range of probabilities against an unknowable future to determine more easily what I must pay to buy these assets cheaply—to determine more easily my downside or margin of safety. This is what value investors, in our delightful jargon (who is immune?), call optionality. That is, paying so little for the asset that you have in effect bought a free or low-cost call option on those assets at some point being priced higher—reverting from the abnormally low mispricing to the mean. This is expressed as a ratio of potential reward for the risk, the reverse of the odds at a race track. Where 12:1 odds on a nag in the fourth race is an unlikely win and bad odds at the track, 12:1 for us means 12 times upside for the estimated downside. If we see 10 percent downside—a margin of safety—we estimate a 120 percent potential upside. This is terrific optionality, but good luck finding such a situation. I look for at least 3:1, enough so that good results more than compensate over time for the inevitable poor results.

It is impossible to calculate the odds with precision because, make no mistake, hard assets are not guaranteed. (Nothing in investing is, and those who flog it are selling. For example, cash is a hard asset, but can be horrible to hold in inflationary times and terrific in deflationary ones.) If a company's business starts to decline, any cash can disappear quickly.

Commercial real estate had better be in locations that present barriers to other developers building spiffier competition next door, or watch the rental advantages evaporate. Even the best-located shopping centers with little or no competition today can fail, because neighborhood demographics change all the time.

It's also important to understand that real estate values, like corporate earnings, ebb and flow. To calculate a range of values of an asset, it is necessary to stress-test them—in a range of possible economic and market conditions that will enable you to make an informed decision about whether a stock's market price to tangible book is low or high and about whether to buy, sell, or avoid a stock accordingly. A major stress test would be whether the real estate investment could withstand the complete unavailability of credit, as in 2008 and for some continuing today. The right company plans for this uncertainty, because it will happen.

Consider another hard asset. Agricultural land must be well located and produce what's in demand at a price providing profits to producers and market prices to consumers. But pests can and will devastate certain agricultural output and may become immune to the latest generations of pesticides. Even farmers with decades of experience must hedge like crazy against uncertainties of weather and market supply. Good weather means that everyone is selling wheat into a buyer's market, bad weather that there is nothing to sell when prices zoom.

But the land itself is very good inflation protection, and it offers long-term benefits. The entry of billions of people worldwide from formerly restricted economies, such as China's and India's, has meant higher earnings, greater food demand, more competition between agricultural and housing developers, and diminishing water resources. All this tends toward scarcer and higher-priced food and increased land prices. Here again, it pays to make a best estimate of the "normal" condition and determine what it's worth under those circumstances. While rising populations, higher incomes, and demand for food will lead to higher demand for agricultural assets—it can also mean that an investor might overpay. It's also good to remember that oil, natural gas, and food prices have all run skyward at various times when some were proclaiming we would run out of them, and then have plummeted when recessions reduce demand. Be wary of the phrase, "This time it's different." Even the premier Canadian resource companies in top-performing investor Eric Sprott's universe diversify. Sprott Resources, which I own today, has invested heavily in agricultural land and production but also in coal, oil, natural gas, gold, uranium, and more.

To value precious metals like gold, silver, and platinum depends on the particular company situation. The discount to reserves—difficult enough to estimate with any confidence—must be good enough against a range of pricing, because the metals so often react to inflation and deflation. Silver in the last several years and gold for much longer have risen dramatically, but they could easily fall. Yet at some price, a company with precious metal assets priced so cheaply will find a buyer, and mergers can be catalysts leading to synergies and higher profits.

Gold is nevertheless always tough. Silver and platinum, along with base metals such as aluminum, copper, zinc, nickel, lead, and tin, have industrial uses and therefore some intrinsic value. Gold really has been worth only what people say it is, reflecting fears over world stability, inflation, and deflation, for example. Emotion rules gold more than supply and demand. That's why I will only invest (and even then only rarely) in gold companies with specific catalysts and underpricing. And that "underpricing" must meet the test of where the company would stand if it were selling its gold at prices higher, lower, and the same as today's.

Despite these caveats, it's still easier to value hard assets with greater—though not overweening—confidence than it would be to value inventory of plastic rubber shoes, athletic shoes, teen clothing, grocery store goods, digital and analog semiconductors, or, today, scads of social networking initial public offerings (IPOs). It's tough to estimate the long-term value of any consumer technology goods, no matter how popular they are today, because technology changes rapidly and prices routinely deflate. And how can you value clothing and household furnishings dependent on the cost of inputs such as cotton or wood products with wildly varying prices, products that face ruinous competition, are prey to fads, and whose customers are fickle at best?

The footwear company Skechers and its inventory of its new Shape Up shoes, detailed in Chapter 4, exploded and had to be sold at any price or written off. Music-based retailer Hot Topic's Goth focus and other products based on teen preferences died when tastes changed and the preppie look returned. Both companies missed their markets, killed investors, and only today are coming out of their business slumps. Investors such as my Motley Fool colleague Ron Gross saw the inventory turnaround and bought Skechers at a very favorable valuation, bringing profits. But those who bought it or any such company at too high a price relative to assets did not and are unlikely to see a profit soon or ever and at enormous opportunity cost.

I prefer hard assets *in use rather than in storage.* Water rights, vacant land held for residential real estate development, or forests may well increase in value (for example, timber left alone gains rings and value every year), but they usually lack definable catalysts for realizing that value. Someone *may* buy the rights, developers *may* monetize land if they can afford to keep it during collapsing demand value in a financial crisis, and forests *may* grow but risk inadequate regeneration and environmental restrictions. The assets may be good hedges and provide risk management on the long side. But I prefer our short book—not assets that are essentially in storage—to hedge our long-short portfolio. Then, unlike hard asset "in storage," my long investments must have positive, definable catalysts to close the gap between the underpriced assets and the higher price that the market is more likely to pay for them eventually.

Bottom line: Can you value the asset today? And can you buy it cheaply enough so that when that asset changes price down the road—as it will—what you paid can live with the ups and downs? Or just as a bank, can you stress-test it under different pricing scenarios? My practice in this section is an antibiotic, effective in most cases but not able to cure everything.

Low Price in Relation to Earnings (Cash Flow, High Dividend Yields with Low Payout Ratios)

Industries and companies go in and out of investing favor all the time. "Opportunistic value" is simply a way of saying that I jump to buy a business I know well when it goes on sale—when it offers a low price to asset value and also a low price to earnings. Why many, many people who buy goods on sale (like my late mother, who bought exclusively at sales and discount stores such as TJ Maxx, yet looked more like a million bucks the older she became) overpay for stocks is a mystery I'll never solve.

I prefer two metrics over price to earnings (P/E): market capitalization to free cash flow and enterprise value to EBITDA. My experience and the research show that if you buy a steady-state business—a decent business with reasonably recurring cash flows and stable margins—at a multiple of 10 or fewer times market cap to free cash flow (covered in Chapter 5), it's pretty tough to lose money. You buy your optionality—future growth, reversion to the mean, whatever—for low or no cost. This is not far from Graham's calculation in *The Intelligent Investor* to do the same thing with a P/E of 8.5. Graham was demanding an earnings yield of 12 percent (100/8.5) or better, whereas I'm looking for a free cash flow yield of 10 percent (100/10) or better.

Most investors know that market cap is the stock price times shares outstanding. But fewer know enterprise value, which takes into account the company's cash, debt, and debtlike obligations.

$$Enterprise\ value = market\ capitalization + total\ debt - cash\ and\ equivalents$$

"Total debt" must include long- and short-term debt, preferred stock, pension obligations, and any other relatively certain obligations, because a buyer of the business will discount those obligations. Buyers recognize that total debt reduces the value of the enterprise and then may become more aware of what price to offer and pay.

Let's say you are in the market for a lemonade stand (if you are in Frostbite Falls, Minnesota, buy only in winter, for sure). You have narrowed your search to two options in equally attractive locations with equally attractive sales. Although this is akin to the economist's example where you assume a hammer, stay with me.

Sally's stand is fully paid for, and she puts her profits in the bank, but Johnny's mother loaned him $100 for construction, signage, and inventory. His loan remains unpaid. This reduces the price of the lemonade stand enterprise. A buyer would pay for less Johnny's stand, but more for Sally's. And a rational buyer would certainly pony up less if Johnny's putting away cash from the business for a pension for his grandmother, who runs the stand on weekdays when Johnny is at school. That's an increased obligation—a future liability—that will cost any owner more and reduces the value of the enterprise.

Chapter 5 explains the uses of EV/EBITDA, but the point here is the same as market cap/free cash flow, in that you as an investor—a buyer of a business—want to pay a low multiple. The difference is that business buyers today, chiefly private equity firms, will value a business according to what they might earn if they were to buy a public company, take the business private, add debt with its deductible interest, use the cash flows to pay the interest and principal on the debt, and eventually take the company public, again, when investors are paying too much for IPOs. A finance rule of thumb is that, *depending on the debt structure*, a level of cash flow will only cover a limited amount of debt payments.

A business valued in the market at 5 to 6 or fewer times EV to EBITDA increases the possibility that a buyer will snap up the company for more—say 9 to 10 times. Of course every seller wants to get more and every buyer to pay less, but this is the principle for the range of buying and selling businesses with relatively steady and not sexy growth cash flows. (You should know by now that sexy, speculative, and otherwise uncertain growth stocks are not in our long book. So-called "growth stocks" almost invariably end in pain because they attract buyers who pay too high a market cap/free cash flow or EV/EBITDA multiple. It works until it doesn't or it comes with unacceptable opportunity costs.)

Here's an example you rarely see, where the EV/EBITDA rough guide worked almost to the number, according to this valuation thinking. Canadian-based deathcare—funeral, cemetery, and insurance—company Loewen Group joined its industry frenzy to consolidate by buying independent "Mom and Pop" deathcare entities at prices that could only bring adequate return on investment in a fantasy world. Loewen's acquisition debt crushed it and put it in bankruptcy. Eventually, in January 2002, the reorganized Loewen was renamed as Alderwoods and emerged from bankruptcy as a public company again.

Alderwoods resumed trading at $14.50. Investors avoided its bankruptcy taint, selling the stock off in 14 months down to $3.10. The new management, with a long list of prior successful turnarounds, explained the problem to me by saying that "no one could find the checkbook." Loewen had been so complex and disorderly that there were no controls on the cash flow. Expert turnaround managers John Lacey and Paul Houston found the checkbook and spent the cash in the business only where it offered sufficient return.

The stock began to rise as investors found the valuation amazingly cheap where management improved cash flows and managed the debt. I recommended buying at two different times between $8 and $9 for very good returns. Here's how it worked.

Alderwoods' business, when properly run, offered consistent free cash flow, in large part because once management found the checkbook, it was relatively easy to track industry trends and actuarial tables. Along with dependable free cash flow, EV/EBITDA rarely varied from an average multiple per quarter of 6 to 8 from the quarter ending June 2002 to December 2005. Then the stock moved up. When the EV/EBITDA multiple hit 9 and then 10, there was no longer the upside to justify a holding with limited growth potential, heavy through declining debt, and static cash flows.

In a marvel of poor timing, I advised a sale on a Friday. The following Monday, the company announced a sale to industry leader Service Corp. at 11 times EV/EBITDA. This missed 10 percent of the potential gain, but as Bernard Baruch is reputed to have said, "I never buy within 20 percent of the bottom or sell within 20 percent of the top, but I can make a lot of money in between." Note that you only get this kind of accuracy with very predictable businesses and cash flow, but it's still a good guideline. Because for many investors this was the first success resulting from the dead of the 2000–2002 crash, they were very pleased with this contribution to portfolio exhumation. Like Orson Welles in *Citizen Kane*, intoning "Rosebud" on his deathbed, I'll likely choose—after the name of the love of my life, of course—"Alderwoods."

But in this case and as with every company, it must pass this book's earnings quality tests. Alderwoods and another company I recommended at the time, Oxford Health Plans, sported earnings quality about as good as it gets. Revenues and inventories showed no signs of aggressive accounting, cash flows were solid, EPS and free cash flow tracked each other, and any acquisitions were textbook examples of the few successes.

And still positive results were never guaranteed. A company selling for 5 times EV/EBITDA can go to 2, from 10 times market cap/free cash flow to 5, particularly if it's a bad or declining business or its earnings are rounding a cyclical peak. Ask those investors in newspaper stocks selling at single-digit multiples to cash flow, who were confident of the printing press hard assets, or ask home builders in 2007, who were sure of the need for homes, ignorant of the buyer's ability to repay loans, and confident in the land value's ability to survive tough times. The music can stop playing, sometimes abruptly, and then, every investor is fighting for the same escape hatch. Cash flows must be tested against a range of scenarios. "Growth" companies—especially newer ones with more revenue growth than actual cash flows—offer the least possibilities for accurate testing and evaluation of risk.

But if the business is steady-state or better, the stocks generally won't stay at fire sale prices forever. There will be reversion to the mean—the stock price will come back to "fair value," to some average, whatever you want to call "nonextreme"—whether through market recognition, a buyer, or an activist investor stepping in. Buy low, sell high.

Pattern of Insider Buying (and Company Share Repurchases)

This is where I most depart from the strict belief that company insiders are in the best position to evaluate company health, that their investment decisions are the best predictors of company success or decline, and that we should buy or sell when they do. All this can be true, but there is no inherent reason that an executive is a good investor. Except in extreme cases where management is buying hand over fist or selling like crazy— and sometimes even then—they may make poor investing decisions.

I apply a different method to the same end: seeing if successful outside investors have bought the stock heavily and then piggybacking on them. Outsiders often bring a rational perspective and disciplined investment process because they have one goal: make money on the stock. Executives are subject to all sorts of incentive compensation schemes that increasingly make me find their purchases and sales less valuable information.

About that compensation. The research data on Tweedy Browne's five investment attributes might well be different today, given the increasing tendency for companies to use stock options as incentive compensation. Then they use company cash, in effect stealing investor money, to repurchase stock to cover up the share count increase from the options. The majority of companies repurchase stock, not because they see it as an opportunistic value (Chapter 5), but rather to increase the value of their options or shares they are selling or plan to sell.[7] Research in the last decade increasingly supports the view that repurchases benefit management, not shareholders.

Yet if you can find the tiny group of executives who apply value thinking to repurchasing company stock, buy when they are buying. The idea is simply to apply the thinking in this chapter: Buy back company stock when it is selling at such a large discount to intrinsic value that it is as good as or better than any other investment to be made with that cash. This is investing gold, and it's all public information. You can look in SEC filings, see the prices they've paid, and loosely speaking, make a determination as to whether share repurchases have generated value for shareholders using the same valuation techniques in this chapter to determine whether *you* would invest.[8]

In the end, nothing has changed Warren Buffett's simple buyback rule: "When companies with outstanding businesses and comfortable financial positions find their shares selling far below intrinsic value in the marketplace, no alternative can benefit shareholders as surely as repurchases."[9] My difference is that I don't need the business to be outstanding, but only to satisfy other investment criteria and for the shares to be selling far below intrinsic value.

After looking for the rare case of repurchases at true discounts to value, I take the point that those in the know are buying for good reasons but that executives can't be assumed to be more "in the know" than outsiders with successful investment records. To find those special investors, I regularly follow a handful of important activist firms and the Schedule 13D filings they must file to indicate activist intent. "Successful records" and "important" mean that an investment firm has more often than not improved shareholder returns at companies before. Such activist firms may pursue their goal of increased shareholder value via casual chats with management to outright battles for board seats. When I see the investors buying, it's a clear sign to me to piggyback and profit, provided that the price has not risen above my estimates of value. That can happen if others follow the same activists and buy quickly when they see the moves I do.

An insider may know things are looking good ahead, and the company might actually buy back shares according to Buffett's dictum—as would a value investor at a discount to asset value or earnings and cash flow—but activists with successful histories do not put their own money or their investors' money into a situation planning to lose money. They push for change gently, aggressively, and, sometimes, with no other choice, with war. Often the goal is simply to improve earnings quality in ways we obviously believe are important to making money. *They work for us with power we cannot have.*

Activists today with track records I respect include investment firms ValueAct (I hold its investment EnergySolutions); Starboard Value (I've bought Regis Corp., a recent Starboard endeavor); Pershing Square (Bill Ackman, currently active at J.C. Penney, Canadian Pacific, and bringing Burger King public again); JANA Partners (currently active at McGraw-Hill and did a lot of good at Charles River Laboratories); and public company Biglari Holdings (which I've owned since the CEO's activism at Steak 'n Shake, which Biglari Holdings now owns). The more aggressive and public Carl Icahn is one to watch closely as well, because Icahn and two other top investment firms currently are benefitting shareholders at

Chesapeake Energy (which, yes, I also own). Please note that "I hold" is not to brag—some of these won't work out and others haven't already—but I've always made it a practice to own whatever I recommend that others buy. ("Eat your own cooking" is my rule. Think of the King's food taster.)

I also back "jockeys," CEOs with successful track records who start or head a new company for whose business their prior success is relevant. But the key is still not to buy at just any price. Today I own a number of jockey-led companies. Newer company Heckmann Corp.'s CEO Richard Heckmann built and sold U.S. Filter for great shareholder profit. Bank expert Gerald Ford has a lifetime of waiting for just the right banks in distress and paying low prices. I've tagged along with him on his recent 16-month investment in California bank Pacific Capital Bancorp. That announced sale yielded shareholders, such as me and those who followed the recommendation, 60 percent from prior close to announced sale price. And I'm with him in his investment firm Hilltop Holdings, growing value through strategic purchases of financials.

There is also shopping center REIT Retail Opportunity Investments Corp. with CEO Stuart Tanz, who built and sold a similar entity in the 1990s that delivered over 700 percent returns to his investors. In mining and natural resources, I own Sprott Resource, one of jockey Eric Sprott's family of companies and run by one of his proven hard asset investors, and Joe Conway of IAMGOLD success at Primero Mining. There have been and will be others. Wouldn't you buy a new venture apart from Berkshire Hathaway headed by Buffett and Munger? But no matter the jockey, don't buy at just any price. The less you pay, the more optionality you get at a low or no cost. No jockey, just as no company, is a buy at any price.

Activists and jockeys are the equivalent of what insider buying and share repurchases are in the best of cases: signs that greater shareholder returns may lie ahead. Why not be what the economists call a free rider? We let the activists and jockeys ride for us, while we sit in the stands with winning tickets and mint juleps.

A Stock Price That Has Declined (Reversion to the Mean)

This requires only a short discussion. The reason we get the chance to invest in companies satisfying the prior three attributes is almost always that their prices have fallen, leading to low ratios of price to assets, price to free cash flow, or enterprise value to EBITDA, and the presence of an activist or jockey. Value investors like me say we "buy opportunistically," but this is just another way of saying that we buy when we see these opportunities to buy cheaply—contrary to the market's view—and on the side of activists and jockeys. What else would rationality counsel?

Tweedy Browne's studies show that stocks with prior declines outperform because they revert to the mean, that stocks hammered in recent periods outperform in later ones. DeBondt and Thaler's study is also very compelling. It basically shows that buying underpriced losers outperforms buying consummate winners.[10]

Sometimes the market decides that a company or companies ought to be underpriced because they are losers *right now*. No opportunity is greater than a major event that leads to sell-off in a whole industry. Investors deep-sixed stocks of all the drilling rig companies after the Gulf of Mexico spill, even if some of them had few or no drilling operations there and faced no liability for the spill. I recommended Ensco, which had few drilling rigs and therefore low exposure to the market's emotional desertion. I don't claim genius—many did well choosing Ensco and even the rig's owner Transocean and lessor BP, for the same contrarian reasons. While these are swift and massive emotional market sell-offs, more often the catalysts for sell-offs are not so clearly emotional or immediate. Rather, they can take place quietly over years until the stocks are suddenly cheap—somewhat like the writer who works for years and is rejected many times, only to publish and be hailed as an overnight sensation.

Emotion is at once the enemy and friend of the investor. It can compel you to make very poor decisions, but if you're calibrated differently—if you have the temperament to be patient during an uncertain time horizon and the gumption to do and believe in your own work—it can provide great opportunity. If we can manage emotions while those around us are succumbing to theirs, we can not only find that a stock has declined contrary to our view of its intrinsic value, margin of safety, and optionality, but we can buy it confidently.

Small Market Capitalization

Without a doubt, along with a low price to assets ratio, small caps are a huge standout in the research leading to Tweedy Browne's collected attributes. The research—as with all that Tweedy Browne presents—is adjusted for all the statistical problems, such as survivorship bias and so on across the board, and points to outperformance of small caps selected by value criteria.

All sorts of reasons may underpin this. Small caps often come with less liquidity—fewer shares in dollar volume available to buy or sell each day—which can make it hard to accumulate a meaningful position. But smaller liquidity also means less news coverage. The financial media need your attention to sell advertising and consequently choose well-known companies—and therefore those far less likely to be efficiently priced. Smaller businesses, if they succeed, provide investment gains out of proportion to large caps—they simply start off a smaller base. And so on.

I own and have recommended in recent years only a handful of companies with greater than $1 billion market caps, and the majority under $500 million, with many under $250 million or even $100 million, the realm of so-called micro or even pico caps. In a nod to my friends in science, I have coined "Angstrom caps" for the really small ones—under $50, $25, or even to the single-digit millions. Studies by O'Shaughnessy and others find that the lower you go to the Angstrom world, the higher your returns. But the smaller stocks' liquidity limits their availability to investors.

A Sixth Attribute: Special Situations/Catalysts

Many value investors, including me, add to the five attributes one more: event-driven situations that are, as much as is possible, separated from the economy.

Let's say a company spins off one of its business units as a separate company. Beforehand, the value of the business to be spun off might be opaque, because the parent doesn't break out its numbers. Or the stock may trade lower than the sum of its parts—a conglomerate discount—because each part is not publicly traded, the true company value isn't realized in the marketplace. That can give you an opportunity to buy before the spinoff and gain two parts worth more than the whole. Or investors might prefer the original company they own, selling off the spun-off company, giving you a chance to buy the spinoff cheaply. But the event itself may bring investor gains, regardless of the broader market or economy.

Another fertile field includes companies out of bankruptcy or those recapitalized, which are shunned as damaged goods. Investors often can't see through the complications to find that reduced debt, slimmed-down cost structures, and fresh-start accounting make these companies stronger and very good investments indeed. Emerging from bankruptcy can be an identifiable and strong catalyst for increased value. At Alderwoods, the price plummeted after emergence, offering investors great opportunistic value.

Though few acquisitions add shareholder value, the rare one may if we know that the acquirer has a value orientation and makes only good deals. Plus, because acquisition accounting can obscure earnings profiles, another catalyst for good returns to those who can find the deal value and purchase at low price to assets, free cash flow, or EBITDA. But you have to know the numbers and the players to determine if the acquisition is among the minority—estimated by some as between 15 percent and 20 percent—that will truly add value. The odds are against you, and, as we have shown earlier, serial acquisitions are the brightest sign to stay away, almost always obscuring poor earnings quality.

These few special situations only prove the point already made, that each of these attributes rarely appears alone in a stock worthy of value buying. The more you see, the better.

The Big Kahuna: Why Long-Short?

No serious, furrowed-brow value investor likes to admit it, but investing is gambling. Not as in all the games where the odds favor the house—craps, roulette, blackjack, and the worst—slot machines!—where, if you play long enough, the house takes your money. Rather, this gambling is as in poker, where the professionals and best amateurs know that if you take the best odds and limit your losses, you will be a winner.

Again, these tactics require patience, a time horizon, nerves of steel, and gumption. They are all about being willing to take favorable odds—that buying cheaply generally leads to profits, declining valuations today generally lead to higher ones later, activists and proven managers generally keep succeeding, and small caps outperform larger ones. In short, you need to invest where your downside is smaller than your potential upside. This is why I never lose sight of minimum odds. I look for situations where I can estimate that the worst-case downside, say 20 percent from the current price, comes with three times or more potential upside—in this case 60 percent, for odds of three to one (3:1). This is "gambling" with information and odds on your side—you *can* beat the house. Take these odds over and over, and you cannot fail to grow wealth.

That's the long side, but it's not enough. You never know when you'll be faced with declines, how disastrous they might be, or what outcomes you'll face. Here's a personal example to drive home why a long-short portfolio can help with these uncertainties.

In 1929, my maternal grandmother was a widow in her 40s with a 13-year-old daughter, my mother (yes, my parents had me really late and really accidentally!). Her husband had died of pneumonia six years before and left my grandmother with the family drug store. Unable to manage it herself, she sold out to her husband's partner and invested the proceeds mostly in bonds, the investment vehicle then far more prevalent with individual investors than stocks.

That July, she cabled—from way uptown down to Wall Street—her broker wanting to cash out and asking his opinion. Here is his reply:

SCHUYLER, EARL & COMPANY
Members of the New York Stock Exchange
Six Wall Street
New York

July 25, 1929

Dear Mrs. Candow,

Answering your question [whether to sell], it would be well to wait for a break in the market if one comes, but I must confess I cannot see where a general break is coming from and believe the stock market should not be considered as a whole and that investing in stocks to-day is a matter of selection of companies and not a study of market conditions.

Sincerely yours, Ralph Waldo Earl

(Yes, Ralph Waldo Earl, and yes, my mother's maiden name was Candow. No way can you make these things up.) I have this letter and read it every year or so. She didn't sell.

First, ol' Ralph had one solid point. A lot of value investors would agree that investing in the market at large is not a winning proposition, and that success is about choosing the right stocks. Also, while my grandmother, as a widow, had bonds almost exclusively in what were viewed as widows-and-orphans companies, bonds were on their way to getting destroyed too. While in bankruptcies such as those that would follow the crash, bond investors do indeed have greater claims on a company's assets than the common stock owners, there must be *some* underlying business capable of paying *something* on the value of those bonds. Countless companies found themselves in bankruptcy with little to no asset value. And even among those companies that would survive the disaster, many lacked sufficient cash flows to pay the interest on the debt.

Now let's give Ralph even more credit and forget hindsight where he dismisses "market conditions." It's easy to see *now* that market conditions were insane, volatile, historically anomalous, whatever. (Reminds me of the Nasdaq in December 1999.) But let's say that, like Ralph, you have no idea, that you ignore the teachings of the next two chapters, and that you truly are a long-only, long-term investor with sound principles adhering to a Tweedy Browne's-study-based strategy. Is that good enough? *No.*

You can only hold your stocks if you do not need the money. It's wonderful to repeat the ultimately useless anodyne that "you should only invest in stocks the money you can afford to lose." But can *anyone* really ever afford *to lose it all*? And can you really invest in a 401(k), say, or a child's college fund, or any retirement fund that is not tax-advantaged, with the thought that "I could lose it all and be fine"?

Obviously, not. Using this long-side investing strategy *alone*—the one proven more than any other to deliver outperformance over time and not with increased risk—you could still potentially lose it all if you are long only.

Think about it. Let's say you are a good, solid value investor, and you bought cheaply before the 1920s explosion upward, and for some reason you forgot to sell to enthusiastic buyers. Maybe you were imprisoned or on a boat without a telegraph, on an African adventure with Bogart and Hepburn without media access. "Well, that's no problem, just hold! Wait for reversion to the mean! I've got all the time in the world!"

You can only hold if you don't need the money, and you will need it unless you are a Gates, Buffett, or Carlos Slim (I exaggerate to make the point). In times of extreme crisis—not 1973–1974, even, but the late 1800s or the Great Depression—you almost always *will* need the money. You *do* withdraw from your 401(k). You *do* cash in anything else you can get your hands on. Because if you don't, you may well lose your job or your house. Or someone close to you may lose theirs, and you're family, after all. Ironically, the Crash of 1929 would have finished off Benjamin Graham, before he founded value investing, were it not for the help from a relative (the ultimate surrender, eh?). What better example?

It all comes back to the famous dictum attributed to Rothschild to "buy when there's blood in the streets." That's only possible if it's not all *your* blood streaming into the sewer drains. And who of us is a Rothschild? Easy for him.

This is why a sound value small cap long book needs short exposure—a long-short portfolio strategy. Having *any* short exposure mitigated complete capital loss in the many end-of-the-world-or-close-to-it scenarios and will continue to do so in the ones certain to come, though at unknown times.

Let's look at combining John's short and my long individual returns in three of the most volatile years in the last—hmmm, 60 or 70 years: 2007, 2008, and 2009.

Table 6.1 shows our separate returns, and then applies them to a long-short portfolio adjusted for three long-short percentages that John would choose according to his view of risk at the time. Compare the results to the S&P 500 for those years.

Now, Table 6.2 shows the theoretical investment of $100 (Tweedy Browne's study always uses $1 million. Love it.) at the start of 2007 in

Table 6.1 Tom and John at Three Long-Short Percentages versus the S&P 500: Annual 2007–2009*

	John (Short)	Tom (Long)	S&P 500	100% Long/ 30% Short	120% Long/ 80% Short	50% Long/ 50% Short
2007	12.6%	(11.4%)	5.5%	(7.6%)	(3.6%)	0.6%
2008	94.4%	(56.6%)	(37%)	(28.3%)	7.6%	18.9%
2009	(29.0%)	69.3%	26.5%	60.6%	60.0%	20.2%

*Including dividends.

Table 6.2 Tom and John at Three Long-Short Percentages versus the
S&P 500: Cumulative 2007–2009

	S&P 500*	100% Long/ 30% Short	120% Long/ 80% Short	50% Long/ 50% Short
Starting Value	$100.00	$100.00	$100.00	$100.00
Value at End of 2007	$105.50	$92.38	$96.40	$100.60
Value at End of 2008	$65.41	$66.25	$103.73	$119.61
Value at End of 2009	$82.42	$106.41	$165.92	$143.72
Percentage of Total Return	(17.6%)	6.4%	65.9%	43.7%

*Including dividends.

these allocations and compares the cumulative results against the S&P
500 in those same years. Combining our long and short results in typical
hedge fund percentages handily outperformed the S&P 500.

Now Figure 6.1 presents the same data in chart format:

Employing the strategies in this book—quality-of-earnings analysis
for both of us with a short-side profit mindset for John and small cap value

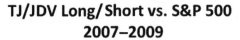

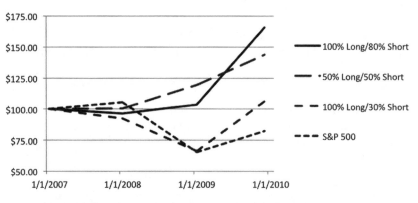

Figure 6.1 Tom and John at three long-short percentages versus the
S&P 500: Cumulative 2007–2009.

for Tom—would have far outperformed the S&P 500 in either manic or panicked years. These are our actual results and the actual long-short percentages from which we would choose in combining them.

Conclusion

No one knows what the market will do today, next year, or in a decade. To be long only works over time, but at any moment the statistical outlier can appear and risk complete loss of capital—and frankly, hand you your head.

It could be Taleb's Black Swan[11]—the thing that we haven't seen so we don't believe it exists—except that it very much *has* existed and we'll see it again. It's the extreme wrong end of the bell curve, the event that is improbable but still can happen—and happens. Taleb directed many of his readers, including me, to the great mathematician and finance researcher Benoit Mandelbrot's work in support. He examined cotton prices back to 1900 to conclude that *extreme events and volatility occur far, far more commonly than statistical tendencies would indicate.*[12] The bell curve is fine unless you get the wrong end of the curve, in which case you are wiped out. It's false comfort.

Long-short portfolio construction and management according to this book avoids losing everything when the once-in-a-lifetime event happens—and history shows that, except for the "great moderation" years before the 2008 crisis, most investors will see *more than one* in their lifetimes. And that's assuming that the chain of events begun in 2008 is over, which it may very well not be. Today we're obviously in a world of great market uncertainty, with Europe at the center of crisis and other countries at the periphery but in danger. Reinhart and Rogoff's work[13] tells us that a credit crisis of recent intensity can take five to eight years to work off *on average.* In 2012, we're only in the fourth year of eight, and that's if what's happened is "merely" *average.*

The market is a history of excesses, of cycles of manias, panics, and crashes. They were routine in the 1800s—at least one a decade. In the mid-1800s, whole blocks from the East River to the Hudson contained squatters heating and cooking with fires and keeping animals. In the 1907 panic, J. P. Morgan was the version of 2008's Hank Paulson, gathering the biggest bankers—those with the power to stop the catastrophe—in a room until they worked out a deal.[14] The 1973–1975 recession was the deepest since the Depression. The S&P 500 rose 4 percent from

November 1968 to July 1982—almost 14 years—but in real (inflation-adjusted) terms, that index lost 64 percent.[15] On and on.

So okay, the steamroller will come when you don't see it, while you are bending over to pick up nickels. With our long-short strategy, you don't have to bend over or be flattened. You don't have to know if it's 1929 going on for many years or a 2008 that persists, or one of the once-a-decade (or longer) value-destroying panics of the 1800s, a routine drop, or a 20 percent bear market. This long-short strategy avoids permanent capital loss when the nuclear bomb drops, but it also avoids devastating portfolio paper losses along the way. Those explosions are psychologically jarring. Long-only investing may still leave you with money, but set you back so much that you need many more years to grow your money where it needs to be. We can reset our investing clock only so often, while our life clocks relentlessly tick.

I'll close with what those poker players know without having any exposure to over a century of commodity data, stock market history, or long-short investment strategies. Professional cash-game poker players use it every time they play a hand. If a given hand in a certain situation is a 99 percent probability to win, they still *never* bet their entire bankroll—the entire cash available to them to pursue their profession. Because they've all seen it, where the hand offering 99 percent probability of winning comes face-to-face to the 1 percent event, and the all-in cash game player is completely wiped out. Don't go all in, and you will survive to play another day. Manage your risk with short exposure.

This book's long-short solution avoids the outlier event far more commonly than we've been taught, and it puts you six feet under. Why not sleep well, alive, and above ground?

Chapter 7

Stock Charts: Know When to Hold 'Em, and Know When to Fold 'Em

The Most Controversial Chapter

This is going to be the most controversial chapter in the book, because technical analysis is one of those things that people use or don't use, are for or against, and, as with the current state of U.S. politics, can or can't understand and work with the other side. Fundamental investors analyze the balance sheet, cash flows, and income statement to find hidden value and mispricing at the rare times when downside risk is limited (this is what Tom does in Chapter 6). Technicians review the price action on a stock chart. This not only improves entry and exit timing, but also risk management, creating greater awareness of how the stocks that compose the portfolio are trading relative to each other and the broader market.

But rarely do investors take classes at both schools. While most investors sign up at *either* the Academy of Fundamental Analysis *or* College for Technical Analysts, I (meaning John here) use the best of both. So far, we have discussed fundamental analysis warning signs that portend doom for shareholders. But the technician's ability to analyze a stock chart is also valuable in determining whether a stock is likely to rise or fall in the future. While both schools misunderstand each other, I'll bet the technician is least understood. However, what I practice managing portfolios and trading stocks daily is the simplest, least jargon-filled technical analysis method. My short-side management employs—requires—both fundamental and technical analysts' tools.

A stock is nothing more than a vehicle to express a bullish or bearish bet—a way to make money. While many people will tell you that they are investors for the long term, they are in the minority, and their volume makes less and less difference to stock prices each day.

For example, Netflix in November 2011 traded approximately 5 million shares per day, with a float of 50 million shares. Thus, the shareholder base was turning over once every 10 days. Netflix at the time was a vehicle for speculators to make bullish or bearish bets, and most of it was done in the short term. In other words, the *stock* of Netflix was nothing more than a commodity, while the *business* was, of course, not that at all.

The idea that you are part-owner of a business when you buy Netflix or any other stock is a fiction sold to investors to encourage them—rightly—to evaluate their holding as a business owner, learn financial statement analysis, and evaluate management. But a long investment in Netflix requires proof that management acts in your interests, either by paying you through dividends and buybacks at opportunistic prices, or if there is an activist investor putting management's feet to the fire, allowing you to benefit as a fellow shareholder. The rest is trust that someone will pay you more for your shares later.

Think like an owner of the business on the long side. Demand tangible benefits. Trust, but verify. But on the short side, think like a technical analyst to time entry and exit for trades. I've found many companies with serious earnings quality issues, but not shorted them, due to timing and technical issues.

Several simple principles can be used to sharpen your ability to see weakness in shares before they collapse. Below, I discuss several of the primary factors I look at repeatedly when managing a portfolio.

Principle 1: Keep It Simple

Ockham's Razor suggests that simpler explanations are, other things being equal, generally better than more complex ones. Consider the conventional wisdom that technicians use sophisticated computer systems, secret formulas, a protractor with grid paper, or the phases of the moon to observe changes in a stock's trend. Some do, but I don't. A simpler approach is better.

Pull up the chart of a stock that you want to analyze. Print it out. Tape it to the wall. Stand six feet away from it and ask yourself "Is the price going up, down, or sideways? For how long?" Let's look at three clear examples.

The chart of Chipotle Mexican Grill shows the stock in an uptrend from October 2010 through September 2011 (see Figure 7.1). Even during an exceptionally volatile period for the stock market and world economy, Chipotle persistently marched higher in price. Burritos resisted downgrades of U.S. debt and concerns over Greek defaults. Patient shareholders who rode the trend were well rewarded.

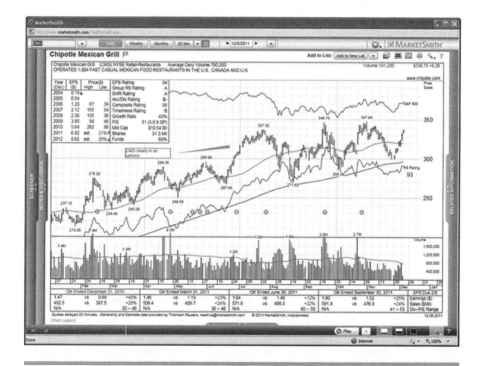

Figure 7.1 Chipotle: Upward trend.
Source: *WONDA® Copyright © 2012 William O'Neil + Co., Inc. All rights reserved.*

Conversely, shares of EBIX were a total disaster during the same timeframe (see Figure 7.2) and were mired in a downtrend for months. Investors seduced by the prospect of higher growth rates have found nothing but frustration in lower prices for EBIX's shares. Only investors in more recent months have seen gains.

Figure 7.3 shows that shares of Coinstar have been range-bound—trading within a range of upper and lower prices—for months. Even though there are dramatic peaks and valleys, the sideways price action is clearly visible from a quick look at the chart.

There's an old adage among traders that "the trend's your friend until it ends." If the chart you printed out shows the stock price climbing, it's likely to continue doing so until some force acts upon it to change that trend. The opposing force that shifts the trend is changed expectations about the company's prospects. This may include a poor earnings report or reduced forward guidance. A negative news article or downgrade from

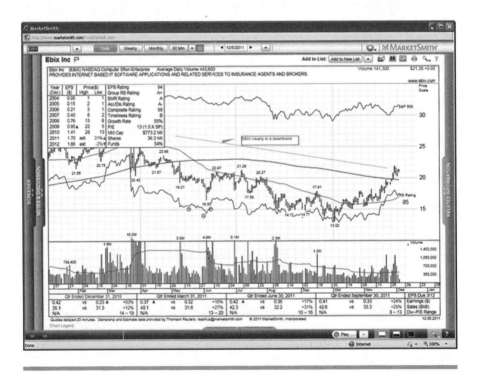

Figure 7.2 EBIX: Downward trend.
Source: *WONDA® Copyright © 2012 William O'Neil + Co., Inc. All rights reserved.*

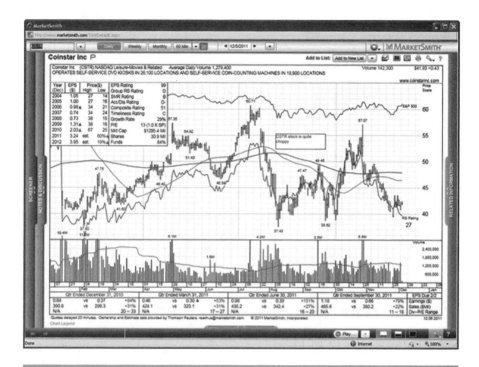

Figure 7.3 Coinstar: Range-bound stock.
Source: *WONDA® Copyright © 2012 William O'Neil + Co., Inc. All rights reserved.*

a Wall Street brokerage firm can also deflate a stock's momentum. But since the event is unknown until it happens, the simplest assumption is that the stock price will continue on its current trajectory until it something causes changed expectations.

When the trend reverses, get out of the way. It seems simple, but behavioral finance wouldn't exist if people were rational. For example, during the Internet bubble, why did investors ride companies all through the uptrend and not sell when the trend turned?

Their mistakes were in not taking advantage of a clear upward trend and not thinking beyond it—believing instead in a paradigm shift, new era, or some other bubble-headed nonsense that seemed to confirm the glossy hype of business-to-business software, fiber optic networks, Internet infrastructure, biotech drugs not even in trials, and new valuation methods. Emotion clouded judgment so that, instead of simply following the trend up and selling at any point for a super profit, investors held when the trend turned south, convinced that everything would turn around because of the good-news stories, which really were just nonstop trains to bankruptcy. No matter your strategy or tools, a stock is a vehicle for a bullish or bearish bet. Investors confused the two.

Investors must separate themselves from the emotion of thinking XYZ is a good *company* and therefore a good *stock*. A good company doesn't necessarily make it a good stock. For years, Microsoft has been a good company. It changed the world by introducing software to make computers more useful, creating millions of jobs, boosting productivity, and enriching the lives of countless people around the globe. Microsoft generates an unbelievable amount of free cash flow, much more than it could ever need or invest. It carries billions in cash on its balance sheet and no debt, with regular dividends, special dividends, and massive buybacks. Yes, Microsoft has been a great company, but its stock has done

Figure 7.4 Microsoft: Good company, not so good stock.
Source: *WONDA® Copyright © 2012 William O'Neil + Co., Inc. All rights reserved.*

zilch in the past 10 years (see Figure 7.4). Good company. Not so good stock.

Therefore, when looking at a stock chart and determining a trend, it is important to focus on price action only and not other factors, such as management team, dividend yield, sector, free cash flow, P/E, or anything else that might obscure the picture. Those items are appropriate for fundamental analysis, but using them here is like taking your grocery list to Home Depot. You go home empty handed. These are not for technical analysis.

Technical analysis gets a bad rap, because it is associated with complex indicators. But indicators are derived from price. So, why not begin with price and analyze price trends, without muddying up the process by throwing mathematically complex indicators on the charts?

Principle 2: The Laws of Supply and Demand Will Not Be Repealed[1]

The same principles of Economics 101 supply-and-demand curves hold true for stocks. When supply is increasing, the share price will be under selling pressure. When demand is robust, the share price heads higher. I live by the tenet that there is always someone who knows more about a stock than I do and that what people say and what they actually do are sometimes two different things. The best way to figure out what the well-informed investors are actually doing, rather than just what they say they're doing, is to analyze supply and demand for shares by simply following the volume traded. You do not need to be a geometry whiz to draw wedges, triangles, squares, wiggles, or any other type of chart-pattern analysis. Volume trends are clear on the stock chart.

To study supply and demand, I use two indicators available on MarketSmith charts produced by William O'Neil + Co., Inc.: up/down volume ratio and accumulation/distribution rating. Up/down volume ratio is pretty straightforward. If a stock price is down for the day, all of the volume traded that day is assigned to down volume. If a stock price is up, then the volume is assigned as up volume. Compare the up and down volume sums over the prior 50 days to create a ratio of up to down. A ratio of 1.0 means as much volume was traded on up days as on down days: the volume patterns in the stock are evenly balanced. Anything greater than 1.0 means there is more buying power than selling pressure, and anything less than

1.0 means heavier selling than buying. Figure 7.5 shows this metric for OpenTable, which at the end of 2011 had a score of 0.6, showing far more selling than buying.

Large institutions buying or selling stock have the ability to move that stock over a period of time. All of the action doesn't happen in one day. Institutions such as Fidelity or Putnam or even the largest hedge funds are simply moving too much capital around to complete their orders in one day. Therefore, the up/down volume ratio provides an easy way to grasp the trend of where the buying power and selling pressure of stocks in the market are occurring.

As a short seller, I like to see the up/down volume ratio trending lower in conjunction with other technical signs discussed in this chapter. Therefore, a ratio below 1.0 is not necessary, although it may be preferred. More important is a ratio declining from 1.5 to 1.2 and ultimately dipping below 1.0. That signals increasingly intense selling pressure from large institutions.

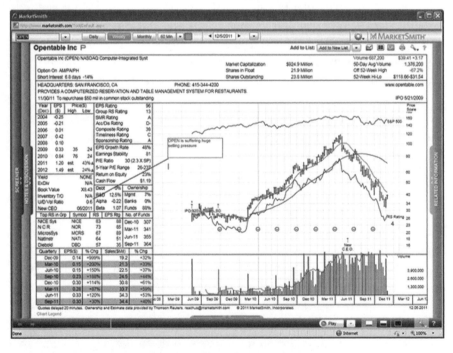

Figure 7.5 OpenTable: Up/down volume ratio of 0.6.
Source: *WONDA® Copyright © 2012 William O'Neil + Co., Inc. All rights reserved.*

The second indicator is the accumulation/distribution rating, also a proprietary metric from William O'Neil + Co., Inc. Generally, I am skeptical of using proprietary indicators, because I can't be certain of the math behind them. However, because the accumulation/distribution rating relates to supply and demand for shares of stock, it's highly probable the inputs reduce the chances for error. It's worth using as one tool, so long as it's not the only one. The rating systems runs from "A+," indicating substantial demand—accumulation (buying) far in excess of distribution (selling)—to "E" for heavy selling of shares—distribution that dwarfs buying. Figure 7.6 shows this for Ciena, which has a rating of C–, showing considerable distribution.

Similar to the trend in up/down volume ratio, I like to see the accumulation/distribution rating weaken in the stocks I'm following. I have no strict criteria, but all else being equal, I am likely to allocate less capital to shorting a stock with a rating of B than one with a D. When both the up/down

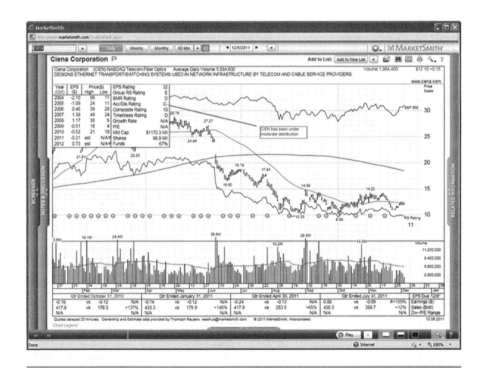

Figure 7.6 Ciena earns a C–, showing considerable distribution (selling). Source: *WONDA® Copyright © 2012 William O'Neil + Co., Inc. All rights reserved.*

volume ratio and accumulation/distribution rating deteriorate, I am more confident that the stock price is likely to come under pressure to drop in the intermediate term, because selling is heavier than buying. While fundamentals may rule in the long term, think of this as shorting with the catalyst of supply and demand.

Principle 3: Be Alert for Divergences

Divergences occur when the stock price and an indicator do not confirm each other. For example, there's divergence when the price makes a new high and an indicator fails to make a new high.

Relative strength is a measure of the stock's price performance over a period of time. William O'Neill + Co. weight it more toward recent prices. The scale is 1 to 99, with 99 indicating a stock that has done better than 99 percent of stocks and 1 indicating a stock that has done worse than 99 percent of stocks.

I look for two primary divergences. First, I analyze the relative strength line—a weighted moving average—in comparison with the price action of the stock. If the stock price is breaking out (rising dramatically in relation to previous flat or range-bound performance) and the relative strength line is lagging, that is a divergence. Although the price is reaching new highs, the performance of the stock relative to the rest of the market is weakening: For some reason, other stocks are performing better. This is a negative divergence for the long buyer and positive for the short seller.

The opposite divergence occurs when the relative strength line is breaking out to new highs, but the price of the stock is lagging. The performance of the stock is accelerating relative to the market even though it's not yet reflected in the price. This is a positive divergence for the long buyer and negative for the short seller.

For example, Figure 7.7 shows that WMS Industries made a new high on the weekly chart May 7, 2010, yet the relative strength line failed to make a new high and surpass the level from October 23, 2009. Then, as WMS rallied again on December 10, 2010, the relative strength line was in a clear downtrend. Each time the stock attempted to push higher, the relative strength line lagged by a greater amount and eventually fell off a cliff. Increasingly, the stock was coming under selling pressure relative to the rest of the market, even though this was not yet reflected in the stock price. That's positive for the short seller and negative for the long investor.

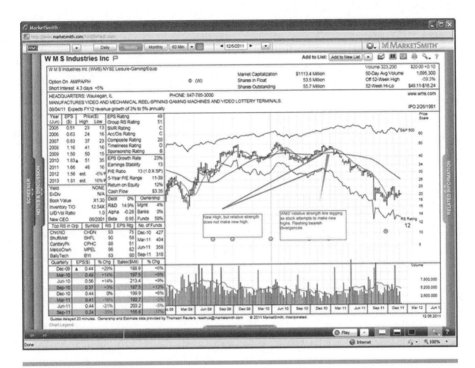

Figure 7.7 WMS Industries: Relative strength line lagged compared to stock's new highs.
Source: *WONDA® Copyright © 2012 William O'Neil + Co., Inc. All rights reserved.*

I also look at the slope of the relative strength line—the "falling off a cliff" at the right side of the chart. If the relative strength line is trending down, but the price of the stock is on an uptrend that is a bearish divergence: the relative strength of the stock is not confirming the move in price. For WMS, by February 2011 as the stock was just starting to break down, dropping significantly compared to its previous action, the relative strength line was already in a clear downtrend with a dramatic slope, a leading indicator of lower prices ahead.[2]

The second divergence relates to the price action of the stock and its volume. If the stock is breaking out to new highs or out of a base (a period of flattish prices), but on weak volume, substantial buying power is probably not supporting the stock. I define weak volume as volume below the 50-day moving average of volume or lower than prior breakouts on the chart. In order to sustain their upward trajectory, stocks need more and more buyers to drive the price higher. Unless and until large institutions decide to support the price of a stock—indicated by up/down volume, accumulation/distribution, and divergence that's positive for the buyer— I'm dubious of an upward trend.

Because the laws of human nature have not been repealed, individual investors are still often late buyers. They latch on to a trend because they hear more and more about the "hot stock" or "can't-fail business." Their volume can boost a price at high levels because no one is selling yet and their smaller volume has an effect. They are the paradigm of the average investor's experience of buying high and selling low. They are the last to know that trouble is just around the corner, because they are buying a story and the price rise is a classic example of confirmation bias—"everyone else is doing it, therefore I must be right." Large institutions are more than happy to unload their shares to individual investors at inflated prices.

An underlying truth has never been better expressed than in O'Neil's analogy of a large institution to an elephant in a bathtub. All these indicators and their divergences matter, because in the intermediate term, large institutions have such significant assets under management that when they buy and sell a stock, it is impossible for them not to influence the price. They are elephants that, no matter how poised while bathing, splash water all over the place. Plus, they too may operate in herds, subject to confirmation bias. The more they buy, the more the stock rises. But when they start selling, look out below. A sure sign is when individual investors pile in, often indicated by rises on low volume. This is bearish for the long investor and bullish for the short seller. After all, the elephant also splashes water all over the place when it gets out of the bathtub.

Let's see all these factors at play in shares of Green Mountain Coffee Roasters. As they pushed higher in 2011, they did so on less and less volume (see Figure 7.8). By the time the stock price leveled out in September 2011, the up/down volume ratio was just 0.80—a ratio of less than 1.0, showing prior 50-day selling volume greater than buying. The accumulation/distribution rating also flashed warning signs with a D score. More selling volume (likely from institutions with large blocks of stock) was occurring on down days than volume when the stock was up (likely from individual investors late to the party). While the relative strength line was 99 and Green Mountain was outperforming all other stocks in the market, chinks in the armor were forming. Volume was not sufficient to sustain a push higher. Unless something changed that altered the fundamentals

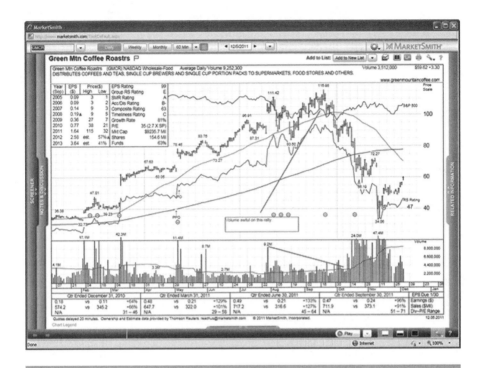

Figure 7.8 Green Mountain Coffee Roasters: All indicators bearish.
Source: *WONDA® Copyright © 2012 William O'Neil + Co., Inc. All rights reserved.*

favorably and brought in new buyers, shares of Green Mountain likely were in trouble. Because of this, I dramatically increased my short position. Figure 7.8 shows that the stock blew up on its earnings announcement and set off a domino effect of company problems and further stock price collapse.

The unknown is always a risk. The long investor insists on a margin of safety, rationally fearing a negative, fundamental change in the business that can reduce the value of the stock. The short seller also must consider that something *favorable* can alter his short thesis. Just as individual buyers may buy once the good news is long gone and before institutional buyers sell, private equity firms or other acquirers have been known to overpay. Using these technical tools reduces upside risk, just as Tom's deep-value investing on the long side reduces downside risk. *Perfect timing is not the goal. Reducing the risk of wrong timing most definitely is.*

Principle 4: The 50-Day Moving Average Is the Maginot Line

It should be clear that it is not necessary to have a plethora of indicators, moving averages, and gadgets on a chart to figure out the trend in a stock. They are nothing more than derivatives of price, which any of us can see if our eyes are open. However, one derivative I do value is the 50-day moving average (50 DMA) of price. Fifty days are long enough to eliminate much of the noise around prices but short enough to capture intermediate trends. By the time a stock breaches (falls below) its 200 DMA, for example, the price may have fallen considerably, leaving insufficient reward for the risks to take a short position.

I call the 50 DMA the Maginot Line of stock prices. Before a big move to the upside or downside, it is the last line of defense against those wishing to suppress prices or push prices higher. Once it is breached, up or down, a stock can move considerably further in that direction.

There is one fact about the 50 DMA and 200 DMA that is worth noting. Any stock that has ever fallen to zero has breached both levels. This may seem obvious to most readers, but it's a sign to sit up and pay attention. When stocks is below both levels, it's most important to concentrate on understanding the fundamentals on the long side or short side. You might think "it's already so far down," then take a gain, but it could be poised really to die. The 50 DMA tells the current trend and potential future of a stock price. With a short candidate, I want to see significant volume when the stock breaks below its 50 DMA, preferably hundreds of percent higher than the 50 DMA of volume. Such a massive volume shows that institutions are shedding shares with reckless abandon.

The 50 DMA is a tool of the short side, but it's no magic bullet. A stock may pierce the average to the downside only to bounce back and resume its upward trend. However, persistent selling around the average over time is an indicator of potential future weakness. Therefore, I analyze volume patterns not only around current price action at the 50 DMA, but also around what occurred in the past—such as the last 12 months. Imagine that stock price is an onion. Every time it breaks below the 50 DMA on high volume, a few layers are peeled away, until nothing is left. There's no buying power to support the stock, and ultimately it plunges sharply lower.

Trading around the 50 DMA may require taking many small losses before ultimately capturing a large profit. It may be the eighth trade before it works as expected. So it is more about what you do with a trade once it's on, once you've found the trade idea in the first place. Juniper Networks in early 2011 (see Figure 7.9) shows the small-loss-before-big-gain process well.

We looked at Juniper Networks in Chapter 2, highlighting how a change in revenue recognition policy pointed toward overstated growth. This is a classic example of a stock that started to break down before the deteriorating fundamentals were well known. The stock broke below the 50 DMA on January 20, 2011 on volume 188 percent greater than the 50 DMA volume. But the stock quickly rebounded toward a 52-week high by early March.

On March 18, the stock broke the 50 DMA on heavy volume, and, yet again, Juniper rapidly rebounded and attempted another comeback,

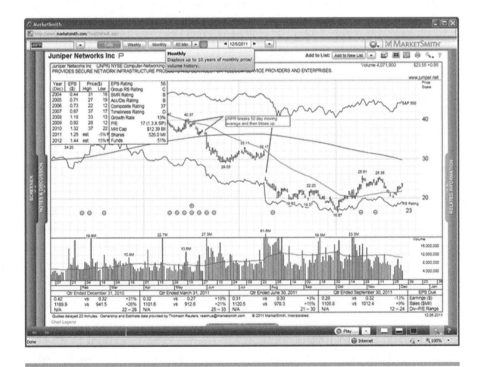

Figure 7.9 Juniper Networks: Trading around the 50 DMA, a few small losses and then the big drop.
Source: *WONDA® Copyright © 2012 William O'Neil + Co., Inc. All rights reserved.*

but this time it did not set new highs. The third time was the charm. On April 4, Juniper shares broke the 50 DMA on greater than average volume, closing off 3.6 percent near its lows for the day. The stock was already weak. And then on July 27's profit warning, the stock ripped apart, falling 21 percent on nearly five times average volume. It extended the drop to 35 percent in eight more trading days and, as of December 5, 2011, had not closed above the 50 DMA.

The 21 percent gap down in price was the confirmation of the Juniper revenue recognition thesis. Yet, the stock was already showing signs of weakness before the fundamentals became well known in the market place. This underscores the value of paying attention to both the fundamentals and the technicals: Oftentimes, changes in momentum precede changes in the fundamentals.

It is easy to get caught up in the minutiae of moment-to-moment changes in stock prices. One day you see that there's a bailout of a major economy that sends stock prices soaring, only to find that the next day the same or another economy is in the tank and stocks come crashing to earth. Intraday, the swings can be even wilder, especially with the advent of computer programs such as high-frequency trading. Even the most rational investor can't hide from media fear and greed or up-to-the-minute stock quotes. This noise can lead investors to believe they have a feel for the market, lulling them into making decisions against their strategy and beyond their competence. They drop the most important thing any investor has—a disciplined, repeatable process—and flail in the wilderness, losing money.

I used to stare at a quote machine all day long. After my blood pressure reached 160/120 it just wasn't worth the stress. Today, with no loss of performance, I pay virtually no attention to intraday prices. The closing price is what matters, and it is more important the longer the timeframe.

I can see everything I need to know on daily, weekly, and monthly charts. If a stock is at an all-time high, then it doesn't really matter what it did each nanosecond before it reached that high. If a stock breaks out to the upside on a monthly chart after years of sideways action, that is far more important than what happened during the last few days or hours.

The myth is that technicians live like day traders, trading pennies by rapid fire. Some do, some don't. I don't. I focus on a few metrics that matter and prefer charts over a longer timeframe. The orders of precedence I give stock charts are monthly, weekly, and daily. I prefer all three to be headed in the same direction. If the daily chart is breaking down but the weekly chart is still firmly in an uptrend, then I give more weight to the weekly charts. and so on for the monthly. Confirmation among the three provides more confidence that my trade may be profitable.

Principle 5: Risk Management Is More Important Than Picking Stocks

When you're looking to maximize profit, risk management is key. Controlling losses may not be as exciting as focusing on the upside, but it's crucial to generating winning returns. Most investors focus on the blue skies ahead, but you make just as much (if not more) money not getting drenched in the rain. Many of history's most accomplished investors achieved their incredible track records, not by hitting home runs, but by sidestepping bombs that could have destroyed their portfolios' returns for years. That's why the size of your trades and whether you actively manage them are more important for risk management than simply choosing a stock.

Consider two famous investors' opposite risk management philosophies. First up is the strategy espoused by Bill Miller, famed for beating the S&P 500 for 15 straight years from 1991 to 2006 as fund manager of the Legg Mason Value Trust. His strategy is "lowest average cost wins." Once he has made a decision, and presumably values the security, if its price falls, he is willing to buy more shares to lower his average cost. If his research proves correct and the stock recovers in price, he earns even better returns than if he hadn't averaged down.

On the other side of the spectrum is the strategy used by Paul Tudor Jones, who at Tudor Investments has made billions of dollars for himself and his investors. Jones's strategy is "losers average losers." In other words, if you average down, you will lose more, because you compound your mistakes. Jones doesn't add to stocks that aren't going his way; rather, he cuts his losses and tends to increase positions that are going in his favor. He employs technical analysis.

Which strategy is correct? In my opinion, Miller's strategy is risky and overconfident. Buying more on the way down assumes that you know something the market doesn't and that handsome rewards await you once your analysis proves to be correct. That sounds good in theory, but what happens when you own shares of businesses that seem top-notch—companies like Enron, WorldCom, Wachovia, Bear Stearns, AIG, and Freddie Mac—and never snap back? Miller owned all of these stocks in his fund, and as he found out, this strategy can destroy performance. He didn't know what he owned.

Conversely, Jones's strategy keeps you in the game long enough for your research to work out and for you to realize higher returns with less risk. When the bottom fell out in 2008, Tudor Investment's flagship fund lost a mere 5 percent while Legg Mason Value Trust lost more than 55 percent—over 11 times more. Miller confused growth with value backed by tangible assets. He averaged financials and other black boxes when he could not know the companies' underwriting and other standards or investments.

In my own fund, I applied Jones's methodology with my own twist.. First, I set a target position size, usually 5 percent for a company with serious aggressive accounting issues. I might only target 2.5 percent for one with fewer red flags. Then, I don't short all at once. For a 5 percent position, I may only short 2 percent initially. If the stock starts to sell off, I add to my position. If my thesis proves correct, and the company misses earnings estimates and the stock price gets clobbered, my position is now maximized for full effect. If the stock moves slightly against me, I might short a bit more, say, from the original 2 percent to 3 percent. However, if the stock continues to move against me, I don't add more until the stock starts to fall again.

I don't employ Bill Miller's strategy on the short side, which would be "highest average cost wins." If the stock continues to rise, I put in a protective stop—a stop-loss order—above the recent high to ease out of the position in case it continues to climb. In my experience, stocks rarely reach new highs and then implode. They reach highs, sell off, rise again but not as high, and then implode. They almost always start to sell off before big problems occur. Individual investors are the last to the volume party, but the institutions—the elephants in the bathtub—have already started selling. You don't have to take this on faith. You see it in price and volume.

Conclusion

With this strategy, my portfolio is always tilted toward what is working in my favor and away from what isn't. I'm willing to take numerous small losses on a stock, if there is a large gain to be had if and when it works out. If I'm completely wrong, I've minimized the damage by having smaller positions in those stocks. Tom and I can control our processes, but not the results.

Sizing and active management are far more important to risk management than your original stock selection. Size one big loser wrong, and you're out of the game. Size positions appropriately, and you can keep playing to win.

William O'Neil + Company is a Registered Investment Advisor providing research and marketing data services, including WONDA®, to more than 350 of the world's leading institutional investment professionals. Founded in 1963, William O'Neil + Company is headquartered in Los Angeles, with offices in New York, Boston, Chicago, and London.

WONDA provides access to over 55,000 global equity listings with key fundamental and technical data laid out in an easy to read proprietary Datagraph®. Additional benefits include time-saving Preset Lists, Quickscreen, and proprietary Ratings and Rankings to find new ideas and monitor existing holdings. For more information visit www.williamoneil.com.

Chapter 8

Market Timing

Like technical analysis, market timing is controversial. Most market timing critics agree that "It's not about tim*ing* the markets, it's about your time *in* the markets."

Every fundamental long-only investing style involves some form of "buy" and "hold." The investor buys, having made a case for the investment, whether one with specific catalysts, or one closing the arbitrage between current valuation and intrinsic value, or both. This chapter is addressed to those who wish to avoid massive bear market losses, or "drawdowns." Drawdown is a money-management term referring to any drop in investment value, no matter how short term. Even if the long-term return is, or would be, acceptable to excellent, drawdowns are scary.

Recall Chapter 1's discussion about Morningstar's analysis of investors in the highly successful CGM Focus Fund run by the extraordinary money manager Ken Heebner. Despite his long-term annualized outperformance, Morningstar concluded that most of Heebner's investors lost money. His drawdowns—periods of substantial and impermanent paper losses—reinforced the average investor's fear of selling at lows, rebuying at times of enthusiasm, and succumbing to bull market good feelings. Confirmation bias leads the average investor to buy high and sell low, losing money, just as in Morningstar's study of the average investor in CGM Focus Fund.

Let's think again about "time *in* the market." The benefit of a long-short strategy using John's short-side risk management and Tom's long strategy is that, while both benefit from the techniques in this book, the long side need not concern itself with either tim*ing* or time *in* the market. It does not require expert technical analysis or market timing if the short book is managed with discipline according to John's practical methods. Why? Because with John's short book management, the long book can have time *in* the markets with the short exposure managed so that any drawdown magnitude is reduced.

In the real world, it is the rare manager who has steadfast clients—usually the result of either well-off relatives or a fabulous first year that provides goodwill for a very long time. If that were not true, no funds would close after a bad year and reopen—with investors incomprehensibly willing to take another ride—so that the manager can attempt a good first year again! It also is the rare investor who has the market-history knowledge, calm, and steadfastness to stick with it in a period of massive drawdown, such as in 2008–2009, 2000–2002, or, even further back, 1973–1974, when drawdowns were massive in both nominal and inflation-adjusted terms.

The long-only investor without the ability to conquer emotion—and/or without permanent capital—has no choice but to use market timing and technical analysis. But the long-short investor can use the techniques in this book to reduce drawdown magnitude, conquer emotion, and increase wealth. Those with lower-magnitude drawdowns will have more assets under management.

And so let's look at how to use market timing to avoid massive drawdowns—peak-to-valley declines—in bear and sideways markets.

Secular and Cyclical Bull and Bear Markets

Bull and bear markets come and go in wavy patterns called secular and cyclical. A secular bull or bear market is a market that trends in a major direction up or down, respectively, for a long period of time, averaging 17 years. A cyclical bull or bear market is a market that trends up or down, respectively, within a secular bull or bear market and lasts a shorter time, one to four years.

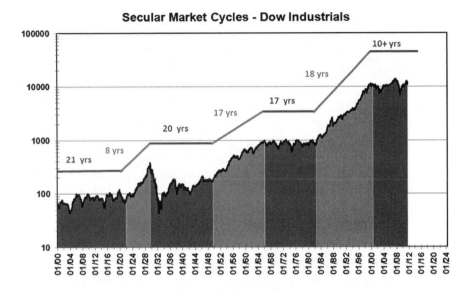

Secular Market Cycles - Dow Industrials

Figure 8.1 Secular market cycles over the last 111 years.

For more than a century, the average secular bull market historically has lasted about 12 years, but the average secular bear market has lasted 21 years. Figure 8.1 illustrates bull markets and bear markets since 1900. The stock market does not go up in a straight line. There are periods of massive drawdowns and sideways markets. Identifying and avoiding those drawdown periods is the first step in market timing.

It is crucial for an investor to understand the stock market's historical major cycles. One of the first key periods in the past 70 years was a secular bull market from 1949 through 1966 (see Figure 8.2), which averaged 14 percent gains each year. Buy-and-hold investors choosing stocks that mirrored the averages—then almost exclusively the Dow Jones Industrial Average (DJIA)—succeeded during this period, especially if they could periodically invest money and reinvest dividends. While lacking the index funds of recent decades and the more commonly used S&P 500, Russell, or Wilshire indexes, investors tended to buy the large, well-known stocks included in the DJIA and were, in effect, linking their returns to the DJIA.

The gains stopped a couple of times, with two large drawdowns in 1962 and 1966. From 1966 to 1982, there was a period during which

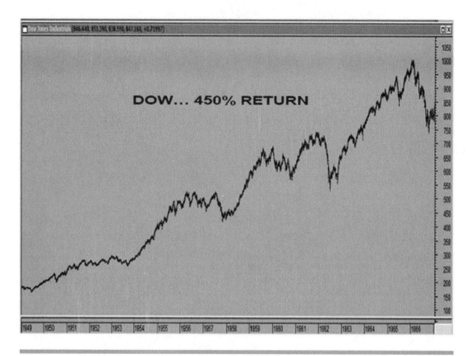

Figure 8.2 Dow Jones Industrial Average—secular bull market 1949–1966.

the market gave buy-and-holders very little, thanks especially to the 1973–1974 bear market and the long-term loss to inflation. Few long investors could withstand 40 percent drawdowns, wiping out years of small gains. Figure 8.3, illustrating the DJIA from 1955 to 2004, shows a superficially sideways market from the mid-1960s to mid-1980s.

Within this seemingly flat trading range are the sharp gains and losses of cyclical bull and bear markets, respectively. The cyclical bull and bear markets within the 1966 to 1982 sideways market are shown in Figure 8.4.

The ups and drawdowns of 1968–1982 reveal what was truly a secular bear market, as shown in Table 8.1.

Cyclical bear declines during this period totaled 146 percent, while cyclical bull gains equaled 211 percent, ending with a 3 percent gain against 50 percent inflation. Periodic investment and dividend reinvestment couldn't make up for this dismal 16-year period, rightly called the "lost decade."

Figure 8.3 DJIA 1955–2004: Sideways market, mid-1960s to mid-1980s.

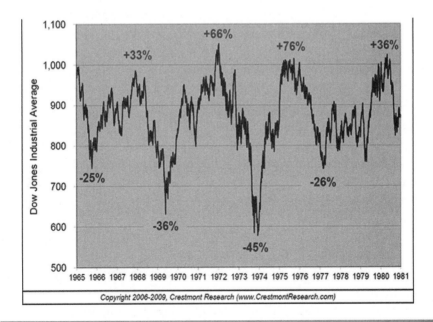

Figure 8.4 The "sideways" 1966–1982 market had sharp gains and losses.
Source: Copyright © 2006–2008, Crestmont Research, www.Crestmont
Research.com.

Table 8.1. Magnitude of Gains and Drawdowns in 1968–1982 Secular
Bear Market

Running Total	Gain/(Drawdown)	Value at Trough
$100	(25%)	$75
$75	33%	$100
$100	(36%)	$64
$64	66%	$106
$106	(45%)	$58
$58	76%	$103
$103	(26%)	$76
$76	36%	$103

Market History Knowledge Depends on Age and Experience

By 2000, a 35- or 40-year-old, with a manageable mortgage, salary covering a 401(k), college fund, and discretionary cash for investing (admittedly a small segment of society, but perhaps the only one fitted for actual retirement someday) was 17 to 22 years old at the beginning of the 1982 bull market. This extraordinary 18-year bull market began with Fed Chairman Paul Volcker's breaking of inflation, the emergence from the recession, and a lengthy bull market in bonds (with declining interest rates—bond prices move in the opposite direction), along with confidence that reduced expectations of inflation.

Most investors knew precious little about the lost 1966–1982 period, and so those investors saw blue skies—with one brief drop in 1987 that only vindicated the new religion of "buy on the dips." The index investor profited hugely from 1982 to 2000, with total returns of 1,100 percent and 2,600 percent, respectively, for the S&P 500 and the Nasdaq. The market rewarded those who stayed all-in with many annual double-digit gains of 20 to 25 percent for the S&P 500. However, investors had to withstand a 35 percent Nasdaq drop in 1998 and a 19 percent drop for the S&P 500, something human nature (and the Heebner example) would suggest didn't happen.

In the late 1990s, individual investors entered the stock market in massive numbers. The investors now used the workplace 401(k) plans that increasingly replaced defined-benefit pension plans, with access to low-commission trades through online discount brokers. With the upward acceleration in market averages, the herd moved in. The 1987 crash, 1990 bear, and the 1998 Asian crisis and Long-Term Capital Management blowup were blips whose wakes only reinforced the mantra "buy on the dips." By 1999, the young adults at the beginning of the 1982 secular bull were in their thirties, fully participating in the mad, final bull stampede—completely unprepared for the balloon's long, slow deflation from 2000 to 2002. It seemed like that was simply a tech bubble—something that didn't really affect well-known large caps, especially when the S&P 500 returned to pre-crash levels in 2007. But with the 2008–2009 crash, all was lost, and despite market rises after 2009, a lost decade-plus had not ended by 2011.

Sure, there were many years of strong returns, such as 2003 and 2009, and noncalendar year periods that did much better. But what really lost index investors the serious money was 2000–2002 and 2008. The

Portfolio Equity

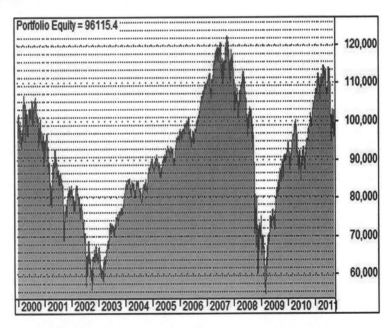

Figure 8.5 SPY: Two major drawdowns, January 2000–October 2011. Source: AmiBroker, www.AmiBroker.com. All charts referenced to AmiBroker are created using their tools and analysis, and by permission.

investor in the S&P 500 index ETF (AMEX: SPY) from the beginning of January 3, 2000, to September 30, 2011, earned an abysmal −6.88 percent, a −0.61 percent compound annual growth rate. Index investors held on to their plummeting portfolios during some of the worst bear market crashes in history, with SPY falling 55 percent from its peak in October 2007 to its bottom in March 2009. The peak-to-valley change in price stunned many who watched their retirement savings cut in half. If they rode out 2000–2002 and stayed the course into 2007, they recovered. After that, though, the ride was seriously over. But the 55 percent loss— requiring a 123 percent gain to return to even—could have been avoided with a little market timing.

Figure 8.5 illustrates the two major drawdowns for the index investor who invested $100,000 in SPY from January 1, 2000, to October 1, 2011.

Underwater Equity

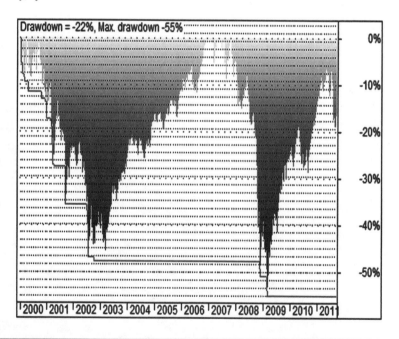

Figure 8.6 The reverse of Figure 8.5, showing the magnitude of drops.
Source: AmiBroker, www.AmiBroker.com.

Profit Table

Year	Jan	Feb	Mar	Apr	May	Jun	Jul	Aug	Sep	Oct	Nov	Dec	Yr%
2000	-3.1%	-1.8%	9.5%	-2.8%	-1.2%	1.6%	-2.3%	6.0%	-5.4%	-1.0%	-7.2%	-2.3%	-10.5%
2001	7.1%	-9.7%	-8.1%	11.3%	-0.3%	-1.8%	-1.6%	-7.1%	-7.7%	4.1%	4.5%	1.9%	-9.5%
2002	-2.5%	1.0%	1.0%	-4.7%	-4.4%	-6.7%	-8.5%	-0.6%	-2.5%	5.3%	4.3%	-2.8%	-19.9%
2003	-5.3%	-2.5%	2.7%	6.8%	5.9%	1.6%	-0.0%	4.4%	-0.3%	3.8%	1.5%	3.9%	24.1%
2004	2.5%	1.9%	-1.7%	-1.4%	0.5%	0.6%	-1.7%	0.2%	2.5%	-0.1%	5.4%	1.4%	10.2%
2005	-1.2%	1.9%	-2.8%	-0.9%	3.5%	-0.4%	3.4%	-0.9%	0.5%	-1.7%	5.1%	0.5%	7.2%
2006	1.3%	0.8%	0.7%	0.5%	-1.3%	-0.3%	-0.5%	3.3%	1.7%	2.8%	2.5%	1.4%	13.6%
2007	2.3%	-2.8%	1.6%	4.6%	3.6%	-1.1%	-3.5%	1.8%	4.0%	-2.1%	-2.2%	-1.3%	4.4%
2008	-3.7%	-4.4%	2.8%	3.3%	-1.6%	-7.1%	-1.7%	1.4%	-8.8%	-16.3%	-15.5%	14.1%	-34.3%
2009	-11.2%	14.5%	15.6%	8.4%	7.8%	-2.0%	8.8%	-0.2%	3.3%	1.3%	6.7%	2.4%	24.7%
2010	-3.8%	2.6%	5.3%	2.2%	-10.6%	-4.0%	9.7%	-3.8%	6.2%	3.4%	2.1%	5.5%	13.8%
2011	2.9%	0.1%	2.1%	2.3%	-3.2%	2.1%	-3.8%	-6.1%	-6.0%	N/A	N/A	N/A	-9.6%
Avg	-1.2%	-2.3%	2.4%	2.5%	-0.1%	-1.5%	-0.1%	-0.1%	-1.0%	-0.0%	0.6%	2.2%	

Figure 8.7 SPY (S&P 500 ETF) buy-and-hold monthly returns, January 2000– September 2011.*

*Monthly results are for that individual month, while the right-hand column—the percentage gain or loss for the year—is cumulative (assuming an initial amount invested and rising and falling monthly).
Source: AmiBroker, www.AmiBroker.com.

Figure 8.6 emphasizes the magnitude of the 2000–2002 and 2008– 2009 drops while Figure 8.7 is a month-to-month performance analysis of buying and holding throughout the 2001 to 2011 period.

Notice the string of months that were consecutive losers, such as September 2008 through February 2009, equal in length from April 2002 through September 2002, but of massively greater magnitude. The more back-to-back losses an investor realized, the worse the negative compounding and drawdown, and the more portfolio destruction.

The Problem of Permanent Capital Loss

Recognizing secular markets is one thing, but recognizing the cyclical markets within them is what provides investors with ultimate gains. If investors can time these cycles—or even come close—they will have the ability to increase returns, reduce drawdowns, protect their capital, and stop buying antacids.

To demonstrate how large drawdowns can truly devastate a portfolio, look at Figure 8.8. It calculates the exponential impact of losses and how hard it is to overcome those losses as they grow. For example, if an investor loses 70 percent of a portfolio, it would take a 233 percent gain to return to the portfolio's original value. The long-term would need to be very, very long indeed.

Figure 8.8 is a more dramatic representation of the concept discussed earlier in the chapter—that a 33 percent gain does not return to even a portfolio that's dropped 33 percent (you would need a 50 percent gain).

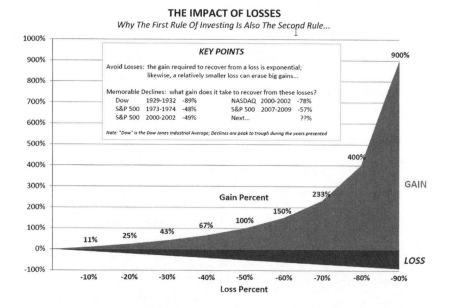

Figure 8.8 The impact of losses.
Source: Copyright © 2009 Crestmont Research (www.CrestmontResearch.com).

Avoiding losses is more important to preserving capital than participating in—or chasing the momentum of—gains.

Limiting Losses Is Far More Important Than Gathering Gains

Value investor Warren Buffett is cited for so much and so often that, if only half of what people said about him were true, he would be a deity. He, Benjamin Graham, and other noted pioneers of value investing have noted that, if you avoid permanent capital loss by buying cheaply—with a margin of safety—the gains take care of themselves. Buffett wrote in his hedge fund letters that he would likely do better than the market in bear markets and the same or a bit less in bull markets. Yet most investors chase gains, thinking that's where the money is made. Where value investors and short-siders find agreement is that keeping the losses to a minimum is where you make the money. This doesn't mean you'll never have losses. It means you should avoid losing capital to such an extent that future returns won't help you in restoring your wealth.

The market timing explained in this chapter provides the advantage of avoiding costly losses so that an attempted comeback will not be so burdensome. However, in order to understand market timing, you must first understand a small part of technical analysis.

Targeted Technical Analysis

As discussed in Chapter 7, technical analysis is based on the premise that market prices for a particular market, such as equities, reflect the fundamental driving forces of supply and demand. Just as market timing is misconstrued as somehow predicting the future, so too is technical analysis. Neither does, but they both follow the truth that prices are determined by supply and demand.

Most technical analysts will examine price action in the form of price charts. By studying charts over different timeframes, an investor can start to recognize patterns of market behavior and apply them toward market timing.

Contrary to popular belief, market timing is not predictive, but rather responsive to market shifts between bulls and bears. Hence, the investor is actually trying to be rational and use tools, rather than being distracted by emotion. Removing emotion is what market timing and technical analysis attempts to do.

Market timing does not care what products a company manufactures or if the CEO is your best friend. Instead, market timing cares only about the price action of the underlying security. Nevertheless, investors who understand risk also understand that making choices is unavoidable. Most of the time, the choices are between greater risk and greater potential reward versus lower risk and lower return. If an investor wants to achieve a maximum return, most of the time he or she will choose the greater risk for greater reward. However, the best investors know that, with premeditated calculation, they can achieve greater returns with less risk. This is really no different from long strategies to calculate potential reward for risk. It just uses market timing and technical analysis to do it.

Investors must consider that, if there are ways of maximizing risk-adjusted return or risk associated with the expected return by participating in bull markets while avoiding bear markets, then they must learn them, practice them, and see if they work. The use of a few technical indicators related to price action can achieve the desired results.

Moving Averages

One important indicator is the moving average, as discussed in Chapter 7. A simple moving average is derived by calculating the stock's average closing price over a certain number of periods. For example, a 50-day simple moving average (50 DMA) is the sum of 50 consecutive daily closing prices divided by 50. As the days move forward, the moving average is recalculated—that's why it's "moving."

Moving averages smooth out price action, so the investor can better interpret a trend. If the moving average is going up, the trend is up. If two moving averages of different period lengths were to cross, it would indicate a change in trend.

The "Death Cross"

A useful though ominous-sounding gauge measuring the shift between bull and bear markets is the "Death Cross." The 50 DMA shows supply and demand for a stock reflected in its price over almost two months, while the 200 DMA does the same over almost seven months. A Death Cross occurs when the 50 DMA breaks below the 200 DMA. This shows that short-term demand is falling relative to longer-term demand and indicates a shift in market sentiment.

The importance of the 200 DMA can go beyond whether the 50 DMA crosses it. Some investors will sell their positions if they move below the 200 DMA, while others will not buy any trading below it. Because many technical investors will not trade in a security below the 200 DMA, it is considered a major support line. If the stock is above the 200 DMA, when the 50 DMA crosses below it, the investor heads for the exit. Moving averages are psychologically important whether applied to an individual security, an index, or a broad market—no matter what the investor is buying or selling.

How well do moving average crossovers—specifically the Death Cross—perform in interpreting the future action of a security or index?

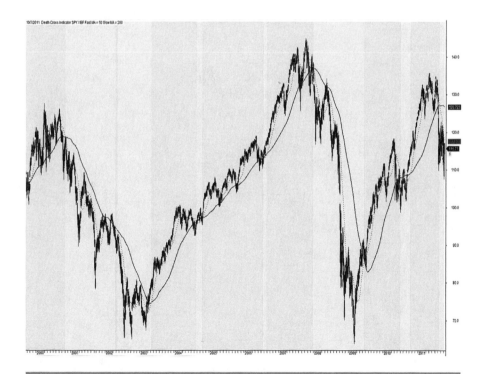

Figure 8.9 S&P 500 using 50 DMA and 200 DMA.
Source: AmiBroker, www.AmiBroker.com.

Figure 8.9 highlights the S&P 500 with a 50 DMA and 200 DMA. When the 50 DMA (dotted line) crosses above the 200 DMA (solid line), you can see the *bull* market uptrend. When the 200 DMA (solid) crosses above the 50 DMA (dotted), the bear market downtrend appears. Overall, the indicator provides a good reference for bullish up trends and bearish down trends.

Recall that the index investor fully invested in this 2000–2011 period lost –6.88 percent for –0.61 percent CAGR. Using the 50 DMA–200 DMA Death Cross signal to move SPY to cash and back again yielded an 81 percent gain with a 5.2 percent CAGR and only a –17.8 percent drawdown. This demonstrates how even the simplest of technical analysis techniques can boost investment results.

In 2004 and 2006, there were brief periods called "whipsaws," periods when the 50 DMA crossing the 200 DMA signaled the trader to exit the market, only to turn around and direct a return to the markets a few weeks later. Whipsaws are frustrating. Expanding the 200 DMA to 250

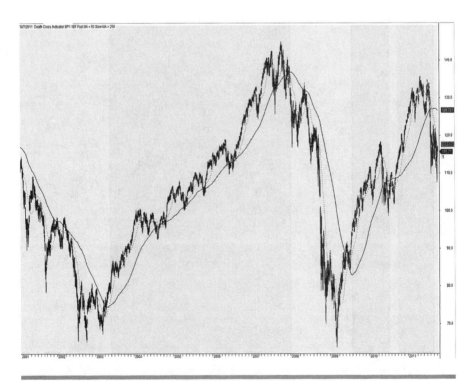

Figure 8.10 Modified Death Cross: 250 DMA.
Source: AmiBroker, www.AmiBroker.com.

days can eliminate the whipsaws and their losses. Figure 8.10 represents a modified Death Cross using a 250 DMA instead of the 200 DMA.

In the modified Death Cross, from January 2000 to October 2011, the investor would have achieved a total gain of 88.5 percent or 5.5 percent CAGR and –17.3 percent drawdown.

Enhancing Performance: Bonds Instead of Cash

Further performance improvements can be achieved, however. Instead of selling SPY and going to cash on the sell signal, sell SPY and buy an intermediate-term bond index, such as the T. Rowe Price U.S. Treasury Intermediate Fund, (NYSE: PRTIX) or the iShares Barclays 7–10 year Treasury ETF (NYSE: IEF), which only began trading in July 2002, limiting a complete comparison for 2000–2011. We'll delve into this more in a bit, but for now, know that, when investors see a greater potential gain in bonds rather than stocks, large amounts of capital move from stocks to bonds. When enough of it does so, this reduces demand for stocks and the broad stock market declines. Switching to PRTIX on a sell signal grows

Table 8.2 Comparison of Results from Four Strategies

Strategy from Jan. 3, 2000, to Oct. 3, 2011*	SPY Switching Between	Fast/Slow DMA	Total Return	CAGR	Drawdown
Index Buy and Hold	SPY as proxy for S&P 500— no switch	N/A	(6.88%)	(0.61%)	(55.2%)
Death Cross	SPY and Cash	50/200	81.0%	5.2%	(17.8%)
Modified Death Cross	SPY and Cash	50/250	88.5%	5.5%	(17.3%)
Modified Death Cross	SPY and PRTIX (Bonds)	50/250	180.9%	9.2%	(17.3%)

*No stop losses employed.

the total gain to 181 percent with a CAGR of 9.2 percent. The drawdown remains at –17.3 percent.

Table 8.2 summarizes the performance from January 2000 to October 2011 of buying and holding the S&P 500 proxy SPY, the original 50 DMA × 200 DMA Death Cross, the modified 50 DMA × 250 DMA Death Cross, and the modified Death Cross switching to PRTIX instead of cash.

Figure 8.11 shows the equity curve and drawdown analysis of a portfolio that invested in the modified Death Cross switching between SPY and PRTIX from 2000 to October 2011. The equity curve demonstrates the growth of the account value starting with US$100,000. Figure 8.12 illustrates the drawdown analysis of Figure 8.11, but also showing percentage dips in account value when holding in the same period. Figure 8.13 shows the month-to-month results over the same time period.

You can see that the returns are much better and drawdown is superior for all Death Cross methods, especially the modified Death Cross switching between SPY and PRTIX.

Portfolio Equity

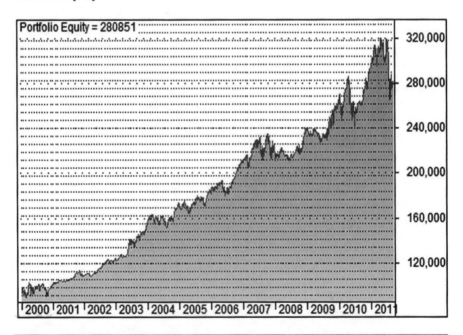

Figure 8.11 Modified Death Cross: Switching between SPY and PRTIX.
Source: AmiBroker, www.AmiBroker.com.

Cash Flows Between Small- and Large-Cap Stocks

Just as the switch between stocks and bonds is important, so too is the switch between small-cap stocks and large-cap stocks. Small-cap stocks serve as leading indicators of directional changes in the market, because investor cash flows into small caps rather than large caps when bond returns are unfavorable. However, because small caps have higher volatility—their relative illiquidity means prices rise and fall more in response to buying and selling volumes—the average investor thinks they are bigger risks than large-cap stocks, which don't experience as much price fluctuation.

But volatility is not the same as risk. For the same reason investors act on emotion at drawdowns, they also tend to withdraw large amounts of capital from small caps when they believe those assets are more volatile and appear riskier. Detecting capital withdrawal from small caps can serve as an early indicator of overall market changes.

Underwater Equity

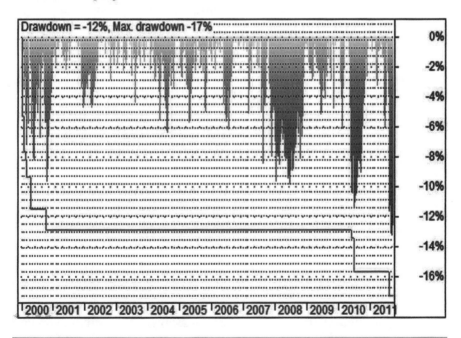

Figure 8.12 Drawdown analysis of Figure 8.11, using percentage dips in account value.
Source: AmiBroker, www.AmiBroker.com.

Profit Table

Year	Jan	Feb	Mar	Apr	May	Jun	Jul	Aug	Sep	Oct	Nov	Dec	Yr%
2000	-3.1%	-1.8%	9.5%	-2.8%	-1.2%	1.6%	-2.3%	6.0%	-5.4%	-1.0%	3.0%	3.8%	5.5%
2001	0.6%	0.9%	0.3%	-0.9%	N/A	0.9%	2.1%	0.3%	3.5%	2.2%	-2.2%	-2.0%	5.7%
2002	1.4%	0.3%	-2.0%	3.2%	1.1%	1.6%	2.7%	2.4%	1.5%	-0.5%	-0.8%	1.5%	13.1%
2003	0.8%	2.5%	-0.5%	N/A	6.5%	1.6%	-0.0%	4.4%	-0.3%	3.8%	1.5%	3.9%	26.6%
2004	2.5%	1.9%	-1.7%	-1.4%	0.5%	0.6%	-1.7%	0.2%	2.5%	-0.1%	5.4%	1.4%	10.2%
2005	-1.2%	1.9%	-2.8%	-0.9%	3.5%	-0.4%	3.4%	-0.9%	0.5%	-1.7%	5.1%	0.5%	7.2%
2006	1.3%	0.8%	0.7%	0.5%	-1.3%	-0.3%	-0.5%	3.3%	1.7%	2.8%	2.5%	1.4%	13.6%
2007	2.3%	-2.8%	1.6%	4.6%	3.6%	-1.1%	-3.5%	1.8%	4.0%	-2.1%	-2.2%	-1.3%	4.4%
2008	-1.1%	1.0%	0.2%	-1.4%	-0.8%	0.2%	0.8%	1.6%	0.2%	-0.4%	5.8%	1.7%	8.0%
2009	-0.6%	-0.2%	2.1%	-2.0%	-1.7%	0.6%	0.6%	-0.2%	3.3%	1.3%	6.7%	2.4%	12.5%
2010	-3.8%	2.6%	5.3%	2.2%	-10.6%	-4.0%	6.1%	1.9%	0.9%	4.0%	2.1%	5.5%	11.3%
2011	2.9%	0.1%	2.1%	2.3%	-3.2%	2.1%	-3.8%	-6.1%	-1.7%	N/A	N/A	N/A	-5.5%
Avg	0.2%	0.6%	1.2%	0.3%	-0.3%	0.3%	0.3%	1.2%	0.9%	0.8%	2.4%	1.7%	

Figure 8.13 Monthly results using modified Death Cross switching between SPY and PRTIX.
Source: AmiBroker, www.AmiBroker.com.

Several methods can detect the movement of capital from stocks to the bond market and back. A simple way to see the changes in momentum between the two is to divide a small cap stock ETF index by an intermediate-term bond ETF index and plot the result on a chart over time. By dividing the small-cap index by the bond index, the ratio of the two will fall faster as the small-cap index decreases in price (numerator decreasing) and bonds increase in price (denominator increasing). The movement of the resulting ratio indicates money flowing into equities when the stock/bond spread indicator is rising or money moving out of equities into bonds when it is falling.

To use this as a market timing indicator, a point of reference needs to be established where the spread indicator ratio is above the reference line and small-cap prices are increasing while bond prices are decreasing. This causes the indicator to rise faster. A moving average of the small-cap/bond spread indicator can provide this threshold, as shown in Figure 8.14.

Unfortunately, using an unmodified spread indicator will result in numerous whipsaws, because the indicator fluctuates as stock and bond index prices change day to day. Figure 8.15 shows equity curves for the iShares Russell 2000 Index ETF (NYSE: IWM) of small-cap stocks, the iShares Barclays 7–10 Year Treasury ETF (NYSE: IEF), and the stock/bond spread indicator in the bottom pane.

From July 2002 to September 30, 2011, the performance of switching between the Russell 2000 Index ETF (IWM) and cash yielded a 151 percent gain with a 10.4 percent CAGR and a –17 percent drawdown. Overall performance can be enhanced by switching to bonds via IEF when the timing indicator issues a sell signal of IWM. Switching between IWM and IEF yields a total return of 268 percent with a CAGR of 15 percent and drawdown of –18.5 percent. This contrasts with a buy-and-hold result of IWM for the same time period of 53.1 percent total return, 4.7 percent CAGR, and –59.0 percent drawdown.

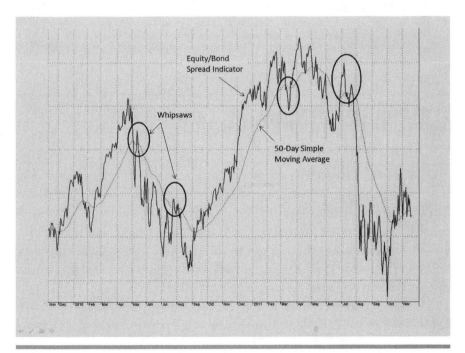

Figure 8.14 Moving average of small-cap/bond spread indicators.
Source: AmiBroker, www.AmiBroker.com.

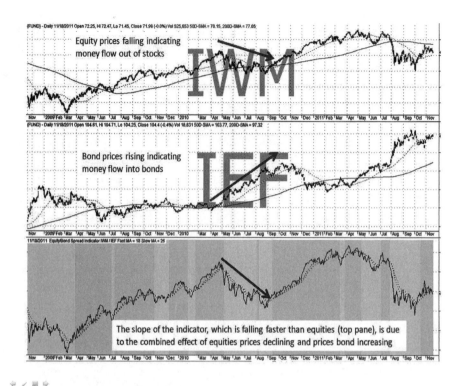

Figure 8.15 Stock/bond spread indicator: IWM (stocks) and IEF (bonds).
Source: AmiBroker, www.AmiBroker.com.

Figure 8.16 shows the equity curve for a portfolio that invested in the stock/bond spread indicator from 2002 to the end of September 2011 starting with $100,000, Figure 8.17 shows the month-to-month results of this system over the same time period, and in Figure 8.18, we see the profit distribution of the trades. Notice how there are more winners than losers, and that the bulk of the losses are moderate and acceptable.

A stock/bond spread indicator can be formed with other major market indexes as well. Table 8.3 summarizes the performance of a buy and hold strategy for IWM, the IWM/cash switch indicator, the IWM/IEF switch indicator, and the SPY/IEF switch indicator (using a short 9 DMA and longer 64 DMA, which research shows as optimal for this switch indicator).

Portfolio Equity

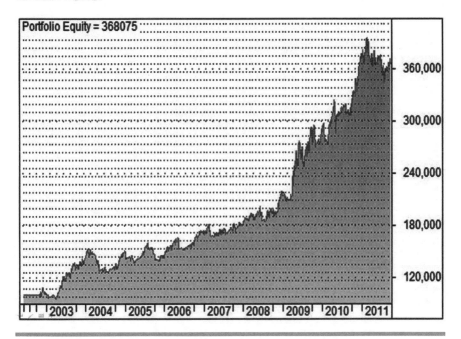

Figure 8.16 Stock/bond spread indicator: equity curve.
Source: AmiBroker, www.AmiBroker.com.

Market timing does not care about emotions. It only cares how the market performs. Measuring how the market performs and creating a system around the data creates a trader's edge. That edge produces success.

Part 1 showed *what* to look for. And Part 2, ending with this chapter, shows *how and when* to act on it. The following and final chapter gives the research supporting the practical advice in this book—but not before our offer to you on market timing.

Current Market Timing Offering

In addition to this chapter's market timing signals, there is another very useful proprietary signal. This market composite signal is derived from several different signals generated on different markets. Combining them into a composite yields still stronger returns with less draw-down, eliminating a number of whipsaws and capturing the majority of

Profit Table

Year	Jan	Feb	Mar	Apr	May	Jun	Jul	Aug	Sep	Oct	Nov	Dec	Yr%
2002	N/A	N/A	N/A	N/A	N/A	N/A	N/A	N/A	N/A	1.6%	6.8%	-7.2%	0.7%
2003	-2.8%	2.6%	-2.8%	8.3%	11.6%	1.3%	4.3%	8.7%	-1.6%	3.5%	3.3%	1.6%	43.9%
2004	3.5%	-0.1%	-2.1%	-8.7%	-3.3%	1.7%	-3.0%	2.7%	3.5%	0.3%	9.3%	0.1%	3.0%
2005	-3.9%	1.0%	-3.9%	2.4%	2.4%	3.3%	6.1%	-2.6%	-4.8%	-5.0%	4.0%	-0.3%	-2.2%
2006	7.4%	1.1%	2.2%	-0.1%	-5.2%	0.0%	1.7%	1.4%	-0.4%	4.6%	4.3%	0.9%	18.8%
2007	2.6%	-2.2%	-3.6%	0.8%	4.5%	-0.7%	-2.0%	2.3%	1.4%	-0.4%	3.6%	N/A	6.1%
2008	2.9%	0.7%	0.7%	0.7%	1.9%	-5.7%	1.0%	3.9%	0.4%	-1.4%	9.0%	2.3%	17.0%
2009	-1.7%	-0.6%	6.1%	14.1%	6.8%	-0.5%	-1.0%	-1.1%	4.7%	-1.1%	1.7%	5.6%	37.0%
2010	-5.8%	1.2%	6.7%	7.1%	-4.1%	2.9%	0.6%	-2.3%	3.3%	2.9%	6.5%	7.5%	28.5%
2011	0.2%	1.1%	-2.4%	1.0%	-1.1%	-1.6%	-6.3%	5.1%	1.4%	N/A	N/A	N/A	-2.9%
Avg	0.3%	0.5%	0.1%	2.8%	1.5%	0.1%	0.1%	1.8%	0.8%	0.5%	5.4%	1.2%	

Figure 8.17 Stock/bond spread indicator: monthly returns.
Source: AmiBroker, www.AmiBroker.com.

Profit Distribution

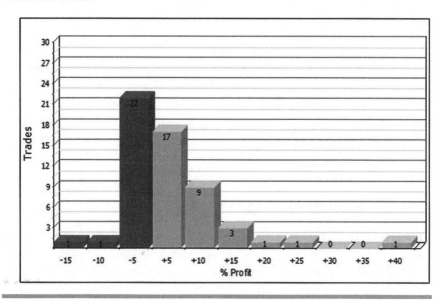

Figure 8.18 Stock/bond spread indicator: profit distribution.
Source: AmiBroker, www.AmiBroker.com.

Table 8.3 Comparing Results from Four More Strategies over a Period from June 3, 2002 to September 30, 2011*

Strategy	Fast/ Slow DMA	Net Profit	CAGR	Drawdown
Buy and Hold IWM	N/A	53.14%	4.67%	(59.03%)
Stock-Bond IWM/Cash	18 DMA/26 DMA	151%	10.4%	(17.0%)
Stock-Bond IWM/IEF	18/26	268%	15%	(18.5%)
Stock-Bond SPY/IEF	9/64	201.3%	12.6%	(11.4%)

*Note: No stop losses used.

intermediate-term trends. By optimizing over a series of various buy and sell combinations, when any one signal goes on a sell, the composite signal will generate a sell. Conversely, when all go on a buy, the composite signal generates a buy order. To receive the buys and sells generated by the composite signal free, please visit our website at www.deljacobs.com.

Chapter 9

Why This Works: The Numbers Behind the Numbers

This book is about risk management: getting out of or avoiding stocks before they destroy portfolio performance and understanding the fundamental and technical warning signs that will help you do that. While our methods draw upon years of experience, don't just take our word for them. The many examples included in these pages emphasize our process, using real-time analysis and decisions, rather than a retrospective look at what we might have found had we been paying attention in the first place.

Experience is crucial, but we also rely on quantitative data to support our process. In Chapter 2, we focused on how companies can manipulate the top line to mask deterioration in their businesses. Often, people use the price-to-sales ratio as a measure of valuation, because of the conventional wisdom that revenue is much less likely to be manipulated than earnings. Every reader now knows that we view this not only as a fallacy, but one that is dangerous to investment returns. However, combining simple rules of valuation with earnings quality supports the point that stocks priced for great expectations founded on potentially aggressive revenue recognition are a sucker's bet.

Stocks Show Investor Expectations

Expectations[1] play an important role in the performance of stock prices over time. A great company may not be a great stock to own, if the market has fully valued its future prospects but investors' expectations remain high. I (John) first learned this lesson as a freshman in college, when I happened to pick up the book *Super Stocks*. If there is a title more appealing to an 18-year-old who wants to make money, I don't know it! So I grabbed it, knowing nothing about its content or author.

First published in 1984, *Super Stocks*[2] was written by Kenneth Fisher, a longtime contributor to *Forbes*, manager of billions of dollars through his firm Fisher Investments, and the son of famed investor Philip Fisher. The book focuses on growth stocks, specifically highlighting the price-to-sales ratio as a way to accurately value companies laboring under high expectations. Fisher advocated buying growth stocks with low price-to-sales ratios and selling them when the ratio exceeded 3:1 to avoid an inevitable "glitch"—the loss of a key customer, a slowdown in demand, supply issues, or virtually any factor that could put the brakes on growth.

Later, I interned for James P. O'Shaughnessy, author of *What Works on Wall Street*.[3] In the decade or so since Fisher's book was published, technology had advanced enough to allow the testing of many common market variables for their effectiveness in predicting future returns. O'Shaughnessy used historical data from Standard & Poor's to do just that. His tests confirmed Fisher's theory, revealing that the price-to-sales ratio was one of the most effective predictors of stock performance.

I assisted in testing some variables, and we broke the results into deciles by performance, with each decile representing one-tenth of the market. The results of the price-to-sales ratio were amazing, because they displayed a perfect stair-step pattern: Each decile performed worse than the one preceding it. So, for example, the companies in the lowest decile of price-to-sales ratio produced the highest returns. The second decile was the second-best performer, and the pattern continued all the way to the most expensive stocks, which generated the worst returns. This makes sense when you consider that the stocks in the highest decile—the most expensive, carrying the weightiest expectations—are often the ones people love to own. They may have intoxicating stories and glossy press releases, but they produce the worst returns over time.

Both Fisher and O'Shaughnessy theorized that price-to-sales is a better valuation metric than price-to-earnings because sales are much harder to manipulate. But after working with Howard Schilit and David Tice and managing a couple of short-selling hedge funds, I found this to be untrue. A company can manipulate sales to mask deterioration in revenue growth in numerous ways, including changing its revenue-recognition policy, offering incentives to customers, and changing the presentation of the balance sheet. This is why we devoted so much attention to revenue recognition before we delved into the three financial statements.

Nothing Has Changed

Recently, we once again tested the theory that the price-to-sales ratio can be predictive of future results. We focused on technology stocks, because they're one area of the stock market that never fails to seduce people out of their hard-earned money. Every year and every decade touts the next big tech thing, with social networking the buzz *du jour* at writing. We tested the performance of all technology stocks in the S&P 1500 over the past 10, years based simply on their price-to-sales ratios. The results were astonishingly similar to both Fisher's and O'Shaughnessy's. Figure 9.1

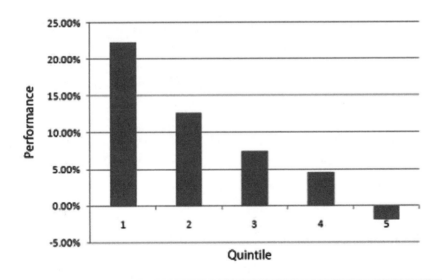

Figure 9.1 Performance of S&P 1500 technology stocks, based on price-to-sales ratio.

illustrates the performance of technology stocks by their price-to-sales ratio quintile.

The quintiles in Figure 9.1 move from left to right—number 1 to 5—from lowest price-to-sales ratio to highest. In the S&P 1500 Index, the lowest quintile by price-to-sales ratio (in other words, the cheapest) returned an average of 22.33 percent over the past 10 years. The next three quintiles returned averages of 12.7, 7.4, and 2.5 percent. The most expensive 20 percent of the technology stocks returned minus 2 percent annually.

The conclusion is simple. Eras change, as do the companies that are traded in the stock market and their management teams. And technology certainly changes; a 5¼-inch disk drive was the latest thing when Fisher wrote the first edition of his book. But human nature never changes. Investors persistently overestimate the future prospects of some companies by bidding their stocks up, relative to revenues, to unsustainable levels. This leads to disappointing returns for shareholders. You can identify these companies by looking for a high price-to-sales ratio, specifically one in the highest decile. So the next time you consider buying a stock, think hard about the expectations already embedded into the stock price. Those expectations can continue to grow for a long time, but they almost always end badly.

Tom notes that consideration of expectations is exactly the mindset of the long-side value investor. When a stock reflects no or low expectations, it has a huge margin of safety. So long as the fundamentals are at least decent—not even good or great—you aren't paying for inflated expectations. Those who pay for high expectations don't understand that they are accepting too little potential reward for the risk that the stock will fail to meet the expectations—and crash. Those who pay for low expectations take on less risk and pay very little for their upside—they have low cost or even free optionality.

The Pressure to Meet Expectations

Adding a second variable, however, can shed light on what happens when the stock is priced for perfection and management stretches to make their quarterly results. The greater the performance expectations embedded in a stock's valuation, the more pressure on management to meet or exceed those expectations. Because no one can know exactly what that pressure consists of—no eavesdropping behind closed doors or reading the CEO's psychiatrist's notes—no one can finish this book without understanding how strongly we rely on days sales outstanding (DSO).

It's so important that it begins the financial analysis in Chapter 2 and takes us out in Chapter 9 with a loud DSO bang, leading to how we use DSO and other indicators in a new and easy way for you to take advantage of the learning in this book. The DSO indicate how long it takes for a company to collect on its accounts receivable. This is important, because the longer it takes a company to collect its dollars, the greater the risks to its business model. Anything can happen until you have that dollar in your hand: Customers may go bust and fail to pay, or cash flow can suffer because revenue has been booked but the money hasn't come in the company's coffers.

In all our financial statement discussions, you learned that our primary concern about any metric is with change over time. So too with DSO, which we also examine over time. Upward-trending DSO can point to the greatest risk of all: aggressive revenue recognition. When companies are under pressure to meet quarterly targets, they often offer incentives—extended payment terms, reduced prices, or both—in order to induce customers to sign a contract today that they may well have signed anyway later, borrowing revenue from the future.

A fertile ground where management feels this pressure is in "growth." Any effort to study market history shows centuries of stock touters seducing investors with high-growth potential. Investors believe that advances in technology promise unlimited possibilities, so of course the companies offering these life-changers must bring stock gains. Right?

Wrong. Investors' expectations are too high in these cases. They expect that subverting old markets and opening new ones will create riches beyond their dreams. The herd instinct compounds overestimating success and brings ever-higher multiples relative to their revenue. CEOs, insiders, and venture capitalists make out like bandits, leaving shareholders holding the bag.

The desire to make out like bandits and disregard for shareholders lead management to do anything to keep the blush on the rose. DSO chicanery is rife, especially among tech companies. Customers know that technology companies book most of their revenue toward the end of the quarter, so they commonly use this to their advantage, waiting to make a purchase and then haggling for better terms. This creates a vicious circle, as more and more customers wait it out, putting greater and greater pressure on the company to make its quarterly revenue estimates.

Numbers Up

Combining the price-to-sales ratio and the change in DSO provides better and more stable returns than using the price-to-sales ratio by itself. So, we're going to rate stocks using both metrics and combine those quintiles into new ones.

Figure 9.2 shows that, in the S&P 1500, the lowest combined quintile—the cheapest stocks by price-to-sales ratio, with the highest-quality credit terms—returned 22.6 percent annually over the past 10 years. The next three quintiles returned 13.2, 6.8, and –1.2 percent, respectively. The most expensive stocks, with the loosest credit terms returned –2.7 percent annually.

Our study turned up a few interesting tidbits. While the lower quintiles in this study resemble those in the simple price-to-sales study above, Figure 9.2 turns negative in the fourth quintile, not the fifth. Also, incorporating DSO into the model is more statistically significant than using price-to-sales alone. The data back up our theory that companies that stretch

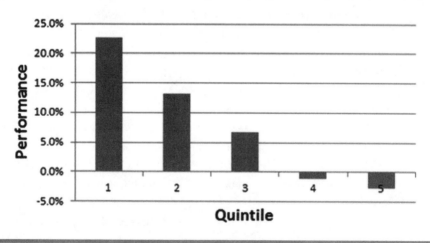

Figure 9.2 S&P 1500 performance, based on combined quintiles (price-to-sales ratio and credit quality).

to make financial targets will falter and suffer a pounding by the market. Because this is statistically significant, it is more likely to yield usable results in the future as well.

Performance is also fairly consistent over time. The only years where the highest earnings-quality stocks underperformed the poorest earnings-quality stocks was 2008—and only by a fraction—and in 2011, by about 5 percent. Interestingly, in the junk rally off the market lows in 2009, the highest-quality stocks outperformed by almost 10 percent. Furthermore, in the liquidity-fueled phase of quantitative easing in 2010, the highest-quality stocks outperformed by approximately 25 percent. One might have expected that easy money would have pushed investors to take excessive risks, boosting the lowest-quality stocks. But no.

If management teams can spackle over a dent in their businesses by offering customers looser credit terms and inflating short-term revenue, they will do so, even as the walls crumble around them. When expectations for companies like that are already high to begin with, take cover.

We provide this analysis to show that earnings quality should be a component of every investor's toolkit. A better understanding of the quality of a company's reported financials will improve your success rate as you zero-in on companies where that catalyst is going to be a significant and sustainable increase in earnings power.

Not all investors have the time or inclination to put the work into picking individual stocks. Instead they invest passively in broad market or sector indexes. There are two problems with this: Indexes include bad stocks as well as good stocks, and most index funds are market-capitalization weighted, tilting toward stocks that have already been through rapid growth phases with some of their best returns behind them.

Investors may then attempt to overcome the problem that indexes include losers. They then know that individual stocks are best, but don't have the time, so they hire active investment managers of mutual funds. But statistics show that most managers fail to outperform indexes over time.[4] This is in part because only a small percentage of stocks are the huge winners in a market cycle. Only 25 percent of stocks accounted for all of the gains in the Russell 3000 from 1983 to 2007. So, if you're not invested in a disproportionate percentage of those big winners (while also getting hammered in the nearly two-thirds of stocks that are underperforming), then you're going to fail to keep pace with—let alone outperform— the market, especially after accounting for fees and expenses.

Some indexes attempt to overcome the market cap weighting issue by assigning weights based on fundamental factors, such as revenue or dividends. But while a stock may have a market cap greater than another stock because of prior success, that says nothing about the future. Most companies make it into the indexes after their heady growth phase is in the rearview mirror. The larger they grow, the harder it is to keep growing at anywhere near the same percentage rates. Other indexes are equal-weighted, to avoid the larger capitalization bias in the index construction altogether, but there is still a threshold to cross in order to be admitted.

Weighting companies based on dividends, for example, attempts to take advantage of the fact that investors may prefer higher yields relative to lower ones, all else being equal. As a result, those higher-yielding stocks may return more in the future. Even so, these indexes still include all of the bad stocks (those that maintain or increase dividends unsustainably, through debt, or where cash flow is declining) as well as the good stocks (whose stable and increasing dividends come from fundamental performance). So, we are back at square one.

Therefore, for internal use, we have created our own index, modestly called the Del Vecchio Earnings Quality Index (sound of Tom applauding).[5] We weight stocks based on their earnings quality, rather than revenue, dividends, or other fundamental factors. Our model differentiates good stocks from bad stocks. We have emphasized that a great company may be an awful stock, especially if the earnings power is being driven by unsustainable sources. The factors I developed are based upon my years of experience in analyzing stocks to short in all market environments. Some are unique calculations that combine fundamental factors in ways previously not considered.

The Power of Earnings Quality

Figure 9.3 illustrates the performance of stocks of the S&P 500 based on their earnings quality, as opposed to market capitalization, dividends, revenue, or other fundamental factors. From this an index can be created that avoids the problems inherent in market capitalization weighting.

What if we then modify the index to exclude the stocks the Del Vecchio model deemed "bad?" Again, most stocks underperform the indexes over time. And only a small fraction of securities account for all of the indexes' gains. Therefore, if we exclude too many stocks, we run

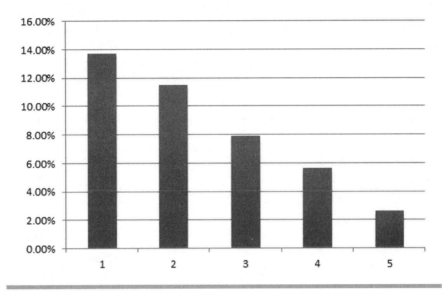

Figure 9.3 S&P 500 performance based on earnings quality.

the risk of leaving out many big winners. However, we know we are going to have a fair share of underperformers as well. So we only exclude those stocks that have the highest propensity for a negative earnings-driven event, such as an earnings miss or SEC investigation. Table 9.1 shows the results.

The DV Index substantially outperforms. Through the lost decade to December 31, 2011, this strategy produced 181 percent absolute return versus the S&P 500's 14 percent loss, and a relative return of 195 percentage points more.

Note, too, that having a subset of the index hold low-quality—but not the lowest quality—stocks is actually beneficial. Why? Because the highest-quality stocks may ultimately outperform over the long run, but there can be significant periods of time where low-quality stocks rule the roost, such as during the massive run-up after the market bottomed in 2009.

The Persistence of Dead Theory and Practice

This new way of thinking about indexing shows what is possible and is particularly useful to institutional investors. An entire consulting industry makes its money advising pension funds, endowments, non-profits, family offices, and more on choosing vehicles for asset allocation. In an era where the Modern Portfolio and Efficient Market theories are dead,[6] they still

Table 9.1 Del Vecchio Earnings Quality Index versus the S&P 500: 2000–2011

Years	DV Index Relative Performance, Percentage Points	DV Index, Return*	S&P 500, Return*	DV $100*	S&P $100
2000	33.4	23.3%	−10.1%	$123.30	$89.90
2001	13.4	0.4%	−13.0%	$123.79	$78.21
2002	6.2	−17.2%	−23.4%	$102.50	$59.91
2003	24.7	51.1%	26.4%	$154.88	$75.73
2004	4.8	13.8%	9.0%	$176.25	$82.54
2005	12.8	15.8%	3.0%	$204.10	$85.02
2006	3.2	16.8%	13.6%	$238.39	$96.58
2007	−10.2	−6.7%	3.5%	$222.42	$99.96
2008	−4.8	−43.3%	−38.5%	$126.11	$61.48
2009	42.3	65.8	23.5	$209.09	$75.92
2010	26.6	28.9	12.8	$269.52	$85.60
2011	4.3	4.3	0.0	$281.11	$85.59
	DV Index Outperformance = 195 percentage points.			181%	(14%)

*Without dividends.

rule large swaths of the institutional roost. Even this industry's consultants recommend to their clients active managers, almost without exception with gazillion-year track records. It's likely that they have far too many assets under management to do anything but buy large caps that, in the end, mimic the averages because, in fact, they *are* the averages.

Most RIAs simply index and asset allocate their clients through mutual funds and ETFs to avoid legal and client troubles for doing anything other than what everyone else is doing. That's why mutual fund managers are incentivized for outperforming usually by only one or two percentage points: if they do too well, RIAs sell their funds when it's time to rebalance the asset allocation. What a racket—you win, you lose!

Institutions and RIAs believe that asset allocation, however performed, and including all sorts of alleged new "classes," such as private equity, reduces drawdowns enough so that clients can distribute whatever they need to pensioners, insureds, university and hospital operating funds, and profligate offspring's trust fund distributions. Why would they need to short? Asset allocation is their baby blanket.

If asset allocation—passive or active—worked, it would have worked in 2008, but it didn't.[7] A long-short strategy would have done well. Putting together our (John's and Tom's) performance over the years shows a long-short strategy that performs consistently. Employ Chapter 6's research and experience-backed value-with-catalysts approach on the long side, the many chapters on the short side, and this book's earnings quality keys on both. It works.

Look, we know you can't change human nature or business. Business is in business to give people what they want. There is nothing to be gained by trying to change the financial decision makers' minds about what scares them or makes them greedy. But it's precisely because human nature is not going to change that those who use the techniques in this book will find it surprisingly easier over time and with practice to outperform in ways they didn't imagine.

The Solution: The Practical Short Side

Current indexing, asset allocation, blah blah blah—they are all just giving the people what they want: mediocrity. Financial industry products, discredited academic theories, and the fact that most people prefer things that are easy and simple may do no harm, but they also provide only mediocre returns. But by thinking in a new way about indexing, investors can start to avoid the blowups and pull in some nice returns.

Most investors spend all their time figuring out long investing for growth, but they never realize that limiting losses is what really matters. What you will not find in books or blogs are more than a handful of resources on avoiding or profiting from the nuclear portfolio bomb, and none as practical as what we've discussed in these pages.

We know: everyone has something to offer. But what we have done, we hope, is present only the tools that matter. We prioritize. You should know now, for example, that if you do nothing else, "DSO trend" should be your last words at night and first in the morning. So this book is designed to be a nuts-and-bolts, practical start, something you can start using Monday morning in a practical long-short portfolio managed according to our principles.

You can also visit our Web site www.deljacobs.com to keep informed of new ways to use the information in this book. For those and everything else, start as soon as you can, and practice, practice, practice—but not just to get to Carnegie Hall. Become the person who can afford the box seats.

Notes

Introduction

1. Just a few of the marvelous books that treat these in depth: Charles Mackay, *Extraordinary Popular Delusions and the Madness of Crowds* (New York: Wiley, 1995, first published in 1841); Niall Ferguson, *The Ascent of Money* (New York: Penguin Press, 2008); A. Gary Shilling, *The Age of Deleveraging: Investment Strategies for a Decade of Slow Growth and Deflation* (New York: Wiley, 2010).
2. Thornton O'glove, *Quality of Earnings: The Investor's Guide to How Much Money a Company Is Really Making* (New York: The Free Press, 1987).
3. Charles W. Mulford and Eugene E. Comiskey, *The Financial Numbers Game: Detecting Creative Accounting Practices* (New York: Wiley, 2002); Charles W. Mulford and Eugene E. Comiskey, *Creative Cash Flow Reporting* (New York: Wiley, 2005).

Chapter 1

1. Blackstar Funds, "The Capitalism Distribution: Observations of individual common stock returns, 1983–2007, http://www.theivy portfolio.com/wp-content/uploads/2008/12/thecapitalismdistri bution.pdf. (Accessed December 10, 2011.)

2. "Historical components of the Dow Jones Industrial Average," http://en.wikipedia.org/wiki/Historical_components_of_the_Dow_Jones_Industrial_Average. (Accessed December 10, 2011.)

3. Peter Lynch, *One Up on Wall Street: How to Use What You Already Know to Make Money in the Stock Market*, 2nd ed. (New York: Simon & Schuster, 2000), 56. "Ken Heebner at Loomis-Sayles Sticks His Neck Out Too, and His Results Have Been Remarkable."

4. Bob Veres, "How to Lose Money in the Top Performing Fund," reprinted in *Financial Symmetry* blog, http://financialsymmetry.com/blog/how-we-see-it/lose-money-topperforming-fund. (Accessed December 10, 2011.)

5. The table and figure are both from "S&P 500: Total and Inflation-Adjusted Historical Returns," http://www.simplestockinvesting.com/SP500-historical-real-total-returns.htm. Table author notes: Figures for dividend distribution rates in Table 1.1 present high uncertainty, of about ±5 percent. Geometric averages were calculated for price changes, total returns, and inflation. Raw data for this work was obtained from the following sources: Standard & Poor's S&P 500, U.S. Department of Labor, Yahoo Finance, and data collected by Robert Shiller, from Yale University, for his book *Irrational Exuberance*, second edition (New Haven: Yale University Press, 2000).

6. Idem. "Reinvesting all dividends from 1950 through 2009 returned 8 times the return of the average alone." But that's a pretty long time for compounding those dividends and it suffers from the same age, wage-earning levels, and behavioral concerns as dollar-cost averaging.

7. Graham, of course, is the founder of value investing and coauthor with David Dodd notably of *Security Analysis*, multiple editions (New York: McGraw-Hill, 1996 and others); he is also the author of *The Intelligent Investor*, revised ed. (New York: Collins Business, 2003) and *The Memoirs of the Dean of Wall Street*, (New York: McGraw-Hill, 1996). His most famous student was Warren Buffett, whom he taught at the Columbia Business School and reportedly awarded his only A+. As recently as the Berkshire Hathaway meeting in 2010, when asked his style of investing by The Motley Fool's Lou Ann Lofton, Tom heard Buffett reply, "Benjamin Graham."

8. Jason Zweig, "If You Think the Worst is Over, Take Benjamin Graham's Advice," *Wall Street Journal*, May 26, 2009, available at http://online.wsj.com/article/SB124302634866648217.html. (Accessed December 10, 2011.)

9. Jeremy Siegel, *Stocks for the Long Run: The Definitive Guide to Financial Market Returns & Long Term Investment Strategies*, 4th ed. (New York: McGraw-Hill, 2007).

10. Jeremy Siegel, "Yes, Stock Data Do Go Back 200 Years," undated, pdf available at http://www.jeremysiegel.com/index.cfm/fuseaction/ Resources.ViewResource/type/article/resourceID/6950.cfm.(Accessed December 10, 2011). In our view, Zweig has the far better argument in the now-classic Zweig-Siegel debate, which Zweig began in "Does Stock Market Data Really Go Back 200 Years?" *Wall Street Journal*, July 11, 2009, http://online.wsj.com/article/SB124725925791924871 .html. (Accessed December 10, 2001.)

11. Jeremy Siegel, "Rough Going for Now, but Stocks Still a Good Bet," *Knowledge @ Wharton*, September 8, 2008, http://knowledge.whar ton.upenn.edu/article.cfm?articleid=2052. (Accessed December 10, 2011.) "And, if you go back 200 years, has it been right to sell in the bear mar- kets? The answer is no. You take the pain, you hold your position, and you will be rewarded in the future."

12. Ross Kerber, "Average 401(k) balance near $75,000: Fidelity," *Reuters*, May 11, 2011, http://www.reuters.com/article/2011/05/11/us -retirement-fidelity-idUSTRE74A0L720110511.(Accessed December 10, 2011.)

13. Idem. "Averages were higher for older workers and those who have added steadily to their 401(k)s. Among those active in a plan for 10 straight years, the average balance at March 31 was $191,000, up from $169,200 a year earlier; within that group, those 55 and older had saved $233,800 on average, up from $203,600 a year earlier."

14. CNN Money Chart and others from "What Should Your Net Worth Be? Net Worth by Age and Income," *Fabulously Broke in the City*, March 21, 2011, http://www.fabulouslybroke.com/2011/03/what-should-your -net-worth-be-net-worth-by-age-and-by-income/. (Accessed December 10, 2011.)

15. Barton Biggs, *Wealth, War and Wisdom* (New York: Wiley, 2008).

16. The Fama-French three-factor model (FF3) is detailed in "Small Cap Value Is Beautiful Again," *Financial Advisor Magazine*, July 2009, http://www.fa-mag.com/component/content/article/1-features/4270 -small-cap-value-is-beautiful-again.html. Its results were especially impressive over the full business cycle following the late 1990s pub- lication of Fama and French's research. The article discusses the economic logic for small-cap value outperformance, defining the stock category as "small companies trading at low multiples to book value and other fundamental measures [that] tend to be distressed firms, even in the best of times." James O'Shaughnessy argues in *What Works on Wall Street* (New York: McGraw-Hill, 2011) that the historic outperformance relies heavily on stocks that are too illiquid, but these

are apples and oranges. Fama and French's data are for valuations and O'Shaughnessy's for absolute market cap and associated liquidity.

17. Christopher Browne et al., "What Has Worked in Investing: Studies of Investment Approaches and Characteristics Associated with Exceptional Returns," (Tweedy Browne paper, revised 2009), http://www.tweedy .com/resources/library_docs/papers/WhatHasWorkedInInvesting.pdf. (Accessed April 8, 2012.)

18. A sad denouement to a formerly stellar career: Sree Vidya Bhaktavasalam, "Legg Mason's Bill Miller Will Exit Main Fund after It Falls Behind Peers," *Bloomberg*, November 17, 2011,   http://www.bloomberg.com/ news/2011-11-17/legg-mason-s-bill-miller-to-exit-main-fund-after-falling -behind-its-peers.html. (Accessed December 10, 2011.)

19. Edwin Lefèvre's, *Reminiscences of a Stock Operator*, annotated ed. (New York: Wiley, 2008).

20. This is a fascinating event in modern investing history because both the CEO and money manager, Whitney Tilson, were willing to put themselves on the line so publicly. These pieces capture this historic exchange, with the two interesting postscripts. Tilson went long in October 2011, quoted in *Business Week* as saying, "The core of our short thesis was always Netflix's high valuation. In light of the stock's collapse, we now think it's cheap and today established a small long position. We hope it gets cheaper so we can add to it." See http://www.businessweek.com/news/2011-10-25/ t2-s-tilson-former-netflix-bear-buying-shares-after-plunge.html (accessed October 25, 2011), committing then two of the shorting sins identi- fied in this chapter—overvaluation (in effect, momentum investing and market timing, see Chapter 6) and poor business model. This is also followed by one writer's excellent post mortem—a writer/investor who endured the pain of being short from $125.00 to the $300.00 top, who then, in his words, ended up with the most successful investment of his lifetime. But everyone seems to ignore that the painful short or long could have been avoided by focusing on aggressive accounting—not the clairvoyance to know a fad, fraud, or business model failure, or exactly when a momentum stock will turn. Whitney Tilson, "Why We're Short Netflix," available at http://seekingalpha.com/article/242320-whitney -tilson-why-we-re-short-netflix (accessed December 16, 2010); Reed Hastings, "CEO Reed Hastings Responds to Whitney Tilson: Cover Your Short Now," available at http://seekingalpha.com/article/242653 -netflix-ceo-reed-hastings-responds-to-whitney-tilson-cover-your-short -position-now (accessed December 20, 2010); Whitney Tilson, "Why We Covered Our Netflix Short," available at http://seekingalpha.com/

article/252316-whitney-tilson-why-we-covered-our-netflix-short (accessed February 11, 2011); "Slim Shady," "A Response to Whitney Tilson's Netflix Flip-Flop," http://seekingalpha.com/article/302726-a-response-to -whitney-tilson-s-netflix-flip-flop (accessed October 27, 2011).

21. David Shook, "Artistic Allusion—Or Delusions—at Human Genome Sciences?" *Bloomberg Business Week*, July 2011, http://www.businessweek .com/bwdaily/dnflash/jul2001/nf20010712_430.htm. (Accessed April 8, 2012.)

22. Consolidated Class Action Complaint, In Re Ambac Securities Financial Group, Inc. Securities Litigation, count 37, p. 16, http:// securities.stanford.edu/1039/ABK_01/2008825_r01c_0800411.pdf. (Accessed April 8, 2012.)

23. Case Study: The Collapse of Lehman Brothers, *Investopedia*, April 2, 2009, http://www.investopedia.com/articles/economics/09/lehman-brothers -collapse.asp#axzz1ZHdnjptAm. (Accessed on December 10, 2011.)

24. See note 21.

25. Reed Hastings, October 24, 2011 Shareholder Letter, *Netflix*, http:// files.shareholder.com/downloads/NFLX/1536753156x0x511277/8 5b155bc-69e8-4cb8-a2a3-22465e076d77/Investor%20Letter%20 Q3%202011.pdf, p. 9. (Accessed December 10, 2011.)

26. Credit must go to the Motley Fool *Pro* and *Options* advisor and portfolio manager Jeff Fischer, a friend, colleague, and former business partner, for writing in an early issue of the no-longer-published magazine, *The Motley Fool Monthly*, that it would be a good idea to sell AOL at the time of the merger.

Chapter 2

1. Financial Accounting Standards Board, *Statement of Financial Accounting Concept 5: Recognition and Measurement of Statements of Business Enterprises* (December 1984) at 30, http://www.fasb.org/pdf/ con5.pdf. (Accessed December 12, 2011.) This is the source of the definitions of "realized," "realizable," and "earned."

2. We realize that some use the actual days in the quarter and average the beginning and end numbers of accounts receivable. That's fine. This simpler formula does the job, so long as it is consistently applied, making comparisons like for like.

3. "EResearch Has Replacement for Esposito," *Philadelphia Business Journal*, June, 12, 2006, http://www.bizjournals.com/philadelphia/ stories/2006/06/12/daily8.html. (Accessed December 12, 2011.)

4. The following is from Note 11 of Quest's 10–Q filing on August 9, 2005:

    "On March 17, 2004, we acquired Aelita. See Note 3. Certain venture capital funds associated with Insight Venture Partners (the 'Insight Funds') previously holding shares of Aelita's preferred stock became entitled to receive (subject to claims against an indemnity escrow fund) approximately $47.6 million in cash in respect of those shares of preferred stock as a result of this acquisition.

    "On May 20, 2005, we acquired Imceda. See Note 3. Insight Funds previously holding shares of Imceda's preferred stock became entitled to receive cash and (subject to claims against an indemnity escrow fund) shares of Quest common stock representing an aggregate value of approximately $48.0 million in respect of those shares of preferred stock as a result of this acquisition.

    "Jerry Murdock, a director of Quest Software, is a Managing Director and the cofounder of Insight Venture Partners and an investor in the Insight Funds. Vincent Smith, Quest's Chairman of the Board and CEO, and Raymond Lane and Paul Sallaberry, directors of Quest Software, are passive limited partners in Insight Funds and, as a result, have interests in the Aelita transaction and the Imceda transaction which are considered to be not material. One analyst's 'not material' related-party transaction can be an earnings quality analyst's red flag."

5. M. Edgar Barrett and Jonathan N. Brown, *Case Study: Stirling Homex* (Boston: Harvard Business School, 1973), http://hbr.org/product/stirling-homex-a/an/173193-PDF-ENG. (Accessed April 8, 2012.) Eleanor Dienstag, the wife of the Stirling Homex executive who blew the whistle, produced a well-written narrative of the personalities and company's rise and fall in *Whither Thou Goest: The Story of an Uprooted Wife* (New York: Dutton, 1976).

6. Michael J. de la Merced, *New York Times*, November 3, 2006, http://www.nytimes.com/ref/business/03computercnd.html. (Accessed April 8, 2012.)

7. U.S. Securities and Exchange Commission, *SEC Staff Accounting Bulletin (SAB) No. 101 – Revenue Recognition in Financial Statements* (December 3, 1999), http://www.sec.gov/interps/account/sab101.htm. (Accessed December 12, 2011.)

8. We thank The Motley Fool for permission to reprint John's Juniper example, © 2011 The Motley Fool:

    "We adopted Accounting Standards Update (ASU) No. 2009-13, Topic 605-Multiple- Deliverable Revenue Arrangements (ASU 2009-13) and ASU No. 2009- 14, Topic 985-Certain Revenue Arrangements That Include Software Elements (ASU 2009-14) on a prospective basis, as of the beginning of fiscal 2010, for new and materially modified arrangements originating after December 31, 2009. Under the new standards, we allocate the total arrangement consideration to each separable element of an arrangement, based on the relative selling price of each element. Arrangement consideration allocated to undelivered elements is deferred until delivery.

"For fiscal 2010 and future periods, pursuant to the guidance of ASU 2009-13, when a sales arrangement contains multiple elements, and software and non-software components that function together to deliver the tangible products' essential functionality, we allocate revenue to each element, based on a selling price hierarchy. The selling price for a deliverable is based on our vendor-specific objective evidence (VSOE) if available, third-party evidence (TPE) if VSOE is not available, or estimated selling price (ESP) if neither VSOE nor TPE is available. We then recognize revenue on each deliverable in accordance with our policies for product and service revenue recognition.

"VSOE is based on the price charged when the element is sold separately. In determining VSOE, we require that a substantial majority of the selling prices fall within a reasonable range, based on historical discounting trends for specific products and services. TPE of selling price is established by evaluating largely interchangeable competitor products or services in standalone sales to similarly situated customers. However, as our products contain a significant element of proprietary technology and our solutions offer substantially different features and functionality, the comparable pricing of products with similar functionality typically cannot be obtained. Additionally, as we are unable to reliably determine what competitors' products' selling prices are on a standalone basis, we are not typically able to determine TPE. When determining the best estimate of selling price, we apply management judgment by considering multiple factors including, but not limited to, pricing practices in different geographies and through different sales channels, gross margin objectives, internal costs, competitor pricing strategies, and industry technology lifecycles.

"For transactions initiated prior to January 1, 2010, revenue for arrangements with multiple elements, such as sales of products that include services, is allocated to each element using the residual method based on the VSOE of fair value of the undelivered items pursuant to ASC Topic 985-605."

Chapter 3

1. Thornton O'glove, *Quality of Earnings: The Investor's Guide to How Much Money a Company Is Really Making* (New York: The Free Press, 1987).
2. O'glove, 1987, p. 109.
3. The Lipman quarters conformed to the calendar (March, June, September, and December), while VeriFone's ended in January, April, July, and October.
4. From *Assay Research*, March 2008, reprinted by permission.

Chapter 4

1. "Behind Salesforce's San Francisco Campus Debacle," SocketSite, May 14, 2012, http://www.socketsite.com/archives/2012/05/salesforces_san_francisco_campus_debacle_insight_and_su.html, accessed June 5, 2012; Jim Finkle and Noel Randewich, "Salesforce's Canceled HQ Project Puzzles Investors," Reuters, http://www.reuters.com/article/2012/02/29/us-salesforce-idUSTRE81S03I20120229, Feb. 28, 2012, accessed June 5, 2012.
2. Charles W. Mulford and Eugene E. Comiskey, *The Financial Numbers Game: Detecting Creative Accounting Practices* (New York: Wiley, 2002), 231.
3. Mulford and Comiskey, 2002, pp. 211–213.
4. Mulford and Comiskey, 2002, p. 204.
5. This chapter frequently refers to salesforce.com, where, as with every company, the negative catalyst of aggressive accounting may not—as is true on the long side with positive catalysts—result in the desired stock price result. There is a risk at salesforce.com. CEO Marc Benioff held management positions at Oracle Corp. under CEO Larry Ellison from 1986 to 1999. Oracle, a serial acquirer, has bought software companies started by former execs before. In 2006, it closed the purchase of Siebel Systems, whose founder and CEO Thomas Siebel held a management position at Oracle from 1984 to 1990. Oracle and Ellison might someday moot the negative catalyst for salesforce.com stock by paying a higher valuation to acquire it; we have no evidence that Ellison is a value investor. Ellison has shown that energetic public criticism from competitors is no barrier to acquisition. Benioff is among his most vocal critics.
6. Floyd Norris, "AOL Pays a Fine to Settle a Charge That It Inflated Profits," *New York Times*, May 16, 2000, http://www.nytimes.com/2000/05/16/

business/aol-pays-a-fine-to-settle-a-charge-that-it-inflated-profits.html. (Accessed December 11, 2011.)

7. ASU 2009-13, "Multiple Delivery Revenue Arrangements," October 2009, Revenue Recognition, (Topic 605), issued by the Financial Accounting Standards Board (FASB), http://www.fasb.org/cs/Blob Server?blobcol=urldata&blobtable=MungoBlobs&blobkey=id&blob where=1175819938544&blobheader=application%2Fpdf. (Accessed December 11, 2011.)

8. There is no better analysis of the credit cycle than Charles Kindleberger's *Manias, Panics and Crashes: A History of Financial Crises* (New York: Wiley, 1978), or of the duration of, damage by, and recovery from credit crashes than Reinhart and Rogoff's exhaustive academic study *This Time Is Different: Eight Centuries of Financial Folly* (Princeton: Princeton University Press, 2009).

9. Rob Bluey, "U.S. Rivals Japan for World's Highest Corporate Tax Rate," *The Foundry*, September 25, 2011, http://blog.heritage .org/2011/09/25/chart-of-the-week-u-s-rivals-japan-for-worlds-highest -corporate-tax-rate/. (Accessed December 12, 2011.)

Chapter 5

1. Financial Accounting Standards Board, "FASB Issues Final Statement on Accounting for Share-Based Payment," December 16, 2004, http:// www.fasb.org/news/nr121604_ebc.shtml. (Accessed December 12, 2011.)

2. Michael Rapoport, "Options Rule Also Hits Operating Cash Flow," *DowJones Newswires*, May 15, 2006, *Cash Flow Analytics*, http://www .cashflowanalytics.com/news.php?articleID=114 (accessed December 12, 2011); BDO Seidman, March 2006, http://www.bdo.com/publications/ assurance/finrptnl/fr_april_06/cashflows.asp. (Accessed December 12, 2011.)

3. Reprinted by permission of The Motley Fool. © 2011 The Motley Fool, Inc.

4. James Montier, KPMG, "Value Investing, KPMG survey of global M&A," report, October 15, 2008, p. 269.

Chapter 6

1. Christopher Browne et al., "What Has Worked in Investing: Studies of Investment Approaches and Characteristics Associated with Exceptional Returns" (Tweedy Browne paper, revised 2009), http://www.tweedy

.com/resources/library_docs/papers/WhatHasWorkedInInvesting.pdf. (Accessed April 8, 2012) at ii–iii ("Tweedy Browne study").

2. http://www.incademy.com/courses/Ten-great-investors/John-Neff/ 9/1040/10002.

3. Warren E. Buffett, "The Superinvestors of Graham-and-Doddsville," Columbia Business School, 1984. Available at http://www4.gsb.columbia .edu/null?&exclusive=filemgr.download&file_id=522, p. 15.

4. For excellent summaries of these two theories, their proponents, and the ascent of their critics, see Wikipedia, "Efficient-Market Hypothesis" at http://en.wikipedia.org/wiki/Efficient-market_ hypothesis. See also "Modern Portfolio Theory," accessed June 5, 2012.

5. Justin Fox's *The Myth of the Rational Markets* (New York: HarperBusiness, 2009). A great listen on Audible, too.

6. Among others, see Deborah Brewster and David Swenson on "The Campus Endowment Legend Likes to Keep It Simple," http:// www.ft.com/intl/cms/s/0/a8d3be62-1c34-11de-977c-00144fe abdc0.html#axzz1wvEf2lDF. (Accessed June 5, 2012.)

7. See, e.g., Bens, Wrong, and Skinner, "What Drive Companies to Repurchase Their Stock? The Relationship Between Employee Stock Options and Stock Repurchases," paper (Chicago: University of Chicago Booth School of Business), Fall 2003, http://www.chicagobooth.edu/ capideas/fall03/stockrepurchases.html, accessed June 1, 2012; Zahn Bozanic, "Managerial Motivation and Timing of Open Market Share Repurchases," *Review of Quantitative Finance and Accounting*, May 1, 2010, http://papers.ssrn.com/sol3/papers.cfm?abstract_id=1979781, accessed June 1, 2012. ("Firms attempt to manage earnings upward through the use of repurchases," and other conclusions other than that the repurchase represents better allocation of capital according to value principles.)

8. David Ikenberry, Josef Lakonishok, and Theo Vermaelen reported in their 1995 study that "the highest returns [from stock buy backs] were from the "value stocks" (those with the highest book value relative to the share price of firms that had repurchased shares). "Market Underreaction to Open Market Share Repurchases," *Journal of Financial Economics* (October 1995), http://www.nber.org/papers/ w4965. (Accessed June 1, 2012.) Apparently value-oriented management knows value at its own company when it sees it.

9. Berkshire Hathaway 1984 Annual Report, available at http://www .berkshirehathaway.com/letters/1984.html. (Accessed June 1, 2012; no page numbers provided.)

10. Tweedy Browne, 2009, pp. 39–40.
11. Nassim Nicholas Taleb, *The Black Swan* (New York: Random House, 2007).
12. Benoit Mandelbrot and Richard L. Hudson, *The Misbehavior of Markets: A Fractal View of Financial Turbulence* (New York: Basic Books, 2006).
13. Carmen Reinhart and Kenneth Rogoff, *This Time It's Different: Eight Centuries of Financial Folly* (Princeton: Princeton University Press, 2009).
14. Robert F. Bruner and Sean D. Carr, *The Panic of 1907: Lessons Learned from the Market's Perfect Storm* (New York: Wiley, 2007). Carr is the reader on the excellent Audible version.
15. A. Gary Shilling, *The Age of Deleveraging: Investment Strategies for a Decade of Slow Growth and Deflation* (New York: Wiley, 2010), p. 23 ("deepest recession") and p. 29 ("S&P 500 Index rose 4 percent, but in real terms plummeted 64 percent").

Chapter 7

1. Relative strength, up/down volume, accumulation/distribution, and more of the metrics in this chapter are available from William O'Neil + Co., their daily newspaper, *Investor's Business Daily,* and other sources at www.williamoneil.com.
2. Reprinted by permission of The Motley Fool. © 2011 The Motley Fool.

Chapter 9

1. Thanks to The Motley Fool for permission to reprint. Copyright © 2011 The Motley Fool, Inc.
2. Kenneth Fisher, *Super Stocks* (New York: McGraw-Hill, 2007).
3. James O'Shaughnessy, *What Works on Wall Street*, third edition (New York: McGraw-Hill, 2005).
4. Everyone disagrees about whether it's 85 percent over five years or more, or percent, or whatever, but we've been unable to find any source that contradicts this statement.
5. For more information, visit our site, www.deljacobs.com.
6. Justin Fox, *The Myth of the Rational Market: A History of Risk, Reward, and Delusion on Wall Street* (New York: HarperBusiness, 2009).
7. This is deliberately provocative, because 2008 is hotly debated. See in particular James J. Green's "The Failure of Asset Allocation" in the December 2008 issue of *Investment Advisor*, http://advisorone .com/2008/12/01/the-failure-of-asset-allocation. (Accessed December 13, 2011.)

Index

About the Authors

John Del Vecchio is the cofounder and comanager of The Active Bear ETF, a fund dedicated to shorting individual stocks with fundamental red flags. Previously, he managed a hedge fund for Ranger Alternative Management, L.P. In addition, he worked for well-known short seller David Tice and famed forensic accountant Dr. Howard Schilit. Del Vecchio coadvises the *Motley Fool Alpha* long-short newsletter.

Tom Jacobs, portfolio manager of *Motley Fool Special Ops*, applies this book's earnings quality tests to his value and special situations long side to form a long-short portfolio. He is managing partner of holding company Complete Growth Investor, LLC, principal of The Marfa Group, Inc., and a real estate investor.

Authors' Note

The authors would like to thank William O'Neil + Company for permission to reproduce many of the figures used in this book.

William O'Neil + Company is a Registered Investment Advisor providing research and marketing data services, including WONDA®, to more than 350 of the world's leading institutional investment professionals. Founded in 1963, William O'Neil + Company is headquartered in Los Angeles, with offices in New York, Boston, Chicago, and London.

WONDA provides access to over 55,000 global equity listings with key fundamental and technical data laid out in an easy-to-read proprietary Datagraph®. Additional benefits include time saving Preset Lists, Quickscreen, and proprietary Ratings and Rankings to find new ideas and monitor existing holdings. For more information, visit www .williamoneil.com.